The FamilyPC Guide

to COOl

CAUTION
Do Not Demagnetize

PC

Projects

SAMUEL MEAD
&
SERIES EDITOR
ROBIN RASKIN

 HYPERION

 FamilyPC
B O O K S

NEW YORK

CO-PUBLISHED BY
Hyperion & FamilyPC
114 Fifth Avenue
New York, New York 10011

Copyright © 1996 FamilyPC

ISBN 0-7868-8207-7

First Edition

10 9 8 7 6 5 4 3 2 1

Vice President and Publisher: Bob Miller
Executive Editor: Rick Kot
Manuscript Editor: Susan Pink
Technical Reviewers: Eric Brewer and Judy McKinley Brewer
Cover Design: Jim Phillips
Interior Design/Layout: Carol Rumbolt
Proofreader: Peggy Richard
Indexer: Liz Cunningham
Book Packager: Trudy Neuhaus

Contents

Foreword

In this world of consumer conveniences, the handmade has become something of a lost art. We run the risk of raising a generation of children who think that storebought products are all that's available. And as computers and high-tech gear dominate our lives, there's some concern that we might forget how to do anything that involves creatively making things with our hands.

In fact, nothing could be further from the truth. With some encouragement and help from their parents, kids can turn the computer into a wonderful tool for unleashing their family's creativity. More important, using a computer as a creative tool does not mean you need to spend hundreds of dollars on specialized software.

Maybe you've noticed that many books of crafts and projects send you on a wild goose chase, hunting down obscure materials and ingredients. We noticed, and we decided to buck the trend. We designed *The FamilyPC Guide to Cool PC Projects* so that families with limited time, limited funds, and limited software and equipment could still have hours of fun and enjoyment creating special, handmade, computer-generated projects.

Most of the projects in this book are built using everyday software and common household items. We encourage you to get fancy and use scanners or digital photography if you like, but you'll be equally successful if all you own are a PC or Mac and some bare ingredients. Word processors, desktop publishing packages, and standard off-the-shelf drawing and art packages are the only tools you need to create more than 60 one-of-a-kind projects from this book. From pinwheels to bookmarks, from cookie cutouts to party invitations — each project can bear your family's stamp of originality.

This book has a personal appeal for me. I've raised three children who've grown up with the computer as a tool — one that helps them accomplish their jobs. When my children have a party invitation or a school election banner to make, they don't have to think about using the computer — it comes naturally. The computer has become a trusted art center that churns out family memories — from the mobile hanging in the hallway to the pinwheels we make for our little cousins. And more often than not, these projects are something we do together, as a family.

My children have learned that they can create things from their own imaginations and with their own hands, even in this high-tech society. That's an important lesson to learn — and this book makes the learning ever so much fun.

ROBIN RASKIN
Editor in Chief, *FamilyPC*

Acknowledgments

I'd like to thank several people who
contributed to this book. Eric, Judy, Daniel
and Matthew Brewer created
the crafts, tested the instructions,
and contributed in countless other ways
to this book and to *FamilyPC*.
Thanks also to Robin Raskin and Dan Muse
for letting me write this book;
Trudy Neuhaus and Susan Pink for
their managing and editing of the project,
and Jim Phillips and Carol Rumbolt
for designing and composing the book.

I'd also like to thank several people
on the *FamilyPC* staff, especially
Si Yegerlehner, Julia Lynch, and Peggy Richard.

Finally, and most importantly,
I'd like to thank my wife, Katie, for her
patience, understanding and encouragement
while I submerged myself in writing
this book for five months.

Getting Started

Whether you've just bought a new computer or you've owned one for years, you probably have everything you need to create some pretty cool crafts — you just don't know it. That's where this book comes in. We'll show you and your kids how to create dozens of projects using your everyday software. With so many projects to choose from, you'll have no shortage of fun. We've listed the projects here to help you find the best ones for your child's age group.

PROJECT	AGE	PAGE
Finger Puppets	2-12	35
ABC's Books	3-6	3
Clip-Art Coloring Books	3-7	22
Wingding Coloring Books	3-7	28
Paper Football Game	3-10	102
Original-Art Coloring Books	3-11	23
Photo Coloring Books	3-11	25
Party Hats	3-12	172
Pinwheels	3-12	51
Birthday Banner	3-15	190
Kid's Calendars	3-15	8
Masks	3-15	170
Cookie Cutouts	4-8	31
Mobiles	4-12	41
Disk Labels	4-14	84
Bookmarks	4-15	74
Bookplates	4-15	72
POGs	5-10	107
Custom Cutouts Invitation	5-10	134
Pull-Tab Card	5-10	148
Bookshelf Labels	5-15	78
Board Game	5-15	127
Buttons	5-15	178
Audiotape Labels	5-adult	90
Fortune-teller Game	6-10	98

PROJECT	AGE	PAGE
Full-Page Wanted Poster	6-11	142
Multimedia-grams	6-12	45
Tri-Fold Card	6-12	138
Classic Pop-up Card	6-12	145
Poppers	6-12	176
Super-Sized Posters	6-15	186
Electronic Cookbook	6-adult	217
Family Calendar	6-adult	13
Return Address Labels	6-adult	86
Nesting Santas	6-adult	154
Christmas Village	6-adult	157
Tree Ornaments	6-adult	161
Baseball Cards	7-12	63
Personal Notepad	7-adult	112
Personalized Paper	7-adult	116
Custom Envelopes	7-adult	120
Pumpkin-Carving Templates	7-adult	195
Stencils	8-adult	57
Travel Booklet	8-adult	247
Family History Map	10-adult	223
Multimedia Greetings Card	10-adult	231
Holiday Greetings Postcard	10-adult	229
Newsletter	12-adult	237
Coaching with Your Computer	15-adult	205

You don't need to be a computer whiz or an aspiring artist to do these projects. All you need are some basic computer skills, the software that probably came with your computer, and this book.

We've designed these projects to be made using software running on a 486 PC and Windows 95 with at least 8MB of RAM; or on a Mac running System 7 or later with at least 8MB of RAM. *The FamilyPC Guide to Cool PC Projects* will lead you through each project in a step-by-step fashion. If the going gets tough, use our Creative Primer. It addresses many frequently asked questions and gives you some computer-craft tips and techniques.

If you're looking for the quickest way to a finished project, check out the CD-ROM that's included with this book. It has a 30-day, full-working model of SmartSketch, a drawing program we've used to create many of the projects in this book, plus more than 20 project templates. Creating homemade crafts with your kids has never been easier!

Projects for Little Hands

There are few things young kids like more than a good art project. With some paper and crayons, they can be content for hours. Now add the computer to the mix, and you'll be amazed at what you and your kids can create in a short time. Calendars, coloring books, pinwheels, puppets, and more: these projects not only are fun to make but also provide hours of entertainment away from the computer. That's right: the projects in this section don't begin and end with the computer. You and your kids will enjoy using the computer together to create these projects, and then you'll enjoy many hours of play with the projects you've made.

ABC's Book

 PREP TIME: 60 MINUTES

Materials

Paint or draw program or clip art • Word processing program •
Print utility (optional) • Printer (color preferable) • Card stock • Copy shop

A is for apple, *B* is for boat, *C* is for cat. What child didn't grow up with an ABC's book? Using your computer, you and your child can create your own version of this classic book that's unique and looks like it was published by a professional. However, instead of someone choosing the pictures for your child, he gets

to pick out the art that represents each letter. Using paint tools or a clip-art package, your child can select whatever images appeal to him — which is as much a part of the learning process as reading the book is. Then you and he can simply take the art and insert it in a word processing document, print it, and compile the book.

Before You Begin

You and your child should make a list of items that correspond to letters of the alphabet (for example, *A* for ant, *B* for bike, *C* for cow). Help your child come up with objects that are easy to recognize. Then you can both get busy creating the art or finding it in your clip-art library. (If you use clip art, you'll have to export the images to your hard drive.) If your child creates the art in a paint or draw program, save each element as a separate file.

Step-by-Step

1. Launch your word processing program.

2. For the title page of the book, begin by creating a text frame for the title. (By using a text frame instead of typing directly on the page, you can move the text easily by clicking and dragging the frame.) Make the frame stretch from one side of the page to the other.

3. Click inside the frame.

4. Choose a fun, easy-to-read font, size, and style (for example, 72-point Comic Sans MS), choose center alignment, and type the name of the book (for example, *My Own ABC's*).

5. Create a second text frame below the title for your child's name.

6. Click inside the frame.

7. Select a font style and size (we suggest using the same font as the title but a smaller size), keep the center alignment, and type your child's name.

8. Drag both text frames halfway down the page. It's easier to find the best position for the frames if you zoom out to 25%. (Usually there's a zoom control window on the toolbar or along the base of the window.) You can also check the page by using the Print Preview option, which is usually located under the File menu.

Use text frames to create your title page.

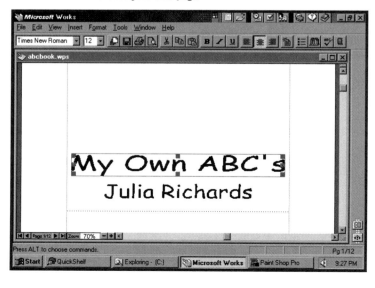

9. Add a page break (Insert, Break) after the second text frame to move to the next page.

10. To create the first page of the book (for the letter *A*), insert the corresponding *A* image that you saved to your hard drive (Insert, File). Or if your child drew the image, open the art file in your draw or paint program, select the image (Edit, Select All), copy it to the Clipboard, and then paste it into your word processing document after the page break.

11. Scale the image so that it is 4 to 5 inches tall and wide.

12. Drag the image halfway down the page to make the page look balanced.

13. Create another text frame that is the width of the page and positioned right below the image.

> **FamilyPC Tip:** *To give your text more pizzazz, put it in a semicircle or a wave using WordArt, a text manipulation tool that comes with most Microsoft word processing products. With WordArt, you can also change the color of letters, give them shadows, and stretch words to the edges of the text frame.*

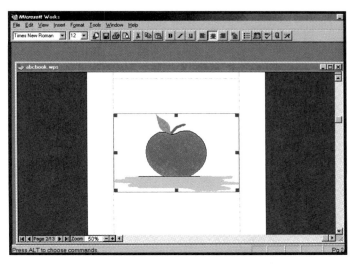

To scale the art, click on it, and then grab and drag one of the corner handles. Drag out to enlarge the image or in to shrink it.

14. Click inside the frame.

15. Select a font style and size (we used the same font as the title page, but a larger point size of 100), keep the center alignment, and type the first letter of the item (such as *A*).

16. Press the Enter key once to move the cursor down a line within the text frame. Select a font style and size (we suggest using a smaller point size but the same font, to avoid making the page look too "busy"), keep the center alignment, and type the name of the image (such as *Apple*).

17. Save the page.

18. Now create the next page. Insert a page break, and then insert the next image

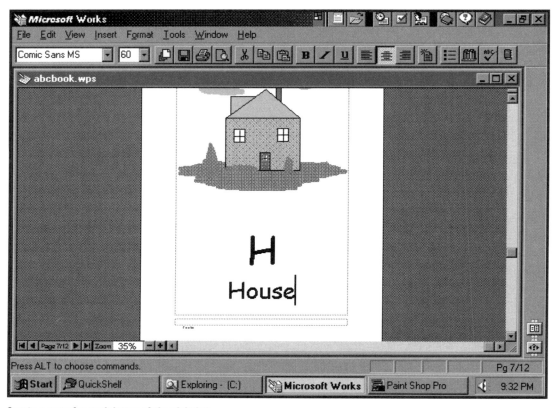

Create a page for each letter of the alphabet.

file you created in your paint or draw program. Then follow steps 11 through 17.

19. When you have created a page for each letter of the alphabet, check your work by printing all 27 pages (including the title page) on regular printer paper.

20. After making any final adjustments, use your word processor to print the pages on card stock or the heaviest paper your printer can handle. If you want a smaller book, and one that has text printed on both sides of a page, use a print utility such as ClickBook.

21. Finish the alphabet book by binding it with plastic spiral for easy page-turning. (Most copy shops provide this service.)

Products You Can Use

Paint or draw program: *CorelDraw, SmartSketch*
Works program: *ClarisWorks, Microsoft Works*
Clip art: *Corel Gallery 2, Task Force Clip Art — Really Big Edition*
Printing utility: *ClickBook*

Calendars

Two projects using original art and photos

 P R E P   T I M E :   9 0   M I N U T E S   E A C H

Materials

Desktop publishing program (or paint, draw, or word processing program) •
Printer (color preferable) • Scanner (for family calendar) • Quality card stock •
Plastic comb binding • Family pictures or your child's art

The first day of school, Christmas vacation, birthdays — these are just a few of the days that are important to your family. Most off-the-shelf calendars will help you keep track of them. But you can make a custom calendar featuring family faces or your kids' colorful art that's more fun to use — for the whole family. That's right:

for the whole family. If you're like most parents, you're constantly compensating for last-minute notices and scheduling conflicts. It's no wonder: kids today have busier schedules than we had. So have them help you keep track. Attach a pencil on a string to your calendar, put it where your kids will see it, and have them jot down their commitments.

Kid's Calendar

Calendars are good for kids of all ages. School-aged kids can use calendars like the rest of us do — to keep track of schedules and remember important dates. And younger kids can use a calendar of their very own to learn the days of the week, the months of the year, and how to count.

Before You Begin

Encourage your child to make a calendar that's truly her own, by creating one that features her in a different picture for each month of the year. She'll need to select thirteen pictures: one for the cover and twelve others to illustrate each month. She might want her first baby picture for the month of her birthday, and a picture of her playing soccer to represent the month of October. Then set aside the pictures for now — they'll be copied into the calendar at the end of the project.

Step-by-Step

To create the kid's calendar, we're going to use Microsoft Publisher for Windows 95. However, you can adapt the instructions for most desktop publishing, paint, draw, or word processing programs. (Some of these programs come with calendar templates, making the process even easier.)

1. Launch Publisher and choose Blank Page, Full Page, OK. This will be the cover page.

2. In this step, we'll set up the page. First, change the orientation to Landscape mode by choosing File, Page Setup, Landscape, and OK. Reset the margins to 1/2 inch all around by choosing Arrange, Layout Guides, and then typing .5 for each margin.

3. Now we need to add twelve pages for the months. Choose Insert, Page, and then enter 12 in the dialog box. Click on OK.

4. Save the file.

5. Create the cover page: turn to page one (use the arrows in the bottom left corner of the document) and draw a WordArt box that fits just within the margins. Let your child select a sans serif font. (We used a font named Kids in the example calendar.) Type the title of the calendar (for example, *Jeremy's Calendar 1996*) and add a space to the end of the name. (You add the space so that the title won't run together when it's made circular.) Click Update Display to see your text in the main window (or update the document automatically by closing the box).

Make the type circular by choosing the Circle shape in the shape box in WordArt. (Click on

Brainstormer

Find pictures of friends and family, pets, sports, kids' artwork, special places, favorite activities, hobbies, seasons

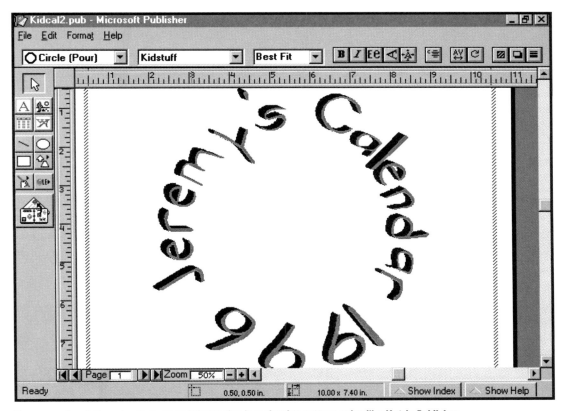

Here, we entered the calendar's cover information in a circular pattern using WordArt in Publisher.

the arrow next to Plain Text to see a list of shapes.) Rotate the circle 20 degrees by clicking on the Rotation tool in the upper right corner (it has a circular arrow on it) and entering 20 degrees. Click on OK.

Still in WordArt, give the cover type some color by clicking on the cross-hatched icon in the toolbar to display a Shading selection dialog box. Set the foreground color to Red (or another bright color) and the style to Solid Color. Click on OK.

Next, give the words a two-dimensional effect by adding a black shadow. To do so, click on the icon with the shadowed box, se-

lect a shadow effect and a black shadow color, and click on OK.

Leave the center space open. (That's where you'll place a picture of your child's face.) Save the file.

6. Create the basic design of the calendar

FamilyPC Tip: *To draw a WordArt box, click on the WordArt icon, and then click near the top left corner of the page and drag to the bottom right.*

pages: turn to page two. Create boxes for the days of the week by clicking on the Table button in the toolbar. Draw the shape of the table by moving the cursor 1 1/2 inches down the side ruler along the left margin. Then drag diagonally across the screen to where the right and bottom margins meet in the bottom right corner. A dialog box appears when you release the left mouse button.

In the dialog box, enter 6 for the number of rows and 7 for the number of columns. Leave the Table Format set to Default and click on OK. Save the file.

FamilyPC Tip: *In Publisher, to watch the effects of your changes as you make them (such as rotating the text in a WordArt box), move the dialog box so that it is not obstructing the object you are altering.*

7. Type the month: assign the table a month by creating a WordArt box that extends from the top margin to 1/8 inch above the table, and out to both side margins. In the box, select a font that matches

The Create Table dialog box lets you define the table format and the number of columns and rows.

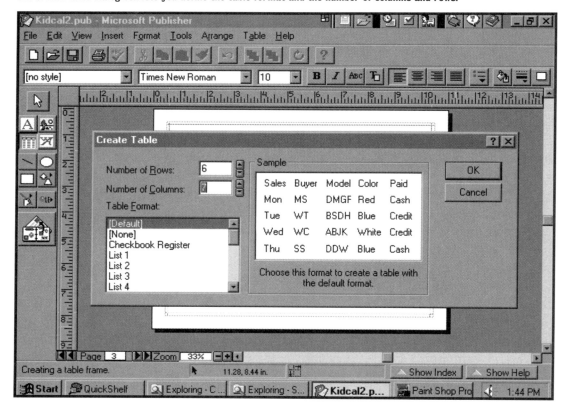

the cover (in this case Kids) and type the word *January*.

8. Type the days of the week: select the entire table (click in the table and hold down the Shift key while you click on the tabs down the left side of the table). Select the font you used in step 9 (in our example, Kids). Save the file.

Now it's time to add the days. Select the top row, set the point size to 14, set the alignment to Centered, and type the days of the week.

After you've created and finished one month of the calendar, select the entire page, copy it to the Clipboard, and paste it into the eleven remaining pages.

9. Format the days of the month: adjust the spacing for the top row as follows. Position the cursor over the horizontal line separating the days of the week from the rest of the calendar. When you do so, an adjustment indicator appears in the left-hand tab. Click and drag the adjustment divider up to just beneath the day names. Now click on one of the bottom handles of the calendar table, and drag to expand the table back down to fill the entire page.

Select the remaining five rows and change the point size to 24. Save the file.

Select the entire calendar (choose Edit, Select All) and copy it to the Clipboard.

Click back on the table and type the appropriate numbers in each row. Save the file again.

10. Create pages three to the end: turn to page three (by clicking on the page arrows in the bottom left corner). Paste

Using Photos in Calendars

If you have a scanner, you can scan your photos for the kid's calendar and save them in a format that can be imported into Publisher (.BMP and .TIF). Then create a 12-page file with the photos placed in the appropriate order. (You'll have to insert the cover photo directly into the cover page.) To print, send the main calendar document through the printer once. Then flip the stack of paper and rotate it 180 degrees. Reinsert the paper manually into the printer (one by one), and print the photos. Note that the quality of the printed pictures will suffer because you must scale them to fill the back of each page. Color images can also require a lot of hard drive space and can take some time to print.

the January template from the Clipboard (Edit, Paste). Type *February* for the month and fill in the appropriate numbers in each row. (Use a printed calendar as a reference, or consult the calendar in Windows (Control Panels, Date/Time). Save after completing each page.

Paste the January template again for each of the remaining months. On each of those pages, type the name of the month (March through December) and be sure to change the numbers in the days of the week as appropriate.

11. Personalize your calendar: add important information to various months, such as school holidays, the first and last days of school, and birthdays. To do so, click on the day of the event, select a small point size (such as 12), and type the information. You can also insert clip art to represent, for example, birthdays or sporting events. (Publisher comes with a full library; just click on the Picture button,

drag the cursor across the screen to create a picture box, and choose an image from the choices that appear. You can scale the clip-art images as necessary.)

12. Print and copy: print your calendar on regular printer paper and check each month carefully for errors. After making any corrections, print the calendar on quality card stock. Take the finished pages to a copy shop and have the pages enlarged and copied onto 11- by 17-inch paper.

To make the pages and the photos fit snugly, they will both need to be enlarged: the months by 130%, and 3 1/2-by-5 photos by 312%. You can have just the months copied in black and white, and the cover and photos in color; or you can have the entire calendar, including photos, copied in black and white. (Note: color copies usually cost $1.50 per copy.)

Be sure the copy shop copies the appropriate month's photograph on the back of the preceding month, or page. For example, the photo for January should be copied on the back of the cover page; February's photo should be copied on the back of the calendar portion of January, and so on. Also check that the photos are oriented so that when the calendar is opened, both the photo and the calendar appear right side up.

Have the copy shop trim the pages with a paper cutter and bind the pages with wire or plastic comb binding.

Use a hole punch to create a small hole in the bottom edge, centered, for hanging the calendar.

Family Calendar

A lot happens in a year. What better way to remember the past and plan for the future than with a family calendar? The key to creating a great family calendar is selecting photos that capture your best and most memorable times. So who better to select them than the whole family? Choose a night, make some popcorn, and bring out the photos. Have everyone choose a few photos they'd like to include. Who knows? Creating the family calendar may become an annual event!

Use the calendar PageWizard in Publisher to create a calendar in a snap.

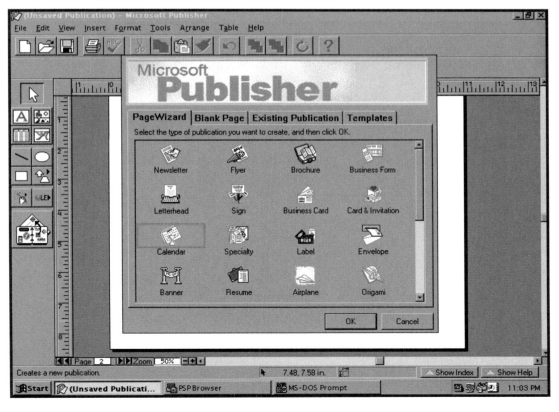

Instant Custom Calendars

Adobe PhotoDeluxe is an easy-to-use photo-editing program with a number of projects that utilize digitized photos; one of these projects is making calendars. To get to this project in PhotoDeluxe, click on the Guided Tours button, and then choose Cards & More. A file called Projects will appear. Click on Calendars (you have a choice of creating a calendar based on a month or a year), and follow the step-by-step instructions for completing the project. If you plan on using your own photos, you must connect a scanner to your computer or find another way to get your photos saved to your hard drive.

You can customize the calendar template in Publisher with your favorite photos.

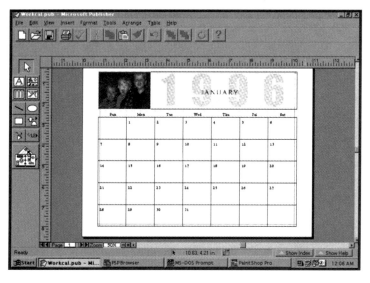

Before You Begin

Thirteen fun photos — that's what you'll need to create the family calendar. Choose one picture for the cover and one for each month. You might choose a photo from the family summer vacation, for example, to represent July or August. And there are sure to be plenty of photos to choose from for December! Then scan the photos and save them in the appropriate format for your software (usually .BMP or .TIF for Windows, or .PICT or .TIF for the Mac). For more information on digitizing images, turn to the "Creative Primer" section near the end of the book.

Step-by-Step

We're using Microsoft Publisher for Windows 95 to make the family calendar. However, you can adapt the instructions for your desktop publishing, draw, paint, or word processing program.

1. Launch Microsoft Publisher for Windows 95 and choose Calendar from the PageWizard choices.

2. Follow the step-by-step setup, choosing these options: Month (for calendars showing each month on a page), Basic (for the style of calendar), and Landscape (for the orientation).

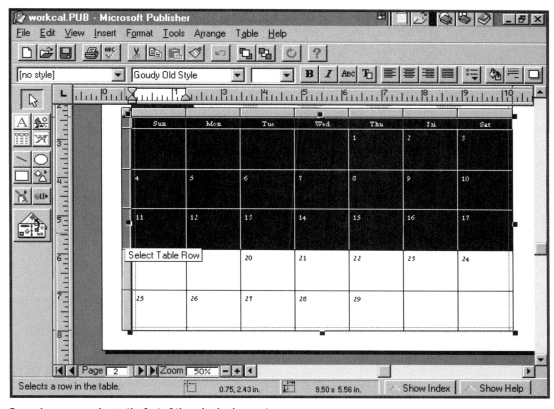

Remember, you can change the font of the calendar in one step.

3. When prompted, do the following:
   - Don't leave room for a picture, but do include space to write
   - Choose the appropriate year
   - Check all twelve months
   - Choose abbreviated day names
   - Select Sunday as the beginning of each week
   - Click on your preferred language (you can choose from eleven, including Portuguese and Finnish)

4. Finally, choose Create It, but don't ask to see the step-by-step procedure, unless you're curious about the process.

5. Delete the year, and then the box it appeared in.

6. Stretch the top frame so that it stretches the width of the calendar and is 1 13/16 inches deep from the top of the print area.

7. Save the file.

8. Create a picture box for a photo or drawing. To do so, click on the Picture icon, and then click at the top and left margins

FamilyPC Tip: *You can quickly re-place an item with the contents of the Clipboard by selecting the item and press-ing Ctrl+V.*

and drag diagonally to 2 1/4 inches down the side ruler and 3 1/4 inches across the top ruler (the black rule's current location).

9. Double-click on the box and insert your picture by locating it on your hard drive using the dialog boxes that appear.

10. Delete the word *January*.

11. Select the WordArt tool and create a text box that extends from 1/8 inch inside the rule and upper right corner of the doc-ument, out to 3 1/4 inches on the top ruler and 2 3/16 inches on the side.

12. Choose the font Impact (or a simi-lar, simple-looking typeface), type the year with two spaces between each number, and then select a light shade of gray from the color palette. Click outside the text box to see the changes take effect.

Group elements of your calendar for better control when copying or scaling. Note the handles shown here.

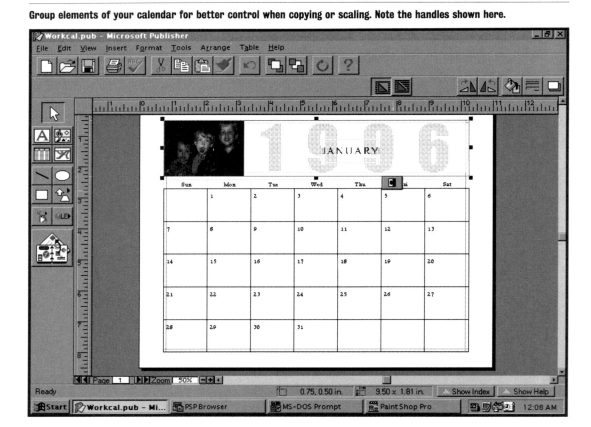

Creating a Calendar in a Draw Program

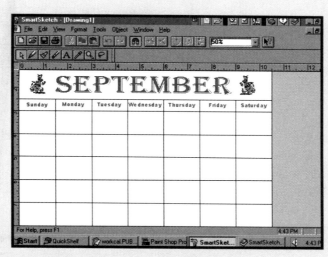

You can use the paint tools in a draw program to create a calendar, though it may take a bit more time than a program with table-making capabilities. To start, you can set up your page in Landscape mode with 1/4-inch margins.

Use your draw or paint program to create calendars.

name of the month. Move down one line, and insert the names of each day of the week. Save the file.

Now select the entire page, and then copy and paste it into eleven new pages. Change the names of the months on each page and insert the corresponding numbers in the five rows below the days of the week. Add photos or clip art. Then print, copy, and bind.

Using the Straight Line tool, draw vertical lines every 1 1/2 inches. Add horizontal lines stretching the width of the page every inch from the bottom of the document up to the 3-inch mark. Move up a 1/2 inch and create an additional horizontal line. Delete all lines above the 2 1/2-inch mark.

Use the Text tool to add the

13. Save the file.

14. Create a second WordArt text box in the center of the year, 1 3/4 inches long and 3/4 inch deep.

15. Type the name of the month (*January* to start) using Goudy Old Style (or a similar serif font) in black.

16. Select all the type in the table (hold

down the Shift key and click on the side buttons of the table), and change the font to Goudy Old Style.

17. Save the file.

18. Select the entire rectangle just above the abbreviated weekdays (including the black border, picture, year, and month). Make sure you include the entire rectangle by starting above and to the right of it and then

Finishing Your Calendars

One way to give your calendars a finished look is to have them copied on glossy card stock and bound with a plastic comb or wire binding across the top. Many copy shops offer this service or one similar to it for as little as $2.45 for small calendars such as our family calendar (10¢ per sheet for black-and-white copies; $1.25 for binding), or $21.25 for larger color calendars such as our kid's calendar ($1.50 per sheet for color copies; $1.75 for binding).

Some copy shops can also work with electronic files. Just be sure that all the elements are placed correctly by printing a test calendar before going to the copy shop.

dragging below and to the left of it. (You should get a rectangular outline of all the information if you do this step correctly.)

19. A grouping icon will appear at the bottom of the selected area. Click on it to group the information. Press Ctrl+C to copy the group to the Clipboard.

20. Move to page two (by clicking on the page arrow near the bottom left corner of the document).

21. Select all the information above the abbreviated weekdays, and press the

Delete key. Press Ctrl+V to paste in the information from the previous page.

22. Ungroup the page by clicking on the icon at the bottom of the selected area.

23. Select all the text from the abbreviated days downward. To do so, just click on any day and the table will appear. Then hold down the Shift key and click the tabs down the left side of the table.

24. Change the font to Goudy Old Style and plain type. (Click off Bold and Italic.)

25. Save the file.

26. Double-click on the picture and replace it with one of your pictures (Insert, Picture File). Or simply select the old picture, delete it, and paste in your new one.

27. Select and change the name of the month.

28. Check the page carefully, fine tuning any details. Save the file.

FamilyPC Tip: *Publisher has a variety of clip art that's perfect for illustrating the seasons. To see it, click on the Picture Tool button, create a picture box, and then select from the choices that appear.*

29. Repeat steps 20 through 28 for the remaining ten months of the year, filling in the appropriate months and different pictures. Save the file after completing each page.

30. Print the document on standard white paper and check each page for errors or inconsistencies. When you are satisfied that everything is just right, save the file, and print it on card stock.

31. Assemble the printed pages, and bind with plastic comb binding (available at most copy shops).

Products You Can Use

Paint or draw program: *CorelDraw, SmartSketch*
Works program: *ClarisWorks, Microsoft Works*
Desktop publishing program: *Adobe Paint & Publish, Microsoft Publisher CD Deluxe for Windows 95, Turbo Publisher*

Coloring Books

Four projects for young artists

 PREP TIME: 45 MINUTES EACH

Materials

Paint or draw program (for Wingdings and original-art coloring books) •
Word processing program (for clip-art and Wingdings coloring books) • Photo-editing
program and scanner (for photo coloring book) • Clip art (for clip-art coloring book) •
Print utility (optional) • Printer • Paper

Coloring books provide fun for kids of all ages. With just a few crayons, kids can entertain themselves and each other for hours. And nothing will keep their attention like a coloring book you and they made together. For young kids, create coloring books with simple objects, such as an apple, a balloon, or a big beach ball. Large pictures will give them plenty of space to color. For older kids, design coloring books with more intricate drawings.

Coloring books make great travel companions, too. Whether you're spending just an hour at the mechanic's or the day at Grandma's, coloring books are easy to take along: simply put some crayons in a bag and go.

Clip-Art Coloring Book

With thousands of images on a single CD-ROM, clip-art packages offer an endless supply of art for coloring books. You and your child can select whatever images strike your fancy. Clip art also makes it easy to create theme coloring books, such as an animal or space coloring book. Or better yet, combine different clip-art images, add captions, and have your coloring book tell a story.

Before You Begin

Peruse your clip-art library for images; if your child wants a theme coloring book, the clip-art library is also a good place to look for ideas. When you've settled on some images, note their filenames and locations (for copying and pasting), or export them from the program to your hard drive.

Step-by-Step

1. Launch your word processing program, and then open your clip-art library.

Clip-art packages, such as Corel Gallery 2, offer thousands of images from which to choose.

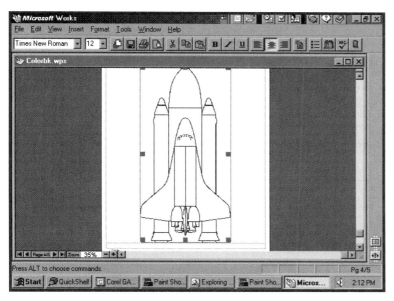

To scale art in your word processing program, click on it to select it, and then grab and move one of the corner handles that appear.

2. In your word processor, open a new document and choose center alignment for the entire document.

3. One at a time, copy each clip-art image your child has chosen to the Clipboard and paste it into your word processing document. (You can switch back and forth between your clip-art library and your word processing program in Windows 95 by clicking on the appropriate task on the taskbar at the bottom of the screen.) Alternately, if you've exported the images to your hard drive, you can now import them by using the Insert command and finding the appropriate image file in the subsequent dialog boxes.

4. Scale each image so that it takes up as much of the page as possible. Then use the Return key and the spacebar to nudge the image down to the middle of the page.

5. To check what the document will look like before you print it, use your word processor's Print Preview mode. Then make any last-minute changes and save the file.

6. Print the pages from your word processing program or from a print utility such as ClickBook.

Original-Art Coloring Book

Making coloring books from original artwork is twice the fun: First your child can help you create the images, and then he or she can color them in. Start with things that are familiar: your house, your child's school, school bus, pet, friends — even a self-portrait. For an educational twist, have your child color the same picture as it looks at different times of the year: color the house in summer and in winter, or add soccer clothes to one self-portrait and winter clothes to another.

Before You Begin

You and your child should make a list of images that you'd both like to draw. As with the other coloring-book projects, you'll have an easier time thinking of individual images if you come up with a theme first (such as animals or vehicles). When your list is complete, turn to your paint or draw program.

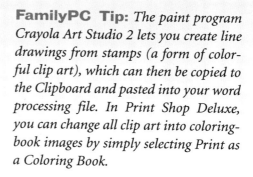

FamilyPC Tip: *The paint program Crayola Art Studio 2 lets you create line drawings from stamps (a form of colorful clip art), which can then be copied to the Clipboard and pasted into your word processing file. In Print Shop Deluxe, you can change all clip art into coloring-book images by simply selecting Print as a Coloring Book.*

Step-by-Step

1. Open a new document in a paint or draw program (such as SmartSketch).

2. Take turns with your child drawing images for your coloring book.

3. If your child wants to remove part of the drawing, select the part and simply press the Delete key. You can also use the Eraser tool, although it's slower and less accurate.

4. Encourage your child to enhance the picture. For instance, have your child add clouds to a picture of a plane, or a lake to a picture of a sailboat.

5. Next, save your masterpiece. You have three choices. You can copy your art to the Clipboard, paste it into your word processing file, and save it. You can also export each image to your hard drive (and import them all to your word processing document when it's time to print them). Or you can simply save the art in your paint program.

6. Then repeat steps 1 through 5 for each drawing to create the pages of the book.

7. Print the pages from your paint program, word processor, or print utility (such as Click-Book).

Learning to Draw

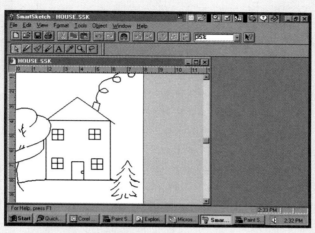

Have your child customize this drawing of a house so that it looks more like your home.

All you need to start drawing are a few tools and a few tips. We'll show you some in this example, where we draw a simple house. Begin by choosing the Rectangle tool. (In many paint and draw programs, you have to click on the Pencil to make the Rectangle tool available.) Set the line thickness to 4 points. Create a tall rectangle by clicking and dragging diagonally. This is the shell of the house.

Switch to the Straight Line tool, and draw a pitched roof on the building. Don't be concerned about how straight your lines are. In many paint and draw programs, you can go back and grab parts of lines and snap them into alignment, or you can just redraw portions of the lines.

Add a chimney using the Rectangle tool or the Freehand drawing tool. Rotate the chimney by clicking on each of its lines, selecting the Rotation tool, and grabbing one of the handles that appear around the image.

Use the drawing tools to add a door, a window, shutters, and anything else your child would like.

Photo Coloring Book

Color your world…literally. Using photos, you and your children can create a coloring book with pictures of your family, their friends, places they've been, or other people, places, and things in their lives. Here's how.

Before You Begin

Make some popcorn, grab a spot on the floor, and spend an evening with your kids going through the family photo album. For the best results, choose photos that contain images with lots of contrast. Then scan your favorite pictures and save them in a format that you can access with your photo-editing software (for example, .TIF files if you use Windows or .PICT files if you use a Mac). If you don't have a scanner, you can get the pictures scanned. See the "Resource Guide" for more information on scanners or digitizing services.

Step-by-Step

To illustrate how to take your favorite photographs and create outline images from them, we're going to use Adobe PhotoDeluxe. If you're using another photo-

Brainstormer

Coloring book themes: animals, vehicles, construction equipment, dinosaurs, letters and numbers, planes, plants, shapes, signs, sports, or symbols

editing program, launch it and then skip directly to step 5.

1. Launch Adobe PhotoDeluxe so that you can open your photographs and manipulate the images.

2. Click on the Guided Activities option to follow the preset steps for completing the project.

3. Next, click on the Transform Photo tab to see the menu

Adobe PhotoDeluxe provides you with step-by-step instructions for converting your favorite photos into digitized images.

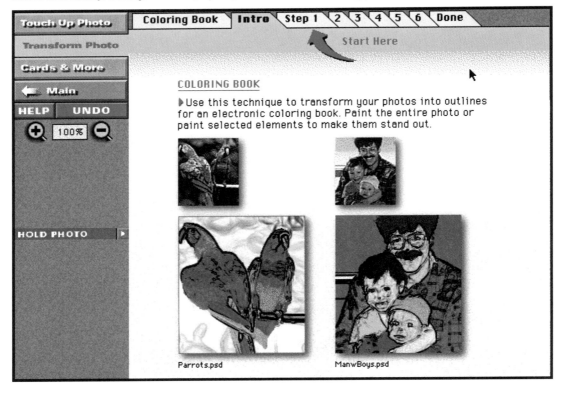

COLORING BOOK

▶ Use this technique to transform your photos into outlines for an electronic coloring book. Paint the entire photo or paint selected elements to make them stand out.

Parrots.psd

ManwBoys.psd

of projects that are available.

4. Click on the Fun tab, and then click on the Coloring Book button.

5. Follow the steps indicated on the tabs in Adobe PhotoDeluxe. The first step is to open the file of your digitized photo.

6. Choose Turn to Black and White.

7. Choose Find Edges.

8. Save the image.

9. Check the image in Print Preview to see how the final image will look when printed. The result should be an image with strong lines around each object and with the colors in the picture faded out.

10. To create another coloring-book image, click on the Coloring Book button and repeat steps 5 through 9.

You might want to remove extraneous lines and shadings with the Airbrush tool.

> **FamilyPC Tip:** *If your photo has a lot of detail, the coloring page will be rather cluttered, even after tracing the edges and fading out the background. Paint Shop Pro lets you adjust the Airbrush tool to "paint" with varying degrees of transparency. Set the color to white and the transparency to a setting between 50 and 100. Then paint out the extra details. You can also adjust the size of the "nozzle" as needed to spray in tight spots.*

11. You have three options for printing the images:

a. You can print the images directly from PhotoDeluxe (or the photo-editing program you are using).

b. You can also copy each image to the Clipboard and paste it into your word processing document so that all the images can be printed at once as a document.

c. The third option is to export all the images to your hard drive and then insert them in your word processing file. From there you can also print the images using a print utility such as ClickBook.

Wingdings Coloring Book

For something a little different, check out Wingdings or other symbol fonts that are standard in most word processing programs. Scale the symbols to fill a page and they become a picture your child can color. They're also handy for jazzing up a page in your clip-art coloring book or adding a decorative border to the pages in your photo coloring book.

Before You Begin

Take a moment and browse through the different symbol fonts in your computer. View symbols in different fonts by opening the Character Map applet located in the Accessories menu. (In Windows 95, the Character Map is located under Start, Programs, Accessories. On the Mac, use Key Caps, which is one of the Apple menu items.) Write down the different key combinations for favorite symbols. After you have listed the keystrokes for specific fonts, start creating your coloring book.

Step-by-Step

1. Launch your paint or draw program.

2. To copy the symbols on the page, begin by selecting the Text tool.

3. Choose the symbol font (such as Wingdings). Set the point size to the largest the program will allow so that when the symbol is scaled it will be less jagged. Type the appropriate keystrokes for the symbol. (Consult your notes.)

4. Select the symbol you've typed by clicking on it or by using a selecting tool (usu-

Use the Character Map to find the keystrokes for different symbols.

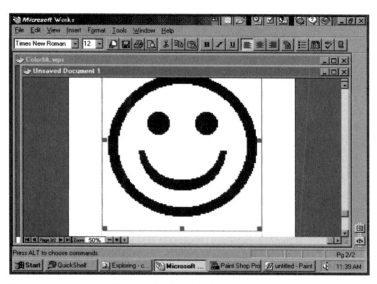

The keystroke for a smiley face in Wingdings is J.

ally a choice on the toolbar.) You can also choose Select All under Edit.

5. Copy the symbol to the Clipboard (Edit, Copy) so that you can bring the symbol into your word processing program.

> **FamilyPC Tip:** *If the Keystroke indicator in the Windows Character Map applet shows Alt+number, use the numeric keypad, not the numbers at the top of your keyboard, to produce the character.*

6. Paste the symbol into your coloring-book document by clicking on your word processing program in the taskbar, clicking on the document in which you want the

symbol to appear, and choosing Edit, Paste.

7. Scale the image so that it fills the page.

8. Center the symbol on the page by selecting it and changing the alignment to Centered. (Alignment is usually available from the toolbar or under Format, Paragraph.)

9. Insert a page break (Insert, Break) to move to the next page.

10. Save the file.

11. Repeat steps 2 through 10 to create as many coloring images as you want in the single word processing document.

12. Print the pages using your word processing program or a print utility such as ClickBook.

Products You Can Use

Paint or draw program: *Corel Photo Paint, CorelTrace (in CorelDraw), SmartSketch*
Works program: *Microsoft Works, WordPerfect Works*
Clip art: *Art Explosion, Corel Gallery 2*
Photo–editing program: *Adobe PhotoDeluxe, Serif PhotoPlus (in Serif Publishing Suite)*
Printing utility: *ClickBook*

Cookie Cutouts

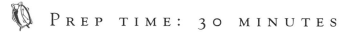

PREP TIME: 30 MINUTES

Materials
**Paint or draw program • Printer • Paper •
Scissors or craft knife • Cookie dough**

Next time your child wants to bake a batch of cookies, add your computer into the mix and you'll never make the same ones twice! Using clip art or paint tools, you and your child can create cutout patterns of snowmen for Christmas cookies or jack-o'-lanterns if it's Halloween. But it needn't be a special holiday; as all kids know, cookies just taste better when they look like a few of their favorite things. So make stars and stripes, bikes and kites, flowers and trees — even bugs. (Remember, these are your *child's* favorite things!) After you print the cut out patterns, your child can trim them, then place them on the unbaked dough, and cut out the cookie shapes. Now you're ready to bake, decorate, and enjoy!

Before You Begin

This one's easy: All you and your child need to do before you start is make a list of the things you want to create. For instance, if you are making Halloween cookies, put ghosts, goblins, and jack-o'-lanterns on your list.

Step-by-Step

1. Launch your draw or paint program.

2. Set up your page so that it will match the shape you'll be drawing: Use landscape mode for wide images, or portrait mode for tall ones.

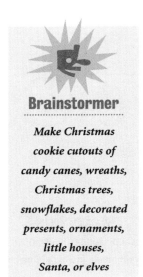

Brainstormer

Make Christmas cookie cutouts of candy canes, wreaths, Christmas trees, snowflakes, decorated presents, ornaments, little houses, Santa, or elves

3. With your child as art director, draw the first cookie cutout shape.

4. If the drawing appears too small when you finish it, try scaling it. (If your program can't scale, copy the image to the Clipboard, launch your word processing program, and paste the image into a document.) To scale the image, click on it, grab one of the corner handles that appear, and drag.

5. Save the file.

6. Repeat steps 2 through 5 for each cookie shape.

7. Print your cookie cutouts.

8. Have your child cut along the outline of the shapes to create the cookie cutouts.

9. By now, your kids are probably clamoring for cookies. Begin by preheating the oven. Then on a lightly floured countertop, roll out the dough from your favorite cookie recipe to about a 1/8-inch thickness. If the dough is too sticky, sprinkle extra flour over the top of it.

Place the paper cutouts on top of the dough. Using a

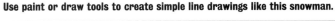

Use paint or draw tools to create simple line drawings like this snowman.

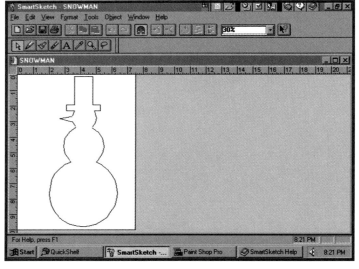

Learning to Draw

At first, using the computer to draw may not seem easy or intuitive. As with most things, however, getting started is just a matter of learning how to use the tools and knowing a few tricks of the trade. It also helps to start with something simple. So here we'll describe how to draw a snowman, but you can apply the principles to any design you'd like to make. And although we'll use SmartSketch, you use any paint or draw program.

Open a new document, and set up the page in Portrait mode. Choose View, Show Rulers.

First, you'll draw the base of the snowman. Click on the Pencil tool, and then select the Oval tool. Choose a line thickness of 2 points. Click and drag diagonally until the circle is the size your child wants. Select the cir-

Save time by copying and scaling objects rather than redrawing them.

cle with the Pointer tool, and drag it to the bottom center of the screen.

Next, make the snowman's middle by copying the circle to the Clipboard and pasting it back into the document. Click and drag the second circle so that it doesn't touch the first circle. Select the second circle and scale it to 60 percent using Tools, Scale by Percent. Save the file.

Now make the snowman's head by copying the second circle to the Clipboard and pasting it back into the docu- ment. Click and drag this cir-

cle so that it is not touch- ing the other two. Scale it by 60 per- cent. Save the file again.

Select the middle circle and place it on top of the largest circle, so that the two overlap about a quar- ter of an inch. Now place the smallest circle on top of the middle one, using the same amount of overlap.

Create a hat and a rim by drawing two rectangles with the Rectangle tool (from the Pencil mode pulldown menu, click on the Pencil tool and then on the Rectangle tool), using a line thickness of 2 points.

Add a carrot nose using the Straight Line tool (another choice available by clicking on the Pencil tool), with a line thick- ness of 2 points. Save the file.

continued on the next page

continued

Use the Selection tool and the Delete key (or Edit, Clear) to select and delete every overlapping line.

Next, we want to group all the parts to create one snowman that can be moved or modified as a whole. Use the

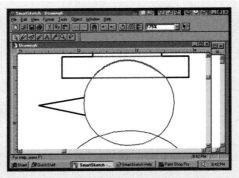

Delete the overlapping lines so that you don't inadvertently cut along the wrong line in your printed cutout.

Selection tool again and drag the cursor diagonally across the entire image to select it. Choose Object, Create Group. Scale the entire image so that it is no more than 5 inches tall (Tools, Scale). Save your file again. Now you're ready to print the snowman and bake away.

knife, cut the dough, following the outline of the template. Remove the paper and the dough that has been cut away.

Set the cookies on an ungreased cookie sheet and bake.

When the cookies are thoroughly cooled, your kids can start to decorate them. Using tubes of decorator's icing (available at gro-cery stores), colored sugar, and other cake-decorating supplies, they can jazz up the cookies by drawing stripes across stockings or adding big goofy smiles to snowmen.

Products You Can Use

Draw or paint program: *CorelDraw, Flying Colors, Paint (in Windows), SmartSketch*

Finger Puppets

How to create a puppet cast and put on a show

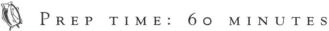 Prep time: 60 minutes

Materials
**Paint or draw program • Clip art • Printer (color preferable) •
Paper • Scissors • Glue • Chopsticks (optional)**

Colorful and easy to make, finger puppets provide instant entertainment for young kids. Whether you're running errands or taking a roadtrip, always keep a few finger puppets with you. They're small, so you can easily fit them inside a jacket pocket or a glove compartment. Then you'll be ready for the inevitable moment when  your kids are restless and wondering, "How much longer?"

At home, finger puppets can provide hours of fun. You and your kids can create a whole cast of puppet characters. Then set up a puppet stage, invite some friends, assign the parts, hit the lights, and let their imaginations do the rest.

Before You Begin

What characters should you and your child choose for puppets? To jump-start your imaginations, scroll through your clip-art library — either a stand-alone package such as Corel Gallery 2, or one that comes with a paint or draw program such as SmartSketch. You can also make your own characters using the paint tools that come with your paint or draw program.

Brainstormer

Make puppets of plants, trees, animals, people, vehicles, buildings, clouds, the sun, or the moon

Step-by-Step

Although we use SmartSketch to demonstrate this project, you can apply the instructions to any draw or paint program with similar functions.

1. Launch SmartSketch or the program you'll be using and choose your page orientation. In SmartSketch, choose Format, Document, and Match Printer.

2. Find your clip-art image. In SmartSketch, open EasyArt Finder (under Help) and select the character you want from the index. Click on the character you want and drag it into your document.

3. Add rulers to the screen (if they are not already visible) by choosing the menu option View, Rulers.

4. Scale the image so that the base is an inch and a half wide (just measure it with the ruler across the top of the page) or large enough to accommodate a child's finger. (In SmartSketch, the Scale command is located under Tools.)

5. Now save the file.

Position the image so it's touching its mirror image.

6. Drag the image to the left side of the page.

7. Next, you'll create the "back" of the puppet. Select the image, copy it to the Clipboard, and paste it just to the right of the original. (You can create a copy also by choosing the Edit, Duplicate menu options.)

8. To flip the new image, select it, and then choose Tools, Flip Horizontal.

Make the figure larger by scaling it.

9. Adjust the placement of the flipped image until it just touches its mirror image.

10. Save the file again.

11. To see how the image will look printed, click on File, Print Preview. If necessary, scale both images so that they both will print on one page. Also, if the images to-

Make a Puppet Show Theater

A large cardboard box makes the perfect beginning of a puppet theater. Start with one that's at least 20 inches wide by 30 inches long by 16 inches deep. Cut out most of one side of the box, leaving about 6 inches of cardboard at the edges and corners. This is the bottom of your theater, through which the puppet masters will hold their puppets. Cut a stage "window," leaving 2 or 3 inches of cardboard on all sides of the window.

Have the puppeteers decorate their theater with things such as wrapping paper, garland, crepe paper, markers, or crayons. Next, using paper and crayons, have the kids create a colorful backdrop for their puppet show. (You can also use your computer to print, in color, a tiled landscape taken from a digitized photo. Print the image on multiple pages.) Tape the backdrop on the inside of the box, so that it hangs down behind where the performance will take place. Then have the kids add a big sign with the name of the featured production.

Finally, use a few flashlights for stage lights or spotlights. (Ask some kids in the audience to act as stagehands and hold the flashlights.) Now you're ready to start the show.

Altering Clip-Art and Making Puppets from Scratch

You can use a draw or paint program to add your own touches to puppets, such as a mustache, a funny hat, or a pattern. Use the Arrow tool to select the image, and choose Object, Edit Object. Then use the tools to make your changes. For example, use the Paint Bucket to change a cow's black-and-white spots to patterned fills to make a calico cow. Or use the Pencil tool to draw a bow on a fairy tale dragon to help the fragile tail withstand the rigors of a puppet show. When you have finished making the alterations, continue with step 4 and scale the image.

To create a puppet from

Use the paint tools in SmartSketch to alter EasyArt images.

scratch (without using clip art), draw the basic outline using the Pencil tool with a smooth, 1-point line thickness. For detailed work, magnify the drawing by 200 or 400 percent. Remember to se-

lect and then delete the parts you don't want, and bend or stretch lines for fun effects. Use the Paint tool to fill the image or colored lines for shading. When your design is complete, continue with step 4.

gether are wider than they are tall, change the orientation of the page to Landscape (under Print Setup). If you do change the page setup, you must select Format, Document, Match Printer again (as in step 1) so that the screen matches your document.

12. Print the puppet.

13. If you are using a noncolor printer, have your child add color with markers, crayons, or pens.

14. Have your child fold the printed images so that one side is directly over the other. Then have

FamilyPC Tip: *If you don't have a color printer, your child can color in the puppets. First, though, you'll need to change your clip art to black and white before dragging it into the document. In SmartSketch, you can change EasyArt to line drawings by clicking on the color mode button in the upper right corner of the EasyArt box.*

your child carefully cut along the outline of the picture except where the images meet.

15. Next, glue the edges of both sides together, leaving just the base open so that your child can easily slide a finger inside the puppet.

16. To make the puppet more rigid, run a strip of glue down the center of the back of one side of the cutout clip art and place a chopstick on it. Then add a small amount of glue around the edges and on the exposed side of the chopstick and press the other side of the clip art into place. Wipe away any excess glue.

Products You Can Use

Paint or draw program: *Flying Colors, Paint (in Windows), Paint module in ClarisWorks, SmartSketch*
Clip art: *Corel Gallery 2, Task Force Clip Art — Really Big Edition*

Mobiles

PREP TIME: 60 MINUTES

Materials

Paint or draw program • Clip art • Printer (preferably color) •
Paper (preferably card stock) • Scissors • Needle and thread • Glue or paste •
Wire, chopsticks, or posterboard

High over head! It's a bird! It's a plane! No, even better, it's a mobile made by your child.

Young kids are fascinated by mobiles so, they're sure to enjoy creating their very own. There's no limit to the mobiles you and your child can make for any occasion. Funny mobiles with clowns or cartoons make great

party decorations; festive ones with seasonal motifs are perfect for holidays.

You can also make mobiles that enhance your child's day-to-day routines, too. A mobile of stars and planets that glow in the dark makes bedtime more fun. And a mobile with letters or numbers is a playful and instructive reminder for any youngster.

Before You Begin

You and your child should decide on a theme for the mobile. If you're having trouble coming up with an idea, explore your clip-art collection. When your child finds an image that's just right, help select other images with the same theme. Note the location of each (for accessing later).

Step-by-Step

The following instructions are for Smart-Sketch, but you can adapt them to any paint

Brainstormer
....

Make mobiles of

planes, planets,

birds, flying insects,

fish, numbers,

letters, trucks,

horses, dogs, cats,

reptiles, or spaceships

or draw program that supports flipping (horizontally and vertically) and scaling.

1. Launch a draw or paint program (such as SmartSketch) and open a new document.

2. Display rulers on the screen so that you can be precise in scaling your art. (In SmartSketch, choose View, Show Rulers if they aren't already on the screen.)

3. Set up your page by choosing Landscape mode for wide images or Portrait mode for tall images.

4. If you are using SmartSketch and a clip-art image from the built-in EasyArt collection, open the EasyArt index, find the image, click on it, and drag it to the right side of your page. Continue with step 6.

If you are not using EasyArt, open the clip-art package and have your child select an image. Export the image to your hard drive as a .TIF file. Then use File, Import to bring the image into your

Use the EasyArt Finder in SmartSketch to locate clip-art images in the program.

paint or draw program. If your art program does not support importing, copy the image from the clip-art package to the Clipboard, switch to your paint or draw program, and paste the image into the document.

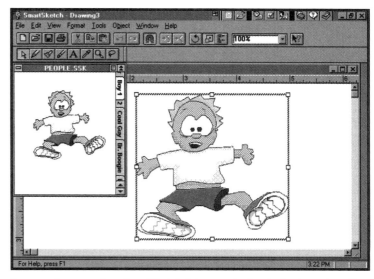

Some programs, such as SmartSketch, let you make images larger and smaller.

5. Drag the image to the right side of your document.

6. View the entire workspace to make sure that none of the image is spilling off the page. (In SmartSketch, choose View, Show Page.)

7. Save the file.

8. Next, you'll create a duplicate of the art so that you'll have a two-sided image for the mobile. Select the image. Then either copy the image to the Clipboard and paste it or, if your program supports duplicating, choose Duplicate. (In SmartSketch, choose Edit, Duplicate.)

9. Flip the new image horizontally. (In SmartSketch, choose Tools, Flip Horizontal.)

10. Drag the duplicate image just to the left of the original, with less than 1/8 inch between the two, and aligned so that one can be folded over the other.

11. Scale the images to an appropriate size for your mobile without overflowing the mar-

gins. (To scale images in SmartSketch, select Tools, Scale.)

12. Save your work again.

13. Print the image using quality paper to get the best possible output. (Heavy card stock prevents curling, but check the maximum thickness your printer can handle.)

14. Have your child fold the paper so that

FamilyPC Tip: *If you have a non-color printer and you are using a Smart-Sketch EasyArt image, you can convert the image to black-and-white line art by simply clicking the Color button above the image before you drag it from the catalog.*

Making a Frame for Your Mobile

You can use almost anything fairly rigid to make a mobile frame. Two crossed chopsticks glued together work well. Or you could use an old wire coat hanger, bent in an S shape or another shape or cut into rods. You can also use heavy paper or posterboard.

For a paper or posterboard frame, use card stock or paper that has at least the thickness of a manila folder. Draw a big spiral on it and cut out the shape. Use a needle and thread to poke holes in the frame and hang the art.

If you use a coat hanger or chopsticks for a frame, tie the ends of the thread (attached to the art) to the frame, spacing the art so the mobile looks balanced when hung.

---

both images are aligned, back to back. Then have him apply glue sparingly to both sides, press the sides together, and wipe away the excess glue. Let dry for 20 minutes.

15. Repeat steps 4 through 14 until all the images have been printed and glued.

Duplicate and flip the art to make a mirror image.

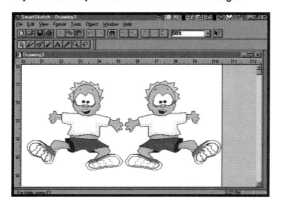

16. Trim the outlines of the images using scissors or a craft knife.

17. Poke a hole through the top of each trimmed piece of art using a threaded needle (with at least 16 inches of thread), and pull the needle through.

18. Tie the threaded mobile to the mobile frame. See "Making a Frame for Your Mobile" (above).

19. Hang the finished mobile using light string, fishing line, or thread. Make sure it's hung high enough so it's out of the reach of infants and toddlers.

Products You Can Use

Paint or draw program: *CorelDraw, Flying Colors*
Clip art: *Art Explosion — 40,000 Images, Corel Gallery 2*

Multimedia-grams

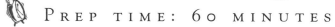

PREP TIME: 60 MINUTES

Materials
Multimedia authoring program • Microphone and sound capability •
Photos • Scanner or digitizing service • Disks or an online service

Ah, for the good old days: sitting with family and friends, flipping through photo albums, and telling the stories behind each picture. With family and friends often at a distance today, this can seem like just another lost tradition.

Now you can keep in touch by sending multi-media-grams: short, two-minute

narrated slide-shows. Collect six to eight photos, and you and your child can show — and — tell Grandpa about your summer vacation or the first day at school. However, no one has to be miles away to enjoy receiving multi-media-grams. Help make one for your child's best friend — even if she's right next door.

Before You Begin

You and your child should decide on a topic. Make sure it's a topic that your child will be happy talking about so she'll feel comfortable as the narrator. Then collect photos on the topic, and have the pictures digitized to make them accessible to your computer.

You'll be limited to six to eight pictures if you want to include sound in your multimedia-gram and still fit it on a disk. So select a topic with a narrow focus: for example, choose a particular event or do a day-in-the life type of presentation.

Brainstormer

Create multimedia presentations of pets, day-in-the-life, Christmas day, birthday party, summer vacation, fishing trip, Little League team, or learning to swim

After your child has chosen the pictures, she should decide what the title screen should look like, and the two of you should jot down ideas for narration. After you feel comfortable with the ideas, jump into creating your slide show.

Step-by-Step

We're using Kid Pix Studio for this project, but you can adapt the instructions for your favorite multimedia authoring program.

1. Launch Kid Pix Studio, and go to the Kid Pix area to create the pages or slides of your multimedia-gram.

2. Open a picture by going to the File menu and choosing Open Picture. If you are bringing in a snapshot from a PhotoCD, use Import Picture. This will be your title page.

3. Add text to the page by selecting the Typewriter tool (called the Text tool in other programs). Choose a big, plain font, click where you want the title to begin, and type your title. Press the Return key and type your child's name using the same font.

Here, several digitized photos and artwork are combined to create the opening title page for a slide show called "My Best Friends."

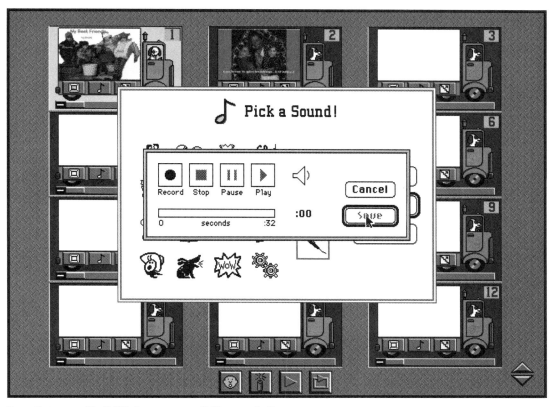

Recording a sound in Kid Pix is as easy as clicking on a button.

4. Save the first draft of the title page. Choose File, Save Picture, and type the file name Page1.

5. To give the page a humorous look, you can add special elements such as a bee flying around one person's head. (You'll find a bee and lots more in Kid Pix Studio's stamps.) Think of ways to use paint tools and some special effects to add additional color to the page.

6. Save the file again after you've made all your changes.

7. Open a new picture; this will be the second frame of the show. Add text and art elements. When you're finished, save the document as Page2.

8. Make additional pages for each frame.

9. For the final frame, include an image that wraps up the presentation.

10. To assemble your presentation, choose File, Return to Studio, SlideShow.

11. To insert each of your saved pages into

its place in the presentation, select the appropriate frame (denoted in Kid Pix as Moving Vans), and click the Picture Frame icon.

FamilyPC Tip: *To help your child deliver a lively narration, ask her to describe the photos as you're both selecting them. Try to keep the descriptions short — sound files can take up large amounts of disk space. You might even run through the photos twice, to make your child more comfortable.*

12. Now it's time for your child to step up to the mic. Click on the Music Note button at the base of each Moving Van, and then select Record a Sound. Make sure the microphone is properly plugged into the computer and functioning, and then have your child give a short narration for each frame.

13. To add transitions between screens, click on the Transition button (to the right of the music note on the Moving Vans).

14. To make sure the screens, narrations, and transitions are working well together,

Kid Pix Studio comes with sixteen transitions.

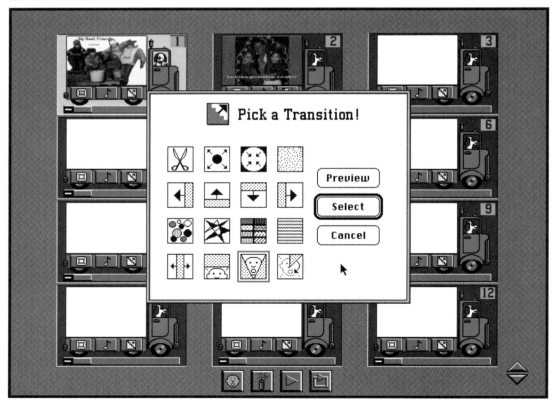

play your slide show. To do so, simply click on the Play button at the base of the trucks.

15. Now it's time to save the presentation as a self-playing file, so that the recipients can play the slide show without having Kid Pix Studio. (They do, however, need to be using a compatible system: Windows or Macintosh.) Choose File, Standalone. Then choose File, Save a Slideshow in case you want to make any further changes before sending off your work. (Standalone shows cannot be edited but Slideshows can.)

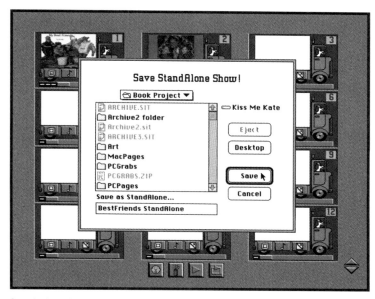

Stand-alone format saves your slide show as a self-playing file.

16. Before you send the file, go to Explorer in Windows 95 (or check the Finder on the Mac) to make sure the file is no larger than 1.4MB, so it can fit on a high-density disk. If the file is too large, consider deleting some sounds — they occupy a lot of disk space compared to photos.

FamilyPC Tip: *If your slide show is larger than 1.4MB and you'd rather not delete sounds or other elements of the presentation, use a compression program to make the file smaller. In Windows 95, you can use a file compression program such as WinZip; on the Mac side, you can use Stuffit. Both programs enable you to make a file that is self-extracting; the people who receive the slide show need only double-click on the file icon and extract it to their hard drive to access the file.*

17. Make an instruction sheet telling the recipient to copy the file to the hard drive and then double-click on its icon to play it. Save the instructions as a Text Only file. If you are mailing the slide show, include a printed version of the instructions with the disk. If you are sending the slide show electronically, send the instruction file as a message.

Products You Can Use

Multimedia authoring program: *Kid Pix Studio, Monstrous Media (formerly Kids Studio), Studio M*
Compression program: *Stuffit Deluxe, WinZip*

Pinwheels

 PREP TIME: 30 MINUTES

Materials

Paint or draw program • **Clip art** • **Printer (color preferable)** •
Card stock • **Thin, approximately 14-inch, wooden handle** • **Tape** • **Pushpin** •
Clear contact paper or plastic laminate (optional)

Pinwheels are one of life's simple pleasures. Their finely curved blades effortlessly turn a passing breeze into a spiral of colors, and all that kids need to enjoy one is to blow with all their might.

You and your child can make some spectacular spinners that are not only unique and colorful, but

also every bit as fun as those you buy. Make quite a few, and your child can share his pinwheels with friends, bring them to a school picnic, set them spinning near the barbecue, or give them out at his next birthday party. For no matter what the occasion, pinwheels are sure to be a crowd pleaser.

Before You Begin

What are your child's favorite colors? The answer and some festive clip art are all you need to create some fabulous pinwheels.

Step-by-Step

We'll be using the draw program Smart-Sketch to make the pinwheels, but you can adapt the instructions for your favorite draw or paint program.

1. Launch SmartSketch. Set the document size to 8 by 10.5 inches (Format, Document, Match Printer) and the page orientation to Portrait mode (the default).

2. You'll need to see the entire page, so choose View, Show Page.

FamilyPC Tip: *To draw a square in SmartSketch, use the Rectangle tool, and as you drag the cursor across the page, watch the rulers at the top and side of the document. Keep the length of the shape equal to the width. When the measurements on the top and side ruler match, a large circle will appear on the cursor. Release the left mouse button.*

3. Create the outline for the blades by drawing a large, 8-inch square. In Smart-Sketch, select the Pencil tool, click on the Pencil mode pulldown menu, and then select the Rectangle tool. Select a solid, black, 1-point line thickness, and draw a square the width of the page.

4. As you'll see in a moment, the blades are created by cutting the paper into four sections, and folding and pinning each section to the center. So to create the cutting lines, draw two diagonal lines extending from the corners to create an X. In SmartSketch, draw the lines by choosing the Pencil tool and Straight Line mode.

5. Save the file.

6. Create a design for the pinwheel using clip art and the paint tools in your pro-

You'll choose the Rectangle tool first to create a square that will mark the outline of the blades.

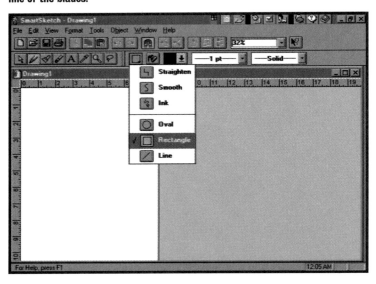

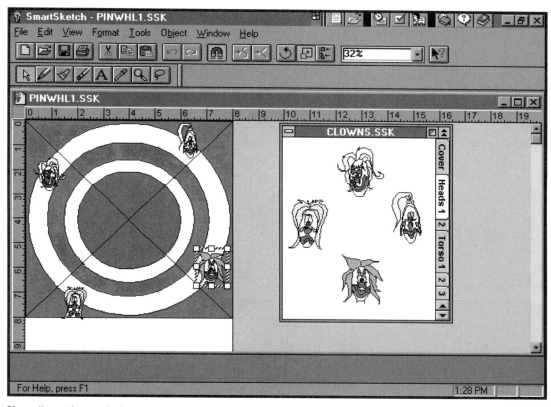

Place clip-art images in the corners of the pinwheel.

gram. To see how we created the pinwheel shown here, see the sidebar "Carnival Pinwheel Design."

7. Next, you'll place clip art in a corner of the square. Have your child select a clip-art image from your clip-art source. If you're using SmartSketch, look in the EasyArt books (located in the Help menu under EasyArt Finder). Drag the clip-art just to the left of a diagonal on the pinwheel page.

8. Repeat step 7 for each corner of the pinwheel.

FamilyPC Tip: *If you'll be making more than one pinwheel design, create a generic pinwheel file by saving the page under both a generic name (such as pw-form) and a new name (such as pw-1) in step 5 in the directions or before adding color in the "Carnival Pinwheel Design" sidebar. Having a pinwheel template will save you time and steps when creating future pinwheels with different designs and colors. Just load the generic file every time you want to create a new pinwheel.*

9. Scale the clip art until your child decides it's just right.

10. If necessary, rotate the clip art so that the images are all pointing out from the center of the square. To do so, choose Tools, Rotate; grab a handle around the image, and then rotate the image clockwise or counterclockwise (either will work). If you are using clip art of faces, for example, keep the chins to the center of the pinwheel.

11. Ask your child whether he or she would like to make any other design changes, such

FamilyPC Tip: *For better control when positioning art elements in Smart-Sketch, choose Tools and turn off the Snap option.*

as deleting lines across white space. (To do so, select the line segment or segments and use the Delete key.)

12. Print samples on regular paper to check the design. If any changes are necessary, make them now.

Rotate your art so that the base of the art is pointing to the center.

Carnival Pinwheel Design

To create the carnival pinwheel, begin by following steps 1 through 5. Next, you'll need four different-sized circles that all share the same center. To draw the first circle, place the cursor in the upper left corner, 2 inches from the left and 2 inches down, on the upper left diagonal. Click and hold, and then follow the diagonal down toward the bottom right corner

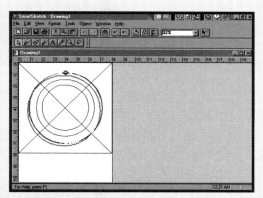

These circles look jagged on the screen, but they'll be smooth when printed.

until you are 6 inches over and 6 inches down. (Watch the rulers!) The result should be a circle, about 4 inches in diameter, centered over the diagonals.

To create the second circle, select all four parts of the first circle (they are technically separated by the diagonals) with your cursor, and duplicate (choose Edit, Duplicate). Drag the second circle directly over the original, choose Tools, Scale by Percent, and enter 125 percent. Click outside to deselect the circle.

Repeat this copy-and-paste process two more times so that you end up with four circles. You may need to use the magnifying glass to zoom in up to 800 percent to make precise adjustments in alignment. Save the file.

FamilyPC Tip: *When placing circles (or squares) on top of one another, watch for a bold, small circle to appear next to the cursor. This circle indicates that the shapes are exactly aligned.*

Fill each ring with color. To add colors in SmartSketch, select the Brush tool, then the Paint Bucket, and finally the color from the Fill Color tab. For this pinwheel, we alternated the colors red and white in the outer rings by clicking with the Fill tool where we wanted the specific color.

Pour in a contrasting color or colors in the center quadrants. (We used blue.) To complete the pinwheel, continue with step 7.

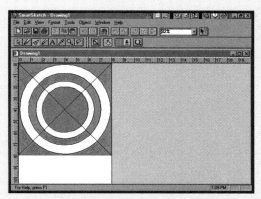

Use the Fill tool to add solid colors to your design.

13. Save the file again.

14. Print the final result on card stock. Flip the printed output and send it through the printer again so that the back will be printed as well.

15. Trim the paper outside the square using scissors. For a more rigid pinwheel, sandwich your pinwheel square between two sheets of clear contact paper or plastic laminate.

16. Cut a slit halfway down each diagonal.

17. Lay your paper on a table. Take the left corner of the triangle at the top of the page and bring it to the center of the X. Tape it in place using a small square of clear tape. Turn the paper clockwise so another triangle is at the top, and fold the corner in.

Brainstormer

Make pinwheels featuring stars and stripes for the Fourth of July; cakes and candles for a birthday; moons, stars, and planets for a sleepover; dolphins and starfish for a day at the beach

Repeat this process for all four corners. For a longer-lasting pinwheel, glue a small washer to the center of the paper design.

18. Mount the pinwheel on a wooden handle (such as a chopstick or a 1/4-inch dowel). Be sure the wood is at least 14 inches long.

19. Use a pushpin pushed through the center of the pinwheel to fasten the blades to the handle. To let the pinwheel spin more freely, leave the pin only partially pushed in.

Products You Can Use

Paint or draw program: *CorelDraw, Flying Colors, SmartSketch, Paint module in ClarisWorks, Paint in Windows*
Clip art: *Corel Gallery 2, Masterclips 35,000 Premium Clip Art Image Collection*

Stencils

 Prep time: 15 minutes

Materials

**Paint, draw, or word processing program • Clip art (optional) •
Printer • Paper • Scissors or craft knife • Stencil brush • Stencil paint • Rags**

Stencilling is an activity your kids will enjoy, whether they're decorating a wall, a door, an old desk chair, or an expanse of poster paper. Poster paper is particularly good to use with young stencillers, and it's all you need to make stencilling a terrific party activity for a slightly older crowd: Just stretch out

rolls of white or off-white paper on the floor or tape it to the wall, and let your partygoers go wild with poster paints and party stencils. Create stencils of simple images such as balloons, flowers, boats, and stars, or just a variety of shapes. Or, if it's a nice day, your budding artisits can try sidewalk stencilling using chalk.

Before You Begin

The most important aspect of stencilling is the subject of the cutout. So help your design expert — your child — come up with a few ideas for templates. (You might want to look through some home design magazines beforehand to see what types of shapes make the best stencils and what combinations of elements work best.) If you're thinking about including stencilling as a party activity, jot down a list of objects that a group of partygoers might like to color in together.

After you both decide on the subject for the stencil, you have a number of choices for sources. Just remember that no matter how complicated a piece of art looks, what's important is the pattern that you cut out with scissors or a craft knife. Try to keep the outline of the shape simple.

FamilyPC Tip: *To create a stencil pattern using clip art, choose Paste repeatedly when you're in your word processing program. To create a stencil with two or more different symbols (for example, leaf-heart-leaf), press the keys in succession while you're still in your paint or draw program. Then select all the symbols and copy them to the Clipboard.*

Symbols fonts

The most basic source for stencil images is the symbol fonts already in your computer (such as Wingdings). Using symbols, you can create, for example, repeating patterns of flowers and vines, a pointing hand, or an airplane. To see the symbols of a particular font, use the Character Map in Windows or Key Caps on the Mac.

Clip art

Whether it's from online libraries or from a CD-ROM, clip art offers a limitless supply of images from which to make stencils. For instance, Corel Gallery 2, which features some 15,000 images, includes fancy stencil art such as curlicues under the category Design, and a number of kid-theme stencils under such categories as Signs.

You can quickly create repeating patterns with symbol fonts such as Wingdings.

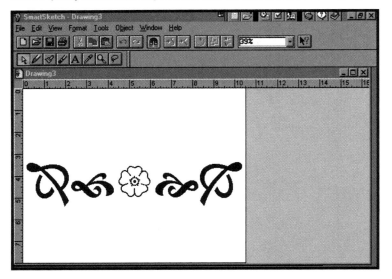

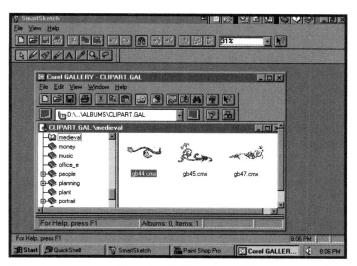

You can copy and paste items directly from clip-art libraries such as Corel Gallery 2 into your stencil document, or export those images to your hard drive and insert them into your document.

FamilyPC Tip: *If you don't like a change you make, you can undo it quickly by pressing Ctrl+Z in Windows or Command+Z on the Mac.*

Original art

For an original look, take advantage of your child's (or your own) artistic talents. Whether it's a stencil as simple as the words Keep Out! or a freehand-drawn pattern, use the text and paint tools in your paint or draw program to create it. One last thing before you start: It's also important that you have a program capable of scaling. If your paint or draw program can't scale, try your word processing program.

Step-by-Step

1. Launch the program in which you'll be creating and printing your image. Then set up the page to match the orientation of the art (Landscape mode for wide images or Portrait mode for long, tall images). If you will be creating a template larger than a standard sheet of paper, be sure to use a program that supports tiling.

2. Find your image (whether it's clip art, symbols, or original art) and insert it into the document you'll be printing.

3. Make any additional alterations to the image, such as flipping it vertically or horizontally, so that your stencil design is symmetrical.

Using Your New Stencils

As with all craft projects, preparation is important. Before you start to apply paint to your stencilling surface, use a ruler and a pencil to lightly mark where the edge of your stencil should be placed. You can use almost any type of paint, but oil-based stencil cremes and paints are good for beginners, and they work on nearly every surface. The trick is to use paints that are thick and won't run under the stencil. If your kids will be helping you paint, choose a nontoxic, water-based paint (for easy cleanup). For party projects such as stencilling long rolls of paper (available at most craft stores), use poster paints (made from powder mixed with water). If you'll be using stencils on your sidewalk, get lots of fat sticks of chalk.

If you're using paint, experiment first on cardboard, using different color combinations and applicators. The best tool for applying paint is a stencil brush with a flattened bottom (available at most craft stores), but you can also use regular brushes or sponges. And you can give the finish a nice textured look if you blot the paint on with crumpled newspaper or a coarse rag.

When you've finished practicing, apply tape across the corners of your stencil to securely fasten it to the surface you are painting. Then apply the paint using light dabbing motions or strokes so that you don't apply too much paint.

As soon as you are finished, carefully peel back the stencil. Lay your stencil on a newspaper, wiping excess paint off the stencil using a damp rag or cloth.

---

4. Scale the image or symbol to fill the page or until your child says When!

5. Print the image or symbol on card stock. Make a copy for each color in the stencil.

FamilyPC Tip: *You can use similar steps to create stencils for names or words. If you want to create a large word stencil, print only one letter on each page. Just be sure that all the letters are scaled to the same size.*

6. Using a craft knife or scissors, cut out the part of the design you'll be painting. If you'll be using a particular stencil repeatedly, you should consider coating each side of the stencil with two or three coats of clear acrylic finish. This way you can use them again and again, cleaning them after each use.

Products You Can Use

Paint or draw program: *CorelDraw, Flying Colors, SmartSketch*
Works program: *ClarisWorks, Microsoft Works*
Clip art program: *Art Explosion — 40,000 Images, Corel Gallery 2*

School Time Fun

Kids aren't the only ones learning during the school year. Parents are, too. We learn with our kids as we help them do their homework, brainstorm with them for an idea for a special project, or watch them perform in a school concert. We know that time spent learning with our kids is invaluable. But you don't learn just by doing homework. And certainly the school year can't be all work and no play! This is what the projects in this section are all about. From bookplates to school time games, these are crafts you and your child will enjoy doing together during the school year. They'll teach both you and your child some new computer techniques, challenge your creativity, and help you have some fun along the way.

Baseball Cards

PREP TIME: 40-60 MINUTES

Materials

Works program or draw program combined with either a spreadsheet or word processing program • Color printer • Scanner or scanning service • Label paper and cardboard (or card stock and glue) • Scissors

Baseball cards are still as popular as they ever were. Some kids would do just about anything for Ken Griffey, Jr.'s rookie card. And to think that their picture would someday be on a baseball card — well, it's something that seems as much of a dream as making it to the major leagues. But there's no reason why your child has to wait

until he makes it to the big leagues before he sees his picture on a baseball card. You and he can make that dream come true today, while he's still in Little League. We'll show you how to create baseball cards with your child's photo. You'll include his stats and make it look every bit as authentic as the cards of your child's favorite players.

Before You Begin

You need the right pictures for the card's cover. Have your child imitate the bat-on-the-shoulder stare of a seasoned veteran or hold up a trophy in triumph. If you've got a great action shot of your child involved in his or her sport, all the better. Then have the pictures scanned and saved in a format that you can access with your computer (usually .BMP for Windows and .PICT for Macs). See the "Creative Primer" section for more information on digitizing photos.

Brainstormer

Make Trading Cards of any other sport (real or imagined), your scout troop or club, Science Olmpiad team, "Outstanding Students", band or orchestra, your favorite teacher

Step-by-Step

We're using ClarisWorks to make the sports cards, but you can use your favorite Works program. Another option is to use a draw program combined with either a spreadsheet program or possibly a word processor.

FamilyPC Tip: *Use scissors to cut out the background before scanning. The result will be a nice, silhouetted image with a white background.*

1. Launch ClarisWorks or the program you plan on using.

2. Begin a new Drawing document by

clicking on Drawing, and then clicking OK. Under Format, click Rulers, accept the defaults (Graphics, Inches, divisions of eight), and click OK.

3. Create a box that's 2 1/2 inches wide and 3 1/2 inches tall. Click on the Paint tool. Then place the cursor in the extreme upper left corner and drag diagonally down toward the bottom right corner. Release the button when the box is the correct size. If you need to make any adjustments, use the Pointer tool (the arrow) to click on the box, and then click and drag any of the image handles.

4. Add a border to the front of the card. Click on the Rectangle tool, and choose a line thickness from the Pen width control (we

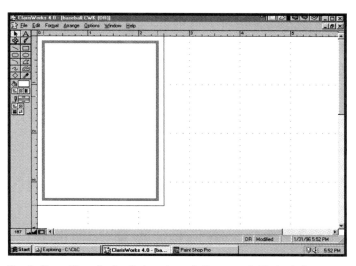

Create the outline of a trading card, ready for your slugger's photo.

used 4 point) as well as a color. (Choose a color that matches your child's team colors.) Click and drag to create a rectangle, making it 1/8-inch smaller than the box you created in the preceding step.

5. Save the file.

6. Now insert your child's picture. Choose File, Insert. Then select your picture file (wherever it is saved on your hard drive) and click on OK.

7. If necessary, resize the picture. (To keep the picture in proportion as you scale it, hold down the Shift key as you resize.) Drag the image into the center of the card's front, keeping the spacing around the image balanced.

8. Change the border of the picture so that it matches (in scale) the existing bor-

der. Click on the Pen width control and choose 4 point (or whatever your border is). Change the color to a second team color.

9. Save the file.

10. Next, you'll insert the team name, using the same team colors that you used for the border. Choose the Text tool, and then click and drag a text box near the top of the page. Make the box about 1 inch long and 1/2 inch wide.

11. Choose a font from the Fonts menu item, a point size from the Size menu item, and a text color from the Style pulldown menu. (We used the no-frills Haettenschweiler font, 26 point, and orange.)

FamilyPC Tip: *If you are using a photo-editing program to touch up the photo, you can copy the finished picture from the program to the Clipboard and then paste it into your document (instead of inserting it).*

12. Type the name of the team. If the letters drop down to the next line in the box, switch to the Pointer tool, click on the text box, and stretch it.

13. Save the file.

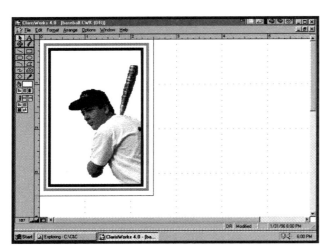

Position the photo and highlight it with the team colors.

14. Add a swath of the second team color (in this case, black) as a design element behind the name. Choose the Rectangle tool, and click and drag a long thin rectangle on the cover, just over the team name.

15. Fill the rectangle with black by choosing the Fill color control just below the Fill icon.

16. Resize the band as necessary.

17. Move the black band behind the team name by choosing Arrange, Move Backward.

18. Save the file.

19. Repeat steps 10 to 18 to enter your child's name and position at the bottom of the card. Use the same font, color, and text style, but a smaller point size.

20. Create the back of the card by repeating step 3, but make the new rectangle's dimensions 2 1/2 inches tall by 3 1/2 inches wide.

21. Add a border to the card by repeating step 4.

22. Save the file.

23. Add personal details for your child athlete using the Text tool and the capability of your Works program to create spreadsheets. Start by creating a text box (as detailed in step 3) that's about 3 inches wide at the top of the card, just inside the borders.

Fill a rectangle around the team name with one of the team colors.

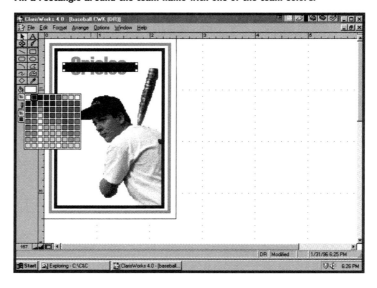

24. Use a plain, sans serif font (we used Arial, point size 6), aligned center. (To change the alignment, choose Format, Paragraph, Align, Centered.)

25. Add two text boxes directly below the one you just drew.

26. In the first new text box, type your child's name and position, using the same font as on the cover (we used Arial, point size 18), aligned center.

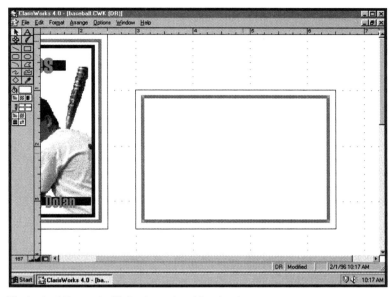

The back of the card will also be enclosed in a border.

27. In the second new text box, type the title of the statistics box, such as *Complete Little League Batting Record.* We used the same font (Arial), but a smaller point size (8), aligned center.

28. Save the file.

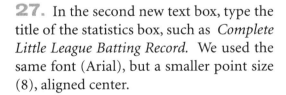

FamilyPC Tip: *To easily move different art elements around on the screen at the same time, hold down the Shift key and click on each element (to select them all), and then choose Arrange, Group to group them. If you need to edit any of the grouped items, just choose Arrange, Ungroup.*

29. Insert your child's statistics in the form of a spreadsheet by selecting the Spreadsheet tool (it looks like a fancy plus sign), and clicking and dragging in the bottom half of the back of the card to create a box large enough to hold fourteen columns, one row for each year played, and two additional rows for headings and totals.

30. Format the table. Click in the top left corner of the table to select the entire table, and then choose Format, Column Width. Set the width to 15 point and click on OK. Set the font to Arial, 6 point, and choose Center alignment. To format the numbers, choose Format, Number, Fixed and enter 0 for Precision.

31. Enter the column headings in the top row of the spreadsheet by selecting indi-

FamilyPC Tip: *If the spreadsheet box you created does not appear to have the appropriate number of rows or columns, click in a cell with the Spreadsheet tool and choose Insert Cells from the Calculate pulldown menu. Click on Insert Cells as many times as you need extra rows or columns. Click outside the table to deselect it, and then click on the table to reselect it as an object. Grab one of the corner handles that appears and move it out to enlarge the table until you see all the rows and columns.*

vidual cells and typing the headings. Enter the following from the left:

What to type	What it means
YR	Year
CLUB	Club, or team
G	Games
AB	At bat
BA	Batting average
H	Hits
2B	Doubles
3B	Triples
HR	Home runs
RBI	Runs batted in
SB	Stolen bases
BB	Bases on balls
SO	Strikeouts
AVG	Average

32. Click on the CLUB cell. Choose Format, Column Width. Set the width to 20 points.

33. In the bottom left cell, type the word *Totals*.

34. Enter the formula for each Totals cell and for the Averages cells by clicking in the particular cell where the result will appear and entering the appropriate formula. (The formula will appear on the entry bar near the top of the screen as you type it.)

For instance, the total of column K (stolen bases) is shown by the following formula:

$$=(K2+K3+K4+K5)$$

In the formula, be sure to enter the appropriate column letter. The formula for figuring the number of hits per times at bat (batting average) is

$$=(F2/D2*1000)$$

where the 2 represents the particular row, or year. (Note: the *1000 multiplies the average by 1000 to show the number as, say, 250 instead of 0.25.)

FamilyPC Tip: *When working with small point sizes, it's easier to see your work if you click on the Zoom-in control in the bottom left corner of the screen.*

In the bottom-right corner cell, enter a formula for the career batting average:

$$=((N2+N3+N4+N5)/4)$$

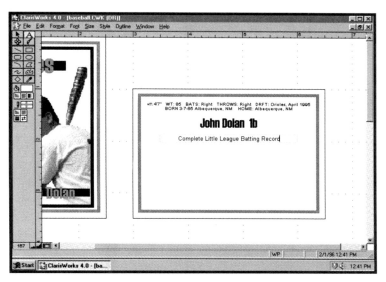

Now it's time to add the statistics, below the biographical information and the title.

35. When you've finished entering all the formulas, save the file.

36. Fill in the spreadsheet cells with the player's statistics. Notice how the numbers recalculate as the information is typed in.

37. Save the file.

38. Make final touches to your child's stats chart. First select the first row. (To do so, click on the "1" that indicates the row number along the left margin of the spreadsheet.) Change the point size to 5 by choosing Format, Size, Other and entering 5. Similarly, change the Totals row to 5 point.

39. Choose Options, Display. Turn off Column and Row Headings, and click on OK.

40. Position the spreadsheet in the center of the back of the card by clicking with the Pointer tool and dragging the spreadsheet.

41. Create a text box at the bottom of the page (see step 3) and include a brief description of the player's best game. (We typed the description using Arial, point size 5, aligned center.)

42. Save the file.

Add the spreadsheet table, but don't worry about squeezing it on the card yet.

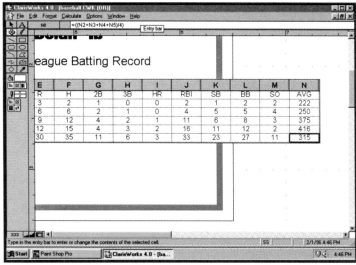

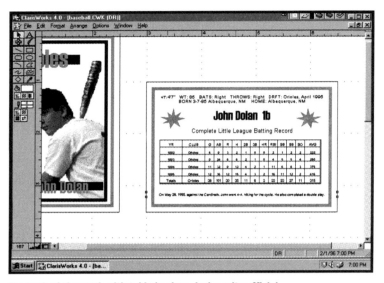

The back of the card, with table in place, looks quite official.

43. If you want, insert pieces of clip art around the name as a final design touch. (In ClarisWorks, look under File, Libraries.) Resize and position the clip art as necessary. (In ClarisWorks, hold down the Shift key to resize without changing the proportions.)

44. Make any final design changes, and save the file again.

45. Print a test copy. Make any necessary adjustments, and save the file.

46. When you are satisfied with the look, print on label paper. Attach each side of the card to the sides of a thin piece of cardboard. (You can also print on card stock and glue the front and back together.)

47. Print several copies. Using this template, you can quickly substitute photos and stats for other team members. Pass them around at the end-of-season team picnic and keep one of each — when a teammate reaches the major leagues, your child can prove he "knew him when..."

Products You Can Use

Works program: *ClarisWorks, Microsoft Works*

Paint or draw program: *Draw module in ClarisWorks, CorelDraw, TurboDraw*

Spreadsheet program: *Excel, Spreadsheet module in Works, Quattro Pro*

Word processing program: *MacWrite, Microsoft Word, WordPerfect*

Book Gear

Bookplates, bookmarks, and other things

 PREP TIME: 15-45 MINUTES EACH

Materials

**Paint or draw program • Clip art • Printer • Paper or card stock •
Label paper (for bookplates and labels) • Glue stick • Clear contact paper •
Scissors • Edging scissors • Hole punch • Ribbon**

Get the school year off to a good start with the right book gear. Custom bookplates will help your child keep track of his books, while personalized bookmarks will help him keep track of his place. And bookshelf labels are a good reminder that books go on a shelf — not on the floor. Now

mind you, none of these is a surefire solution to a messy desk or room: Some books will still be lost, some corners will still be dog-eared, and still other books will find their home under your child's bed. (After all, kids will still be kids.) But you may find that these things happen a little less frequently!

Bookplates

Bookplates are labels that identify the owner of a book. Although they don't guarantee that your kids' books will always come home, they can help — if you follow some commonsense dos and don'ts. Don't replicate the plain, colorless ones you've seen on library books for years! Do jazz them up with your child's favorite colors. And do add some lively clip art. If your child likes the bookplates, he'll use them.

Brainstormer

Bookplate themes: astronauts, flowers, knights and dragons, planes, sports, initials

Before You Begin

You and your child should think about a design for your bookplate. What kind of border do you want to create? How do you want the bookplate to read? What kind of pictures do you want to use to decorate it? When you have some ideas, you're ready to begin.

Step-by-Step

In these steps, we use Smart-Sketch, but you can adapt the steps for another draw or paint program.

1. Launch SmartSketch. Make sure the page orientation is Portrait mode (the default). Also make the on screen dimensions match the printable surface by choosing Format, Document, Match Printer.

2. Choose View, Show Page so that you can see the entire page.

3. Make a sizing guide for your bookplate by drawing a 4-by-5-inch box with a Hairline pencil.

4. Select the Text tool (the button with the large *A*) and create a text box, about 1 3/4-inch wide, in the center of the box.

5. Have your child select a font. (You might want to suggest a font that matches the book, such as the classic Engravers Old English font for a collection of Grimm's fairy tales.) Set the point size (we used 18), and set the alignment to centered. Ask your child what he or she would like written on the book-

A font such as Engravers Old English gives your bookplates a classic look.

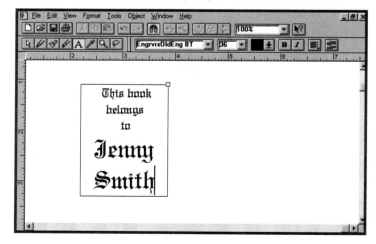

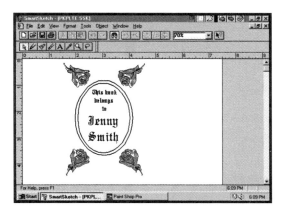

Decorate your bookplate with clip art.

plate, and then type it in. (You might suggest *From the treasures of* or *This book belongs to*.) Switch to a larger point size (we used 36) and type your child's name.

6. Go to the clip-art library and select the image your child wants to use.

7. If you are using clip art in SmartSketch, drag the clip art to your document. If you are using another clip-art library, copy the clip art to the Clipboard and paste it into your document. Rotate the clip art and place each element so that it appears balanced. Note: SmartSketch cannot rotate images pasted or inserted from another source. Instead, you need to rotate the image before you copy it to the Clipboard or import it.

8. Scale the art, if necessary, leaving room for a border.

9. Create a border around the text and around the edge of the bookplate if desired, using paint tools or one of the choices in EasyArt (under Logos).

10. Make any changes your child suggests, such as additional scaling, rotating, and flipping. Save the file.

11. Select the entire image, including the text, border, and art (Edit, Select All). Duplicate the image (Edit, Duplicate). Drag the new image next to the original, and repeat this process until the page is filled with images.

12. Save the file.

13. Print the page on label paper or plain paper. (For paper sources, turn to the "Resource Guide.")

To make the most of label paper, duplicate your bookplates so that they fill the page.

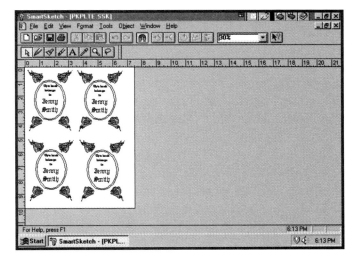

14. Have your child cut out the bookplates. Next, she can peel off the backing or, if you are using paper, apply a thin layer of glue. Finally, have her apply each bookplate to the inside front covers of her favorite books.

Bookmarks

Bookmarks are back in style. Skeptical? Just browse the displays at a Barnes & Noble bookstore. You'll find them with various designs and in a range of colors. Personalized bookmarks can be just as nice, though. Complete with your child's name and his choice of art, bookmarks will help him keep his place, and help him and others (such as teachers, neighbors, and friends) easily identify his books. Bookmarks also make great gifts. Whether it's a birthday party or the class grab bag at Christmas, help your child create special bookmarks for his friends.

Before You Begin

You can make bookmarks quickly and easily using clip art. The key to having your child use the bookmarks, however, is making sure they have a design that your child likes. So

> **FamilyPC Tip:** *You can find free clip art for Mac and Windows platforms in the FamilyPC Software Libraries on America Online (keyword: FamilyPC).*

Brainstormer

Bookmark themes: animals, planets, flowers, fish, initials, names, directions

together, peruse your clip-art library. As your child finds images he'd like to use, copy them to the Clipboard, and then save them to a file. Or you and your child can create your own designs and save them to a file.

Step-by-Step

We're using SmartSketch to create the bookmarks shown here, but you can adapt the steps to your favorite draw or paint program.

1. Launch SmartSketch or the program you'll be using.

2. Make sure the page orientation is Portrait mode (the default). Choose Format, Document, Match Printer so that the screen shows the printable surface.

3. Go to the clip-art library and select the clip art your child wants to use. (In Smart-Sketch, clip art is located under Help, EasyArt.)

Here, we dragged several roses onto a page from the Flowers group of images in EasyArt, and then selected and scaled them individually.

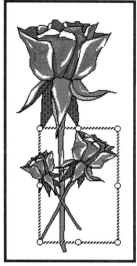

For the second side of the bookmark, we rotated the stems of the three roses so they would cross.

4. Now it's time to create the first side of the bookmark. If you are using clip art in SmartSketch, drag the clip art to your document. If you are using another clip-art library, such as Corel Gallery 2, copy the clip art to the Clipboard and paste it into your document.

5. Using the top and side rulers as a guide, scale the clip art to no larger than 2 inches wide by 4 inches long, leaving about 1/8 inch space all around for fancy edges (to be cut later).

6. Check the placement (View, Show Page), and make any final adjustments.

7. To make the second side of the bookmark, select the image and then duplicate it using Edit, Duplicate. Move the new image just to the right of the original. Save the file before continuing.

8. Give this side a slightly different look by rotating individual elements — let your child be your guide. (Click once outside the selection box to deselect the group of ele-

ments, and then select and move the individual elements.) Note: In SmartSketch, you cannot rotate items imported from another source. Instead, rotate the items before you insert them.

FamilyPC Tip: *In SmartSketch, you can select items by dragging the cursor across them on the screen, or by holding down the Shift key and clicking on them. To deselect a specific item from a group, hold down the Shift key and click on the item.*

9. Make final adjustments to the design, and save your handiwork.

10. Next, make several copies of the

design. Select the entire design (both sides) and choose Edit, Duplicate. (Move the copy so that the items are evenly spaced and not overlapping.) Continue making enough copies of the design to fill the page.

11. Print the page. Use card stock, colored paper, or heavy stock parchment-type paper.

12. Cut out the front and back of your bookmarks with standard scissors. Have your child glue the sides, back

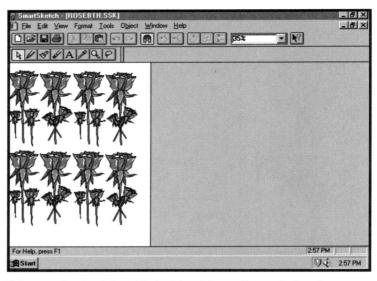

Make several copies of the original art to print more than one bookmark on a page.

to back. Use edging scissors to give the bookmarks a sawtoothed edge.

Handy Helpers

Elmer's School Glue Stick is especially handy for these types of gluing projects because it goes on blue (so you can see your glue coverage) and dries clear.

Edging scissors, by FISKARS (about $5 at craft shops and office supply stores), give your paper projects a professional look with just a few snips. You and your child can choose from a number of edging styles, including wavy and zig-zag. Beware of plastic imitations — they cost nearly as much and will not produce a satisfactory edge for your work, especially on card stock.

13. Finish by laminating with clear contact paper or a laminating sheet, trimming about 1/8 inch larger than the printed paper edge.

FamilyPC Tip: When applying clear contact paper, start in the center. Push air bubbles toward the edges to eliminate them.

14. In the top center of each bookmark, punch a hole. Fold a 6-inch length of narrow ribbon in half and pass the folded end partially through the hole. Tuck the ends through the loop extending out of the hole, and gently pull tight.

Learning to Draw

Clip art is easy to use and can help you and your child create great-looking crafts fairly quickly. But when you draw the art yourself, you know it will be one of a kind. Using a draw or paint program, you and your kids can make bookmarks fashioned

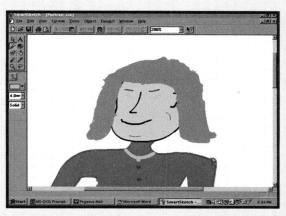

You can do all sorts of things with a simple line, including stretching, shrinking, or bending it.

with drawings of themselves and friends, their home, or their pet.

Usually, the first hurdle to using a paint or draw program is becoming familiar with the different tools and when to use them. Because each is designed to give the artist flexibility, the best way to learn when to use what is by example, and a bit of trial and error. So let's try creating a drawing of your child.

Launch SmartSketch or another draw program. Click on the Pencil tool and choose a line thickness of 2 points. SmartSketch can compensate

for the jagged lines produced by drawing with a mouse: just select Smooth shape. Start by drawing your child's head, eyes, and mouth. In draw programs (such as Smart-Sketch, Windows Draw, and CorelDraw), you can reshape a section of your drawing by clicking on an area and dragging it until it's the shape you want. In paint programs (such as Kid Pix, Flying Colors, and Paint), you can edit a drawing only by erasing or painting over an error, and then re-drawing as necessary.

Draw hair using the Pencil tool, with a line thickness of 8

points and a Smooth shape. Use squiggly or straight lines to match your child's hair.

Change the line thickness to 2 points again, and draw the outline of your child's hands, feet, and clothes. Add color to your drawing by selecting the Paint Bucket tool (in Windows, choose Brush and then Paint Bucket), choosing a color in the Tool palette, and then clicking on the area to be filled. How you add color to an object will vary depending upon the draw or paint program you're using. Spend some time with your program to learn its unique capabilities and methods.

When you and your child are happy with his portrait, the color of his clothes, and so on, you can transform your artwork into bookmarks by picking up from step 4 in the directions for bookmarks.

Bookshelf Labels

Colorful bookshelf labels won't guarantee that all your child's books are always in their rightful places, but they may inspire a sense of organization in your child's life. The best bookshelf labels have clear, easy-to-read text with a splash of color or a small decoration. Brevity is key to making easy-to-read labels. Don't try to squeeze in too much information.

Before You Begin

Decide on a label design for your child's bookshelf. First, choose a font — maybe one like Kids, which looks like a child's writing but is clear enough to read. If you plan on adding clip art, review your clip-art collection with your child to find the best images. (Plan on having one to three images per label.) You might want to create a list of images with corresponding fonts so that you can create a sheetful of labels in one printing.

We used a not-so-fearsome dragon for a Folk Tales bookshelf label.

Step-by-Step

To make the bookshelf labels, we used SmartSketch, but you can use your choice of paint or draw programs.

1. Launch SmartSketch. Make sure the page orientation is Portrait mode (the default). Make the on-screen dimensions match the printable surface by choosing Format, Document, Match Printer.

2. Find your child's choices for clip art.

In SmartSketch, clip art is located under Help, EasyArt.

3. If you are using clip art in SmartSketch, drag the clip art to your document. If you are using another clip-art library, copy the clip art to the Clipboard and paste it into your document.

4. Scale the clip art (by selecting it and then choosing Scale from the Tools menu) so that it will fit on a label approximately 3/4 inches wide and 3 inches long.

Making Book Covers

Brown paper bags are the time-proven choice for making inexpensive, long-lasting textbook covers. Unfortunately, nothing's more boring than a bookbag full of brown bag–clad books. Your kids can give their books a unique and personalized look by adding smart labels that feature large letters and colorful clip art.

First measure the dimensions of the cover and of the spine. (You'll be creating la-

With a bold label like this, your child won't grab the wrong book when it's time to gather her things at the end of a busy school day.

bels for both.) If you have a book that measures 7 inches by 9 inches and is 1 inch thick, your spine label can be no larger than 1 inch by 9 inches, and

the cover label can be no more than 7 inches wide.

Next, launch your paint or draw program. Select the Pencil and Rectangle tools. Click on Hairline thickness and create a box that matches the dimensions of the spine. This box is the line that you will follow when you cut out the labels. Make a square for the cover, keeping the dimensions at least 2 inches

continued on the next page

continued

smaller than the overall dimensions of the book.

Select the Text tool. Choose a font that reflects the subject matter (for example, the Countdown font for a science book), a large point size, black or another dark color, and center alignment. Type the topic of the class. Save the file.

Next, you'll create a 3-D effect. Select the word you just typed, duplicate it, and change the color of the letters in the new text box to a bright color such as red. For a 3-D look, drag the text almost completely over the original text.

Now it's time to duplicate the text to create a label for the spine. Select the text by dragging a box over it with the Pointer tool. Duplicate the text, rotate it, and scale it to fit the spine.

Open your clip-art library and place the clip art on the page. By selecting individual images on the page, you can scale, rotate, and flip each object.

You may want to add clip art to your spine label as well.

When you're satisfied with the design, select the text, and choose Object, Move to Front so that all your text will appear in front of the clip art. Save the file. Print a test copy to see how the objects fit on the textbook cover, and then print on label paper. Use scissors to trim the excess paper.

Carefully apply the labels to the textbook cover. After they are in place, seal the cover (or just the labels) in clear contact paper. Contact paper provides a water-resistant shell over the type, which otherwise may run if the cover gets wet.

5. Type the name of the label by selecting the Text tool (the button with the large *A*). Choose a font (Engravers Old English is great for a fairy-tale label), a point size (20 to 24), and center alignment by selecting each choice from the pulldown menus on the toolbar. Type the name of the label (for example, *Fairy Tales*).

6. Group the elements by first deselecting the text (click elsewhere on the page).

Then click and drag each art element to either side of the word. When all the elements for the first label are in place, hold down the Shift key and click on each element. Choose Object, Create Group. Drag the group to the upper left corner of the page. Save the file.

7. Create a new label using a different font and different clip art. Group the elements and place the group under the first

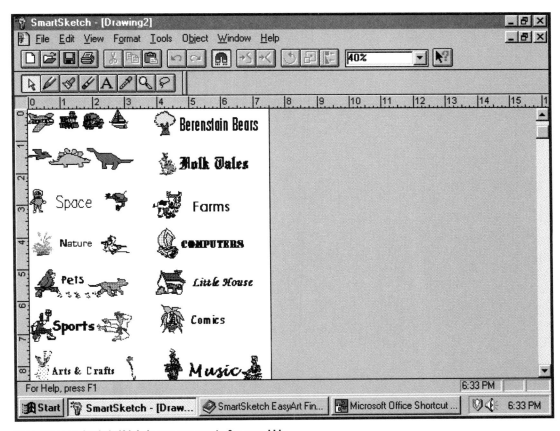

Here are some bookshelf labels you can create for your kids.

label. Save the file. Repeat these steps until you've finished creating all the labels.

8. Print a sample of the labels on regular paper to see how they look. Make any final adjustments, save the file, and then print on label paper.

9. Have your child cut out the labels with scissors and apply them to the front of the bookshelf.

> **FamilyPC Tip:** *If you don't want permanent labels, print on regular paper and use glue that lets you reposition the label (Post-it style).*

Products You Can Use

Paint or draw program: *CorelDraw, SmartSketch*

Clip art: *Corel Gallery 2, Task Force Clip Art — Really Big Edition*

Label It

Three quick label projects

 PREP TIME: 15 MINUTES EACH

Materials

Desktop publishing program (or draw, paint, or word processing program) •
Clip art (optional) • Printer (color preferable) • Scanner (for disk labels) •
Full-sheet adhesive paper • Card stock (for cassette covers) • Sealer (optional but
recommended for items that will be transported in backpacks, for example)

When we were growing up, only our parents could operate special equipment. But today, kids learn early. We find ourselves amazed at how quickly they assimilate new technology, how adept they seem at flipping through menus and finding what they want. But we cringe when we find unmarked floppy disks

all over our desk and unmarked tapes near the VCR. Whose are they? What's on them? Before you wind up with your daughter's book report at your budget meeting, or watching *Sesame Street* instead of your favorite movie, get everyone labeling. Have your kids create their own labels and pre-label some disks and tapes.

Disk Labels

Your child's floppy disks needn't look like every other kid's in her class. In fact, your child's teacher will appreciate it if they don't. Although the most important thing is for your child's disks to be labeled, teachers find it helpful to receive disks that are easy to tell apart from the others in a glance. The secret for the best custom labels: use a picture of your child.

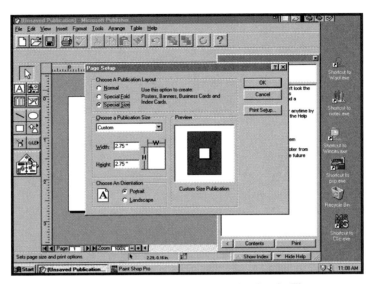

Change the size of your page in Page Setup, located under the File menu.

Before You Begin

Have your child choose an appropriate font and image for the disk. Then choose a photo. School pictures work well, but any candid photo will do. You'll need to have the picture scanned and saved in a format that you can access. For more information on digitizing images, turn to the "Resource Guide."

Step-by-Step

We create these labels using Microsoft Publisher for Windows 95, but you can use a draw, paint, or word processing program.

1. Launch Publisher and click the Blank Page tab. Click on Full Page, and then click on the OK button.

2. Change the size of the page to the size of a floppy label (2.75-by-2.75 inches) by going to Page Setup under File, clicking next to Special Size, entering 2.75 for the width and 2.75 for the height, and clicking on OK.

FamilyPC Tip: *You can use the built-in templates in Publisher to create your labels. Choose Label on the Page-Wizard screen, choose 3.5" Computer Disk, and then click on the Create It! button. Just fill in the appropriate text in the next two dialog boxes, and then click on OK to see the preformatted label. Remember that this template prints in a multipage format. Also, you can customize the design, but if you're going to make significant design changes, it's easier to start from scratch.*

3. Set the margins to zero by choosing Arrange, Layout Guides and entering 0 for all the margin guides. Click on OK. Save the file.

4. Add a border around the label. First click on the Box tool. You can choose both the line thickness and the color of the border by clicking on the Border tool (with the horizontal lines) in the upper right corner, and then choosing More in the pulldown menu. (We chose a red, 2-point border.) Click on OK. Draw the border by placing the cursor in the upper left corner of the label and dragging it to the bottom right corner.

5. Insert a picture of your child. First, create a picture box by choosing the Picture tool and dragging the shape of the picture box

Insert a digitized picture of your child using the Picture tool.

to the bottom right corner of the label. Double-click in the picture box, and use the dialog boxes that appear to find the saved file of your child's picture. Insert it.

6. Crop out the background of the photo by selecting the picture and choosing the Wrap Text to Picture tool. Next, choose the Edit Irregular Wrap tool. Grab the handles that appear and move them as close as possible to the outline of your child's face.

7. Scale the picture so that it is about 1 1/2 inches high. (While holding down the Shift key, grab the top left corner handle and drag toward or away from the upper left corner of the page.) Watch the side ruler as you scale.

You can change the color and size of your border by clicking on the Border tool, choosing More, and then selecting your choices from the Choose a Thickness and Color areas of the Border dialog box.

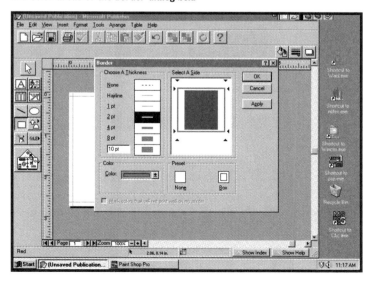

8. Place the picture behind the border by clicking on it and then choosing Arrange, Send to Back.

9. Add text to the label. First click on the WordArt tool and create a text box (just as you created the border and the picture box) to the left of your child's picture. Align the top edge of the box with the top of her head. From the pull-down menus that appear, have your child choose a favorite font and a point size. (We used 12-point Lucida Calligraphy, which provides a refined, personal touch.) Click in the text entry box and type a phrase, such as *Property of:*.

Brainstormer

Make labels that include your child's class picture, decorative initials, a sports symbol

10. Create a second text box below the first. Have it stretch to the bottom of the label. Using the same font as in step 9 but Best Fit as the point size, type your daughter's full name, pressing the Enter key to begin a new line after the first and middle names. Click outside the box. Save the file.

11. Print a test copy of the disk label. (Choose File, Print and make sure that Print Crop Marks is checked.) Make any final adjustments to the page, and then save the file.

12. To print multiple copies of a label on the page, load full-sheet label paper into your printer and click Page Options at the bottom of the Print dialog box. Choose Print multiple copies per sheet. Click OK and then click OK a second time in the Print box.

FamilyPC Tip: *For work that requires attention to detail, such as cropping a photo with the Wrap tool, zoom in to 200 or 400 percent using the + and the - buttons at the bottom of the screen.*

Return-Address Labels

Return-address labels are popular with kids because they're so versatile. We may find them suitable only for letters, but kids will use them for that and many other things. Kids find the size (usually 1/2 inch by 1 3/4 inches or 1 inch by 2 5/8 inches) perfect for tagging all sorts of personal belongings — everything from books and binders, to games and toys.

Before You Begin

Peruse your fonts with your child and have her select her favorites. Then she can either select a clip-art image or create her own using a draw or paint program.

Step-by-Step

For this project, we used Publisher, but you can use any program that lets you manipulate text and images, including another desktop publishing program or a word processing, draw, or paint program.

1. Launch Microsoft Publisher for Windows 95. We'll use its built-in templates to create the labels. (The templates feature preset text boxes and a page setup, so you can make your labels more quickly.) Start by choosing Label on the PageWizard screen. On the Label PageWizard Design Assistant screen, choose Return Address, and then Large Return Address (1″ x 2 5/8″). Choose Next in the subsequent dialog boxes, and then Create It!

2. Type your child's name and address when prompted, and then click on OK. The

Microsoft Publisher for Windows 95 features templates for all sorts of labels.

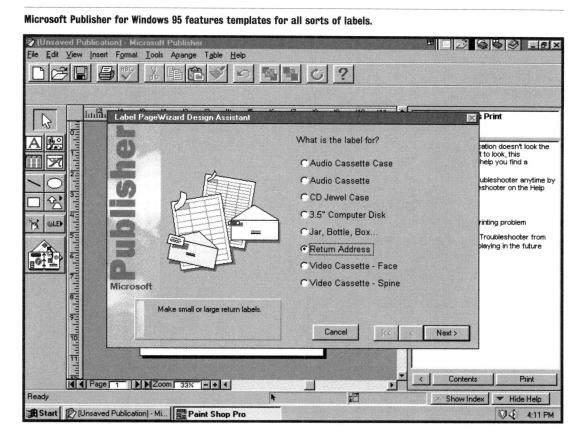

program will create a simple label featuring your child's name and address in the two text boxes, with the text flush left.

3. Nudge the address text box down to give the name box more space by clicking and dragging it. Resize the address box to fill the new space using the bottom middle handle. Drag the edges of both boxes in so that you can just see the colored margin lines all around the label.

4. Change the size and font for your child's name, if desired. (We used a point size of 12 and the Kids font.) Click anywhere on the screen to make the changes take effect. (If Publisher gives you a warning about the size of the text frame at this point, ignore it.) Make similar changes to the address text, using the same font but a smaller type size. (We used 10-point Kids font.)

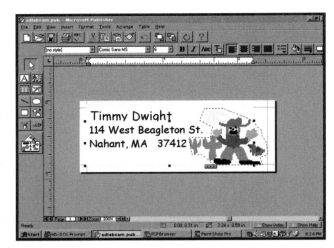

Use the wrapping tools in Publisher to get the text as close as possible to the art.

5. Insert a piece of clip art or original art by copying the image to the Clipboard and pasting it onto the address label, or by using the OLE (Object Linking and Embedding) capability of Publisher to create the art. (For more information on OLE, see the "Creative Primer.")

6. Save the file.

7. Have the text wrap as closely to the picture as possible by clicking on the picture,

Resize the type so that it's large enough to read but still leaves room for clip art or artwork.

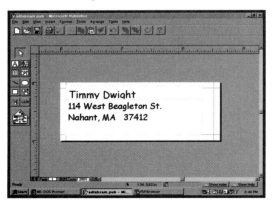

FamilyPC Tip: *To add additional handles, position the cursor over the wrap outline and hold down the Control key. Click where you want a handle to appear. To delete a handle, repeat the same procedure, clicking on the handle you want to remove.*

and then choosing the Wrap Text to Picture tool. Handles appear. Click on the Edit Irregular Wrap button, and move the handles by using the mouse, just as you would if you were scaling the image.

8. Add a phrase along the bottom of the label to give it some humor. Click at the end of the address, tap the Return key a few times to move the cursor down, and type using the same font. Select the new text and change the point size (we used 6), and change the color (we used red).

FamilyPC Tip: *To change the color of the text, click on the Font Color button and choose a color. Use the same steps to change the color of the address text as well, if you want.*

9. Make any final touches to the boxes and the type (by clicking and then dragging or resizing), so that the text and the art are within the colored margins. Then save the file.

For the final touch, have your child add a phrase along the bottom.

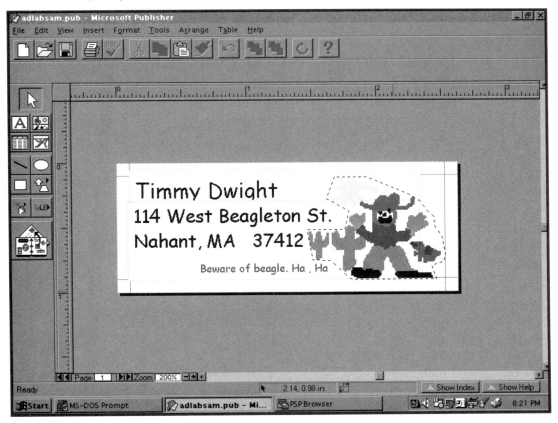

10. In the Print dialog box, check the option for printing cutting guides. Print a test copy of a sheet of labels on plain paper to see how the labels look.

11. Make any final changes to margins or art, and then save the file. Print on full-sheet label paper. Have your child use scissors to cut out the labels.

Audiotape Labels

Despite the proliferation of music CDs, kids still love to record their favorite music on audiotapes. In addition, it's wise to create copies of kids' tapes and conserve the originals because of the "play-and-play-again" nature of kids' listening. Unfortunately, the labels that come with blank cassettes are colorless and boring. You can add pizzazz to those cassettes by using Publisher, which features templates for audio cassettes. These labels — and their matching trifold covers — feature two colors and fun shapes and fonts.

Before You Begin

Colors and unique fonts are the secrets to this design. Take the time with your child before you begin designing to choose one or two fonts that look good together and are easy to read in a small point size. Also find two contrasting colors that will look good together when printed on plain white paper.

Step-by-Step

For the following direction, we used Publisher, but you can use your favorite draw, paint, or word processing program.

1. Launch Microsoft Publisher for Windows 95 and use its built-in templates to create your tape labels. Start by choosing Label

Later, you'll cut out the circles and the rectangle in the middle of the label.

FamilyPC Tip: *If some labels are being cut off when printed, click Print and then click the Page Options button. Click the Custom Options button and choose Automatically calculate spacing. Click OK, and click OK again in the Print dialog box.*

in the selections for PageWizard and clicking on OK. Choose the Audio Cassette template, and click on Next in the dialog boxes that appear. Then click on Create It! and OK to see the template.

2. Your text and background will be different from that provided by Publisher, so you need to clear the text and background

Learning to Draw

What child would settle for just text on her cassettes? Use the Shape tool to add simple art, such as an arrow or a star.

To add an arrow like we did on the sample cassette label, click on the Custom Shapes tool. Choose the Arrow shape, and drag it to the

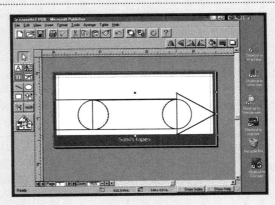

We've scaled the arrow so that it overlays the rectangle and circles.

arrow body the width of the circles and rectangle. Shrink the arrow head so that its base bisects the right circle.

Click on the Border tool and choose None. Click on the Object Color menu and choose a color. Then choose Arrange, Send to Back so you'll

label. Rotate the arrow by placing the cursor over one of the corner handles and pressing the Alt and Shift keys; click and drag the handle so that the arrow rotates 90 degrees clockwise. (The Shift key will restrict the rotation to 90-degree increments.)

Next, grab the front of the

arrow and stretch it so that it reaches the right edge. Extend the back of the arrow to the left edge. Drag the entire arrow down so that it is over the circles. You can adjust the width of the arrow, and even the length of the arrow head, by clicking and dragging individual handles. Make the

be able to see your cutting lines.

Make the tip and the end of the arrow show by selecting the border and choosing Arrange, Send to Back. Also, click on the colored bar along the base and choose Arrange, Send Farther. Save the file and continue in the directions with step 7.

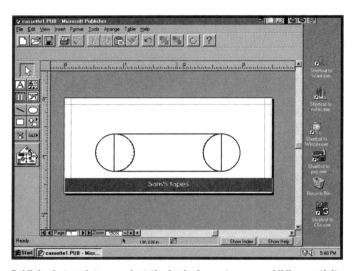

Publisher's templates are just the beginning — tap your child's creativity for the final product.

Color button and choosing a color in the pulldown menu. Change the font size to at least 10 points. If you have a particularly long phrase (such as *Frederick's Funky Favorites*), you may want to left-justify the text.

5. Add cutting lines to the label by using the Circle tool to draw circles where marked on the template. Scale, if necessary. Then use the Box tool to create a rectangle connecting the circles. Once the cutting lines are complete, save the file.

from the top of the label. Click on the text and press the Delete key; then click on the same space (where the text was) and delete the black background.

3. Change the color of the bar at the base of the label. To do so, click once on the black bar at the base of the label to select it, choose the Object Color tool, and have your child choose a color.

4. Change the text in the bottom bar to something like *Sam's tapes* by clicking on the text and typing. Select the new text and change the color by clicking on the Font

6. Add a colored border around the outermost edge of the entire label by choosing the Box tool, the Border tool, More

The final touch is adding "This side:" in a text box in the upper left.

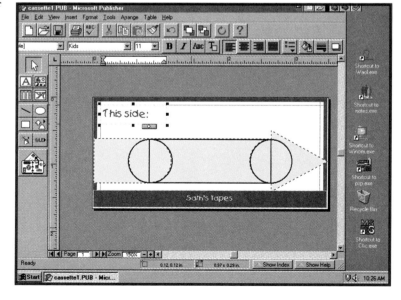

Making Matching Cassette Covers

After you make labels for your child's audio cassettes, take the extra step and make matching covers.

Begin by clicking on the Label icon in the PageWizard dialog box. Then choose the Audio Cassette Case template from the Label PageWizard Design Assistant dialog box. Choose the basic style, and press the Return key (accepting the defaults) through the rest of the dialog box until the cover is displayed on the screen.

Change all the black borders (but not the text frames) to colored borders. To do so, click on each border while holding down the Shift key; then choose the Border tool, More, and a point size and color. Click OK.

Add a colored border to the text box containing only the word *Title*. To do so, select the box, choose the Border tool, More, and a point size and color. Click on OK. Then fill the box with the color using the

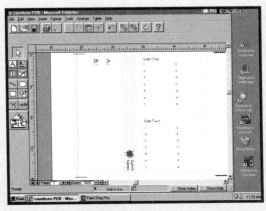

Make cassette covers as funky as your labels using the template in Publisher.

Object Color button.

Delete the text frames where individual songs will be listed (on the right side) by pressing the Delete key. Stretch the remaining boxes in that section to fill the side. Insert a table in the top box by clicking the Table tool and dragging the Rectangle shape to fill the border under the *Side One* text. Define the number of rows (we used 7) and the number of columns (we used 2), and accept the default style. If requested, have the program make the table expand to fit the table box.

Drag down the left tabs of the table (to select all the rows),

and then choose from the toolbar the font, point size, and color. (We used Kids, 6 points, blue.) Click on the table when you're finished. Number the boxes (we used 1 through 14). Resize the box (using the bottom middle handle) back inside the border. Copy the table to the Clipboard and paste it back to the document. Then drag the copy to the lower rectangle for side two.

Change the font, point size, and color of the *Side One* and *Side Two* text as desired. (We used Kids, 8 points, blue.) Resize the table where necessary to fit.

Delete the word *Title* from the long rectangle in the center by double-clicking on the text to display the WordArt editing box and then pressing the Delete key. Click outside the box to complete the operation.

Near the bottom of the rectangle, create a text box and

continued on the next page

continued

type the same words that appear on the colored bar of the cassette label (*Sam's tapes* in our example). Change the font and color. (We used 6-point Kids, blue.) Rotate the text 90 degrees (using the Alt and Shift keys and the mouse). Enlarge or shrink the box to fit the text. Fill the box with color to match the spine. Finally, include a fun shape using the Custom Shapes tool. Choose another color for the shape and its border.

Replace the word *Title* in the left hand box with *A:* by double-clicking on the word and typing in the new text. Change the font as desired (we used Kids) and change the jus- tification to Left (click the Text Justification tool and choose Left). Click the on Shading tool and change the color as desired. (We used blue.) Repeat for *B:* in the top *Performer* text

frame, and then delete the bottom *Performer* text. Save the file. Print a test copy on plain paper. Make any adjustments to the elements of the cover and save the file again.

To print two covers per page, do the following. Select all the items on the page (choose Edit, Select All) and copy them to the Clipboard. Now zoom out for a better view, and then paste and drag the copy so that it is adjacent to the original.

Print on card stock. Cut out the two covers using the outside crop marks as guides. Fold backwards on the crop marks to the left and right of the filled center panel (spine). Fill in song titles and insert the cover into the cassette box with the titles showing through the front of the box.

---

from the pulldown menu, and a point size and color. (We used a 4-point, blue line.) Click on OK. Draw the border by placing the cursor in the upper left corner and dragging diagonally to the bottom right corner. Save the file.

7. Now it's time to add text (such as *This side:*). Click on the Text tool, choose a font and point size from the pulldown menus, and choose a color using the Font Color

button. (We used Kids, 11 points, blue.) Create a text box in the upper left corner by dragging the cursor across the screen. Type the text. Resize the text box so that it is just larger than the words contained in it. You can also adjust the placement of the text by dragging it. Save the file.

8. Print a test copy of just one label on plain white paper by choosing File, Print, Page Options. In the Page Options dialog box, choose Print one copy per sheet, and click on OK. Click on OK again in the Printer dialog box.

9. Make any necessary adjustments to the text, the arrangement of elements, and the colors. Check that your label fits your cassette and adjust your cutting guides accordingly. Then save the file.

10. Print multiple copies on a single sheet of label paper by

FamilyPC Tip: *You can draw circles (instead of ovals) by holding down the Shift key while dragging the cursor diagonally.*

changing the Page Options setting to Print multiple copies per sheet.

11. Have your child trim the labels, peel off the backing, and apply the labels to the sides of her favorite cassettes.

Products You Can Use

Paint or draw program: *Draw module in ClarisWorks, CorelDraw, SmartSketch*

Works program: *ClarisWorks, Microsoft Works*

Desktop publishing program: *Adobe Paint & Publish, Microsoft Publisher CD Deluxe for Windows 95, Turbo Publisher*

School Time Games

Fortune-teller, paper football, POGs

 P R E P   T I M E :   4 5   M I N U T E S   E A C H

Materials

**Draw program • Clip art (for POGs) • Printer (color preferable) • Paper •
Sticker paper, thin cardboard, and scissors (for POGs)**

Even though your closets are packed with board games and your home office stacked with computer games, it's nice to know that your kids still enjoy playing games that are simple and homemade. Fortune-teller, POGs, and paper football are three such games. Kids often play them during homeroom and recess, but they can be just

as much fun on a Saturday with neighborhood friends or at a birthday party. The pieces are made out of common household items, and the rules are few, but the games will entertain for hours.

Fortune-teller

More than a simple yes-or-no awaits in the folds of this fortune-teller (also known as a Cootie Catcher), which sits like a finger puppet over the index fingers and thumbs of one person. When worked by the schoolyard sooth-sayer, it answers those gnawing questions of romance and fortune that all kids have. To play, one child asks a question and then chooses one of the four colors on the outside of the fortune-teller. The soothsayer then opens the fortune-teller — forward, backward, and side-to-side in turn — once for each letter in the color (for example, three times for red). Next, the questioner chooses one of the four numbers exposed inside, and the soothsay-er moves the fortune-teller that number of times. Repeat this process one more time. Finally, the questioner chooses one of the numbers revealed inside, and the soothsay-er folds it back to reveal the answer.

Before You Begin

This fortune-teller should be able to answer almost any question it is asked, so you need to come up with a list of general but humorous responses, such as *Most definitely, Not on your life,* and *Try again.* Also, because your computer lets you access a vari-

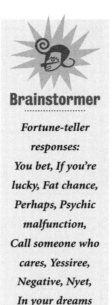

Brainstormer

Fortune-teller responses:

You bet, If you're lucky, Fat chance, Perhaps, Psychic malfunction, Call someone who cares, Yessiree, Negative, Nyet, In your dreams

ety of clip art, don't limit the design to just numbers and colors — add specific images such as a skier, fish, or a flower.

Step-by-Step

We used SmartSketch to make the fortune-teller, but you can use your favorite draw program — just make sure it has on-screen rulers for precise placement.

1. Launch SmartSketch (or your draw program) and open a new document.

2. You'll need rulers as a guide for this project, so choose View, Show Rulers. Then choose Show Page (also under View) to show the entire document.

3. Use the default page setup (Portrait). Choose Format, Document, and Match Printer so that the on-screen drawing area matches the printable area.

4. To draw the outline of the fortune-teller, click on the Pencil tool and choose the Rectangle tool (under the Pencil mode pull-down menu). Draw an 8-inch square. (Use the rulers as a guide.) Save the file.

5. Next, you want each of the four squares to have a diagonal line through it. Choose the Straight Line tool (under the Pencil mode pulldown menu), and draw diagonal lines from the corners to create an X. Use the

Straight Line tool again to bisect the square with one vertical line and one horizontal line. (You can use the bold circle that appears near the cursor to find the exact position for the lines.)

6. Create the last fold line by using the Straight Line tool to draw two vertical lines and two horizontal lines at the 2-inch and 6-inch marks on the rulers. Then make four matching X's by drawing an additional diagonal line through each of the four squares, intersecting the existing diagonal. Save the file.

FamilyPC Tip: *In SmartSketch, you can select multiple elements at one time by just clicking on them. Then you can make a universal change, such as deleting all the elements by just tapping the Delete key. This is handy if you need to make uniform changes to several parts of one design.*

7. Select the diagonal lines in each of the outermost corners — up to where they intersect another line — and press the Delete key.

This is what the fortune-teller should look like after you draw all those lines.

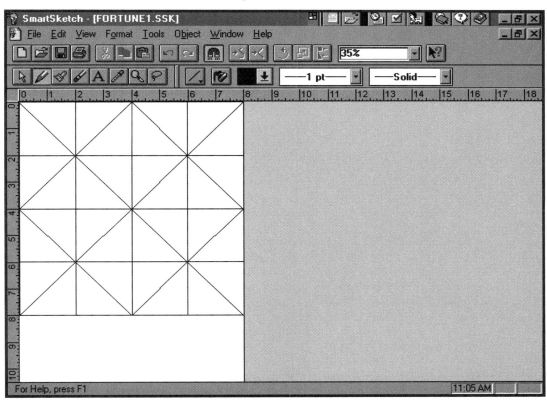

FamilyPC Tip: *You can add varied clip art to each of the different colors in the corner squares.*

8. Add a different color to each corner square by clicking the Paint Brush and then choosing the Paint Bucket tool. Add a single color to the triangles at the center. (All share a common point at the center of the square.)

9. Now you need to add numbers to the fortune-teller. Choose the Text tool and create a text box at the bottom of the page. Type the number 1 using a serif font such as Arial Rounded MT Bold with a point size of 48. Click on the Pointer selection tool and select the number. Rotate the number 45 degrees, and place it in the upper left corner in a triangle adjacent to the colored square. Copy the number to the Clipboard and paste it back in to create a duplicate. Choose Flip Horizontal and Flip Vertical to reori-

Choosing a color is the first step to revealing someone's fortune, so make each square of your fortune-teller a different color. If you're printing in black and white, leave the areas blank for your child to color later.

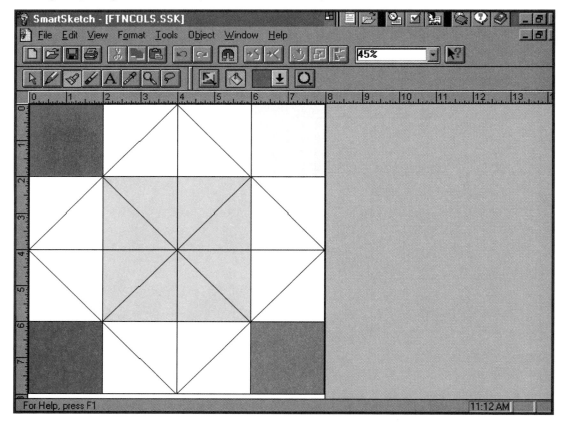

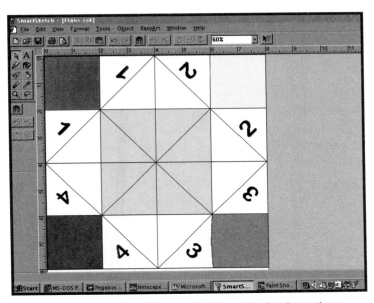

Follow the screen shown here if you need help in positioning the numbers.

13. Check the placement and alignment of type, colors, and lines on the fortune-teller. Make any necessary adjustments and then print. If you have a black-and-white printer, have your child add color with markers.

14. Now it's time to fold your fortune-teller:

a. Fold the square in half diagonally in both directions, creasing to form an X. Unfold faceup.

b. Flip the square over, folding each colored corner to the center to make a square.

c. Turn the smaller square over, folding each numbered flap to the

ent the duplicate, and then move it to the adjacent triangle. (The tops of the numbers should end up pointing at each other.)

10. Work your way clockwise around the larger square, typing 2, 3, and 4 in the triangles next to the colored squares. Type a number, rotate it, and place it; then duplicate the number, flip it, and place it.

11. Type your responses in the triangles in the center of the page using the same font as your numbers but a smaller point size (so the text will fit) and centered alignment. (We used 20-point Arial Rounded MT Bold.)

12. Rotate the answers so that they run along the long side of each triangle.

center, covering the answers in the middle. Carefully fold and unfold along each seam to make the fortune-teller flexible.

d. Fold in half to create a rectangle with the colored sides out, making it easier to insert your fingers. Carefully place your thumb (in front) and forefinger (in back) under the colored flaps on each side and push upward and toward the center, forming points with the colors outside and the numbers inside.

Paper Football

Paper football is an indoor game that two people play sitting at opposite ends of a table. The football, a triangle of folded notebook paper, is slid between the two players.

The object of the game is to send the football skidding across the surface of the table so that when it comes to a stop, a portion of it is hanging over the table's edge.

The opposing player checks a shot by sliding his finger across the edge. If his finger makes contact with the football (usually sending it spinning), the shot is declared a touchdown and the player who sent it is awarded six points. That player can then "kick" for an extra point. To do so, the opposing player first creates field goal posts by pointing his index fingers at one another to form the crossbar, with his upright thumbs forming the posts. The player who scored the touchdown "kicks" by setting the football on one of its edges and holding it in place with one index finger, and then flicking the football with the other index finger. If he puts the football through the "uprights," he gets the extra point. Play continues back and forth between the players up to an agreed-upon score or for a set amount of time.

Draw a series of straight lines to create your original fold lines.

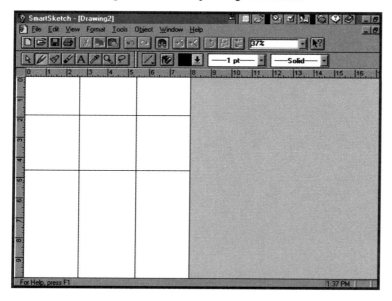

Before You Begin

You and your child should think up a team name and team mascot. You can use your child's favorite sports team or the name of a local team, or the two of you can make one up, perhaps using your child's name

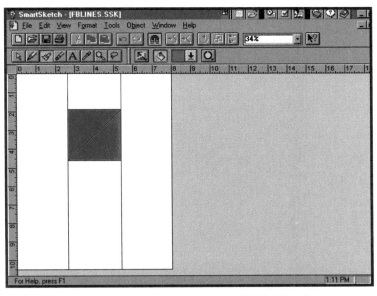

Use the Paint Bucket tool to fill the center square with a bright color.

(such as *Rob's Raiders*). Then draw a mascot or choose one from your clip-art collection, and save it to a file.

Step-by-Step

We used SmartSketch for the paper football, but you can use your favorite draw program — just make sure it has on-screen rulers.

1. Launch SmartSketch (or your draw program) and open a new document.

2. You'll need rulers as a guide for this project, so choose View, Show Rulers. Then choose Show Page (also under View) to show the entire document.

3. Use the default page setup (Por-

trait). Choose Format, Document, and Match Printer so that the on-screen drawing area matches the printable area.

4. Click on the Pencil button and choose Straight Line. Draw two vertical lines, one at the 2 5/8-inch mark and the other at the 5 3/8-inch mark on the top ruler. Draw two horizontal lines, the first at the 1 7/8-inch mark and the second at the 4 5/8-inch mark on the side ruler. (To make it easy to set lines exactly horizontal or vertical, choose Tools, Snap; a bold circle indicates perfection.) Save the file.

5. Use the cursor to select the horizontal lines in the left and right columns, and press the Delete key. Now you should have a single center column with a box in it.

For our team mascot, we used a gecko from the EasyArt collection.

6. Use the Straight Line tool to draw a diagonal line in the 2 3/4-inch square in the center column, extending from the lower left corner to the upper right. Save the file, and then select Save As and give the file a new name. The old file will serve as a template for future designs, eliminating the need to go in and set up the page and the lines again.

7. Choose the Paint Brush, and then click on the Paint Bucket. Select a bright color such as red. Fill the two triangles by clicking on them.

8. Locate the artwork of your child's team mascot. If you are using a clip-art image from SmartSketch, click on the EasyArt Finder under Help. (On the Mac, just look under the EasyArt menu item.) After you lo-

cate your art, click in the small red-and-green square to rid the art of color. If your child doesn't like any of the choices available, have him create his own using the Paint tools.

9. Drag the image onto the red square. Adjust the scale and the rotation of the image as necessary.

10. Now it's time to add the team name. Select the Text tool, drag a rectangle next to the red square, and type the name of your child's team (such as *Gary's Geckos*) in a modern-looking font such as Bauhaus 93, point size 28. Use a separate text box for each word.

11. Select each word, and copy and paste it.

12. Rotate one set of words 45 degrees and place it along the diagonal in the red square. Select the nonrotated mascot name (such as *Geckos*) and rotate it 90 degrees counterclockwise. Place it inside the extreme right edge of the red square. Place the other word (such as *Gary's*) along the bottom edge of the square. Save the file. Then select Save As and give the file a new name. The old file can now be used as a template, in case you want to personalize the football design for other kids.

13. Make any final design changes, and then print on regular-weight color paper. If you have a black-and-white printer, just print the page as a line drawing (without color) and have your child fill in the colors using markers.

Customizing Clip Art

For a bright, colorful mascot, we used the Paint Bucket in SmartSketch to fill the gecko.

For the sample football project, we customized a gecko from the EasyArt collection in SmartSketch. You can adapt the following steps to customize any EasyArt clip art. Begin by selecting the gecko image. Rotate it (choose Tools, Rotate) 45 degrees counterclockwise. While the gecko is still selected, choose Object, Edit Object. Under View, click on Show All so you can see more detail for your editing.

Next, fill the gecko with color. Choose the Paint Brush, the Paint Bucket, and the color purple, and then click inside the gecko.

Choose the Pencil tool, Smooth line (under the Pencil mode pull-down menu), and draw an eye outside your clip art, on the blank workspace.

Now use the Line tool and Paint Bucket to add colors to the eye. Then dupli-cate the eye: select all the parts you've just drawn by clicking above and to the left of the eye and then dragging a box down and to the right to surround the eye. Copy it to the Clipboard and paste it back into the document. Select the new eye and choose Tools, Flip Horizontal. Move the new eye next to the original one.

Select both eyes (use a box again), and then group all the parts by choosing Object, Create Group. Drag the eyes into place on the gecko.

Choose View, Show Page to return to your original work area view. Continue with step 9 in the directions.

Next, we used the Paint tools to add eyes.

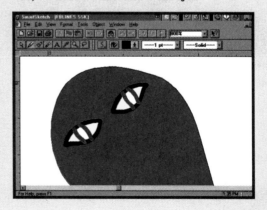

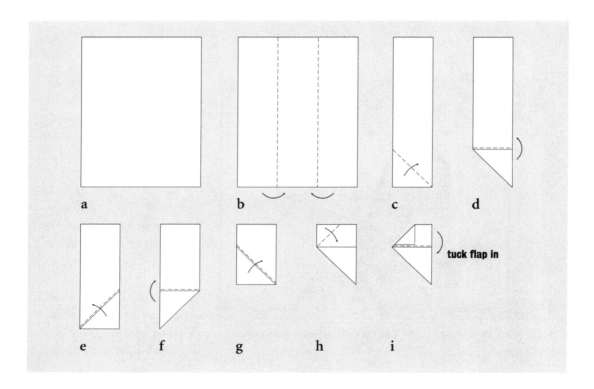

14. The last step is folding your football:

a. Take the printed paper and flip it over so that the red square is facedown and near the top of the page.

b. Fold the right third of the page over, following the black fold line. Then fold the left third of the page over.

c. Fold the bottom left corner up until it meets the right side, creating a small triangle. The edge that was on the bottom should now be flush with the right edge. Crease.

d. Fold the bottom point up, keeping the right edges aligned and maintaining the shape of the triangle. (This is the same folding pattern that you use when folding a flag.)

e. Fold the bottom right corner up to the left side. Keep the left edges aligned.

f. Fold the tip up, following the left side.

g. Fold the bottom left corner along the diagonal (the triangle's long side). Align the right edges.

h. Fold the top left corner down diagonally to meet the edge of the football.

i. Tuck the remaining flap into the fold of the football.

POGs

POGs are game pieces that kids collect. The first POGs were cardboard caps from milk bottles. The object of the POG game is to win as many caps as you can from opposing players. To play, everyone sits in a circle and stacks the caps, decorated side up, into one column

World POG Federation

For more POG information, you can call the World POG Federation in Costa Mesa, California, at 714-548-2600. You can also check out on CompuServe Library 13 of the Trading Card Forum.

for each person, with the same number of caps in each column. The players take turns throwing a special POG called a *slammer* at a stack of POGs, trying to flip as many caps in the stack as possible (by knocking them over). All caps that land blank side up are that player's winnings; all flipped caps remaining art side up are

Here are just a few of the colorful POGs you can create.

restacked into one column. Play continues until the very last cap is won or the players decide to stop.

Before You Begin

Have your child make a list of the images he'd like to put on his POGs. Remember, anything goes: animals that he'd like as pets; the cartoon characters he thinks are the funniest; his lucky number; his favorite sports stars; funny words; letters; shapes; photos — whatever comes to mind. (See the "Creative Primer" for information on scanning and digitizing photos.)

Step-by-Step

We're using SmartSketch to make the POGs, but you can adapt the steps for your favorite drawing program.

FamilyPC Tip: *Tubes of premade POGs are inexpensive, but your kids may find the art on some of them unattractive or boring. Just stick your new surfaces on these "discards" to create perfectly weighted and trimmed POGs.*

1. Launch SmartSketch and set up the page so that the on-screen document will match the printout by choosing Format, Document, Match Printer.

2. Draw a circle 1 5/8 inches in diameter by choosing the Pencil tool, and then choosing Oval in the Pencil mode pulldown menu. Position the cursor in the upper left corner (where the rulers meet) and drag.

3. Select the circle, and choose Edit, Du-

Creating Backgrounds for Your POGs

Would you like to make special backgrounds for your POGs, like we did on the Winger's Stinger POG we created for this project? If so, follow these steps.

FamilyPC Tip: *Clip art will show up best if you use pastel or light colors rather than sharply contrasting colors for the background circles.*

In SmartSketch or a similar draw program, choose the Pencil tool, the Oval tool, 8-point thickness, and a color. Then draw four concentric circles that fit inside one another. To draw the circles, just click on the upper left corner of the circle and drag diagonally, keeping the large bold circle at the cursor's location.

Scale the circles as necessary.

Fill in colors between the concentric circles by choosing the Brush mode, the Paint Bucket, and a color, and then clicking where you want the color to appear. Try contrasting colors.

Save the file using Save As; change the file name slightly for each variation you want to keep.

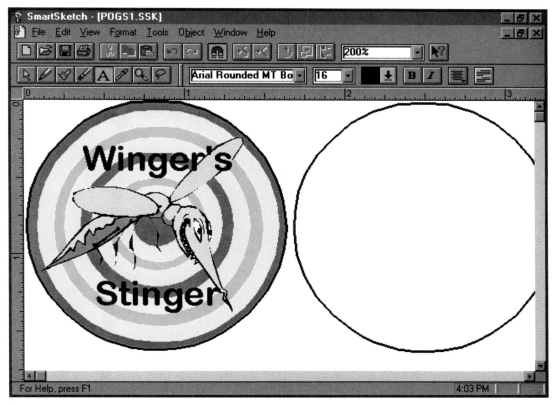

We used two text boxes to add the words to this POG design so we could adjust the placement of the text separately.

plicate. Drag the new circle next to the original one. Repeat two more times, so that you have a row of four circles. Save the file.

4. Add a background color to each circle.

5. Choose a clip-art image, copy it to the Clipboard, and paste the image into your document.

6. Select the image and scale it so that it fits just inside the circle.

7. Save the file.

8. Add text to the POG by clicking on the Text tool (the capital *A*), choosing a font, point size, and text color, and then dragging the cursor to create a text box. Create multiple text boxes if you want to move different words freely around the POG.

9. Add any finishing touches. Print a test copy to see how your POG looks.

10. Move to the next circle on the top row and create a new design.

11. After completing a row of POGs, group

POGware

If you are looking for a quick and easy way to make POGs, try StickerShop Plus (Windows or Mac disks, $39.95; Mindscape, 800-866-5967 or 415-883-3000). The program, which is also great for making buttons and stickers, comes with cardboard discs and adhesive paper. To make a set of POGs, you just select and scale your art elements (choose from premade designs and logos or your own artwork and text) and then print your creations.

the row (choose Create Group on the Object menu) and duplicate it several times down the page.

12. Print the circles on a full sheet of label paper. If you don't have a color printer, have your child color the POGs. Affix the sheet to a piece of cardboard and cut out the circles. If you don't have label paper, you can use regular paper and glue it to the cardboard.

Products You Can Use

Paint or draw program: *ClarisDraw, CorelDraw, SmartSketch*
Clip art: *Art Explosion – 40,000 Images, Task Force Clip Art – Really Big Edition*

Stationery Store

Create your own personal stationery

 PREP TIME: 15-20 MINUTES EACH

Materials

Word processing, desktop publishing, draw, or paint program (for notepads and personalized paper) • **Draw program (for envelopes)** • **Photo-editing program (optional)** • **Clip art (optional)** • **Printer** • **Scanner (optional)** • **Paper** • **Copy shop (for notepads)**

Whether your child is leaving you a quick note before going to play with friends or writing a thank-you letter to grandparents, she'll enjoy using her own stationery. Together you can make different styles of stationery: notepads for short messages, writing paper for letters, or notecards for thank-yous. You can create them using classic designs or funny sayings. And you can change them as often as you like for different occasions, such as back-to-school or summer vacation. Whatever you decide, one thing's for sure: nothing encourages kids to write like their own special paper.

Personal Notepad

What could be handier than a notepad for dashing off a quick note, writing yourself a reminder, or making a To Do list? With these notepads, you and your kids can leave notes by the front door, on the refrigerator, tucked into the bathroom mirror — wherever you and they are sure to see them.

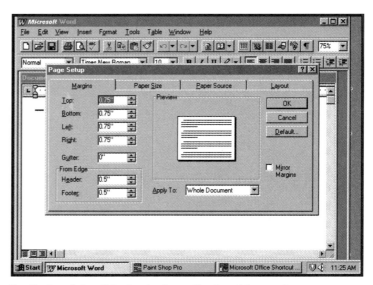

Use the Page Setup dialog box to change the size of the margins.

Before You Begin

Choosing design elements for your pad comes first. The classic scratch pad features slogans such as *From the Desk of..., Red Alert!,* or *Read Me.* You could include something like this, or use your child's or family's favorite saying instead. Notepads often include an illustration as well. To find one for your notepads, peruse your clip-art collection or symbol fonts. Before you begin, you should also choose a size for your notepad; the following directions are for a pad 5 1/2 inches by 8 1/2 inches.

Step-by-Step

We use Microsoft Word in the following steps. However, you can complete this project using the word-processing module in a Works program, or a desktop publishing, draw, or paint program.

1. Launch Microsoft Word. First, you'll set up the page in Landscape mode and expand the printable size of the page. Choose File, Page Setup, and the Paper Size tab, and then choose Landscape. Now choose the Margins tab, and reduce all margins to .75 inch.

> **FamilyPC Tip:** *To make sure your printed document will look the way you want, use the Print Preview mode regularly to view your work.*

2. Make your whole worksheet visible by choosing View, Page Layout. Then change the Zoom control on the toolbar to Whole Page to see the entire document.

3. Next, divide the page with a vertical line down the center so that you can create two notepads on the same page. Click on the Drawing Tools button and choose the Straight Line button. Start at the top of the document at the 4 3/4-inch mark on the ruler, and drag straight down with the left mouse button depressed. Go to Format, Drawing Object. From the Size and Position dialog box, set Horizontal to 5.5" from Page and Vertical to 0" from Page. Finally, click anywhere on the page to deselect your line. The page should be bisected.

FamilyPC Tip: *To move a frame, you must first select it. Then move the cursor near the edge of the frame until the cursor becomes a four-way arrow symbol. Now you can click and drag the frame to a new position.*

4. Insert a frame for your catchy slogan by choosing Insert, Frame. Stretch the frame so that it is about 3 inches wide and 1 inch deep. (You can adjust the size anytime.)

The Kids font is perfect for creating notepads that look like they were handwritten by your child.

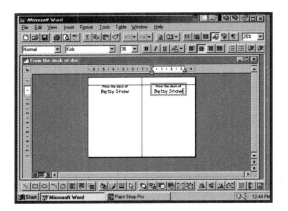

We've copied the original design so that there are two on the page.

5. Click and drag the frame so that it is centered in the left notepad page, with the top edge of the frame flush with the top 3/4-inch margin marker.

6. To make the text frame disappear, choose Format, Borders and Shading, None. To make the frame reappear, simply click in its general area.

7. Add text to the frame by choosing a fun, nontraditional font and typing the slogan. We used the Kids typeface (22 points for the first line and 36 points for the second) and center alignment.

8. Next, copy the text from the page on the left to the page on the right by selecting the frame, and copying it to the Clipboard.

9. Click anywhere outside the original frame to deselect it. Then paste the copy from the Clipboard onto the page and drag the new text over to the right half of the page. Again align the top of the frame with the 3/4-inch top margin marker.

10. Save the file.

11. Create a frame at the bottom of either page to provide a place to insert art by choosing Insert, Frame and then clicking and dragging.

12. Insert a piece of clip art as a design element into one of the new frames. In Word, it's easiest to choose an image from the Microsoft ClipArt Gallery. Simply double-click inside the frame, and then choose Insert, Object. Highlight Microsoft ClipArt Gallery,

Microsoft ClipArt Gallery 2.0 has thousands of images.

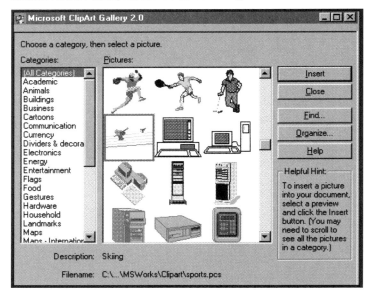

and click on OK. Using the dialog boxes that appear, locate your choice of clip art. Select the art and click on Insert.

13. Scale the art to suit your needs. You'll probably want to make it about the same size as the slogan or smaller. To keep the same proportions as you scale, press the Control key (in Windows) or the Shift key (on a Macintosh). Or experiment and stretch or squash the art. Make any final adjustments to the placement.

14. Select the frame with the clip art and copy it to the Clipboard. Click outside the clip-art frame to deselect it. Then paste the image onto the workspace and drag it to the empty frame.

15. Save the file.

16. To delete the vertical guide, click on

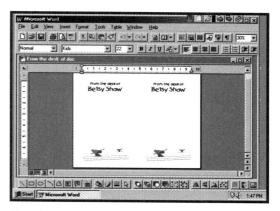

Place large clip art along the bottom of the notepad. Smaller images will look best at the top, alongside your child's name.

the line and press the Delete key. (Keep the line if you'll be cutting each sheet yourself.)

17. Check all the elements of the page one last time for spelling errors and problems with alignment or your choice of clip art. Save the file when you are satisfied.

Stack and Glue Notepads Yourself

Personalized party favors, birthday gifts, stocking stuffers — there's no limit to what you and your kids can do with the custom pads of paper you make with your computer. And if you plan to make a bunch of your own pads, consider getting a jig that lets you clamp and glue your own stacks.

Queblo (800-523-9080), a mail-order paper supply company, offers the Jiffy Pad Making Press in its catalog for $120. Although that's not cheap, the press is built to last. It's a metal frame with adjustable clamps and a removable faceplate. You stack your paper flush against the front section and then clamp it securely into place. Remove the faceplate and slather on the special padding glue. The jig is over a foot tall, so you can make a bunch of pads at one time — just separate each pad with cardboard.

FamilyPC Tip: *If you have color clip art but want a black-and-white print with shades of gray, choose Mono-chrome or Grayscale under the Graphics settings in the Print Setup dialog box or the Print dialog box.*

18. Print the notepad design.

19. Take your printout to a quick-print shop, such as PIP or Kinkos. To create two 50-page pads, have the shop make 50 copies of your printout and cut the pages in half. Then have the shop glue the paper into pads. It costs about $6 to make two pads of 50 sheets each, using regular copy paper and black-and-white artwork. (The price will increase if you want to duplicate color artwork, use a better paper, or make more pads.) If you want to use color paper, make sure it doesn't clash with or obscure your de-sign. For more information on paper and paper suppliers, turn to the "Resource Guide."

Personalized Paper

Offbeat, stylized stationery is perfect for your child's everyday use — whether he's writing to a friend, a pen-pal, or his favorite uncle. Personal stationery is easy to create, too, because the only "must" is that you leave enough writing space. Other than that, let your child's imagination be your guide.

Before You Begin

In the following steps, we'll show you how to create stationery with a saying at the bot-tom of the page along with an illustration. Before you start, you and your child should choose the font and images you want to use. Browse through your font collection and your clip-art or photo collection, and choose a typeface and one or more images. If you choose to use a photo, have it digi-tized. (See the "Creative Primer" section for details.)

Step-by-Step

We use Microsoft Word to create the sta-tionery, but you can use your favorite word processing, desktop publishing, draw, or paint program.

1. Launch Word and begin a new docu-ment. Keep the default page setup (Portrait, 1.25" margins).

2. Insert a frame for your art and your text by choosing Insert, Frame. To create the

FamilyPC Tip: *If your frame appears with a black border, you can remove the border. Simply select the frame and choose Format, Borders and Shading, None.*

Special Effects: Creating Ghosted Images

For one-of-a-kind stationery, create a ghosted image of a favorite photo and use it as your background. First, have your photo digitized. (See the "Creative Primer" section for details.) Next, use a photo-editing program such as Paint Shop Pro to convert the photo into a light-colored, low-contrast, grayscale file.

Start by removing any distracting background. Use the Lasso or Oval tool to encircle the portion of the image you want to preserve. Cut the selected area to the Clipboard and paste it to create a new image. Next, use the Airbrush tool to whiteout the rest of the background and give your image a soft edge. Choose Colors, Greyscale to convert the

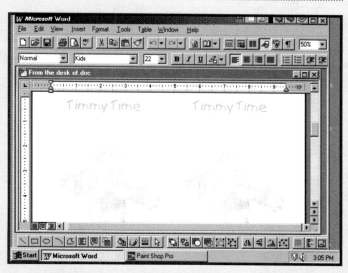

Use a photo-editing program to create a ghosted image for your child's pads.

image to shades of grey. Fade it further by going to the Colors menu and choosing Adjust, Gamma Correct. Set the correction factor as high as possible and click on OK. Finally, use the Image menu to resize the picture.

When doing detailed editing, you'll probably need to zoom in on your picture. Paint Shop Pro lets you magnify an image up to 16 to 1 (the image becomes 16 times larger), so

you can adjust the color of pixels one at a time. The program also has a number of tools and filters for creating special effects, such as blurring the image so that it appears to be moving.

When you are satisfied with the image, create two frames in your word processing document (one in the left part of the page, and one in the right) to create two notepads. Then either insert the picture or copy it to the Clipboard and paste it into place. Add text, align and size all the elements to suit your tastes, and print.

We took the photo on the left and knocked out the background, faded the image to grayscale, and enhanced the edges to create the image on the right.

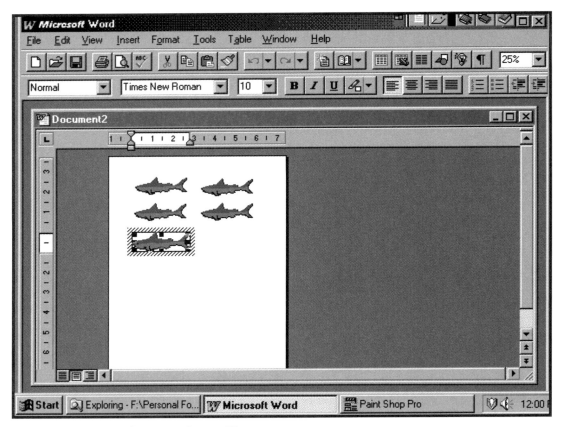

Try copying or combining clip art to make something new.

frame, click on the document and drag across the screen.

3. Click inside the frame.

To insert a clip-art image, first choose Insert, Object. Then choose your clip-art source (in this case, Microsoft ClipArt Gallery) and locate the appropriate file. Choose Insert.

To insert a digitized photo, first choose Insert, Picture. Locate the image file on your hard drive (using the dialog boxes that appear), and choose Insert.

FamilyPC Tip: *If you're using clip art, you can have fun using copies of the same piece of clip art — perfect for creating a school of fish, for example. To reuse the same clip-art image, select the frame with the inserted clip art and copy it to the Clipboard. Click elsewhere on the page to deselect the frame, and then paste from the Clipboard onto the page. You can select any individual fish and scale it to a different size.*

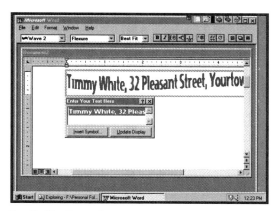

Use the WordArt tool to create exciting text effects, such as a wavy pattern.

4. Save the file.

5. Resize the individual clip-art image or your photo so that it's no more than a 1-inch or 2-inch square.

FamilyPC Tip: *If you don't have WordArt, you can insert plain text into the document, or manipulate text in a draw or paint program and then copy your work to the Clipboard and paste it into your document.*

6. Drag all the art to the bottom of the page, but leave some space between the art and the edge of the paper so that no part of the art will be cut off when printed. (To see how your printed page will look, choose Print Preview.) Save the file.

7. Next, you'll create a frame for your child's name and address. Click on an open

frame or insert a new one, as shown in step 2. Then choose Insert, Object. Choose Microsoft WordArt 3 and type in the name and address information.

8. Select the font your child wants to use. (A sans serif font such as Flexure works well.) Also have your child choose a pattern to make the text look different than text on a standard letterhead. (We used Wave 2.) Then choose Best Fit for the size of the text, and stretch the letters to the extremes of the text box by clicking on the button that has an A and arrows going in different directions. Next, click on the button with cross-hatching to choose a color, and click on the shadow button just to the right to choose a shadow and a color for the shadow. When your child has finished making these choices, Click Update Display and close the dialog box.

9. Drag the text box to the bottom of the page and resize it. (Check to see what the

Change the view to Whole Page to see the combined clip art and text.

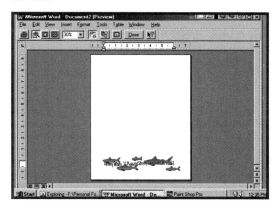

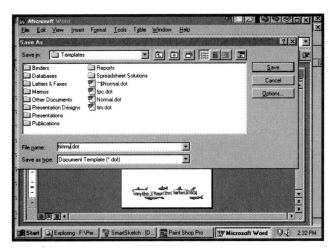

By saving your design as a template, it's readily available when your child wants to compose a letter on the computer.

Custom Envelopes

What better way to send a special letter than in a special envelope? Creating envelopes to match your child's stationery is the perfect finishing touch.

Step-by-Step

These directions are based on SmartSketch, but you can adapt them to any program with drawing tools and on-screen rulers.

printed page will look like by choosing File, Print Preview.) Save the file.

10. Make any final adjustments, save the file again, and print a test copy.

11. Make the document into a template so that every time your child wants to fire off a letter, a new, unnamed document complete with artwork and his name and address will appear. Choose File, Save As, Document Template (one of the choices in the Save as type pulldown menu). Save the template with your child's name.

12. To use the stationery, choose New and click on the template. Then you can print the page immediately and have your child handwrite a letter. Alternatively, have him type the letter on the unnamed document.

1. Launch SmartSketch and leave the default page setup in Portrait mode.

2. Set the working document size to the maximum printable area of a standard sheet

Click the Pencil mode menu to choose the Straight Line mode.

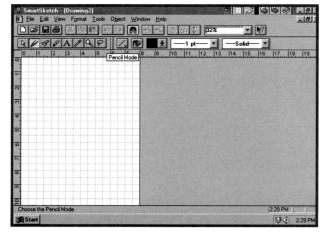

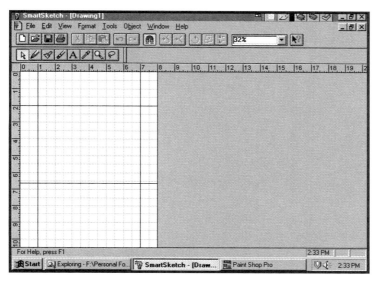

The top area is the envelope's flap; the center area is the envelope's front panel; the bottom area is the envelope's back panel.

of paper by choosing Format, Document, Match Printer. In the same dialog box, click on Show Grid.

FamilyPC Tip: *To see exactly where you are working on a page, change the view to the entire page by choosing Views, Zoom, Whole Page, or by choosing Whole Page on the Zoom pulldown menu on the toolbar.*

3. Choose View, Show Page so that you can see the entire page. The dimensions of the document on-screen should read 8" by 10" or 8" by 10 1/2", depending upon your printer.

4. Next, you'll draw a series of horizontal and vertical lines to represent the outline of

the envelope. Click on the Pencil tool and choose Line from the Pencil mode pull-down menu, which is just to the left of the ink bottle.

Draw vertical lines the full length of the page at the 1-inch and 7-inch marks on the top ruler. Draw horizontal lines the full width of the document at the 2-inch and 6 5/8-inch mark on the side ruler.

5. Taper the top flap and back panel by clicking and dragging the ends of the two vertical lines. Drag each 1/2 inch toward the center of the document. (The lines will snap to the 1/2-inch grid line.) Taper the left and right flaps on both ends 1/2 inch as well.

6. When it comes time to cut out the envelopes, it would be helpful if the areas to

Turn off the grid to see how your envelope will print.

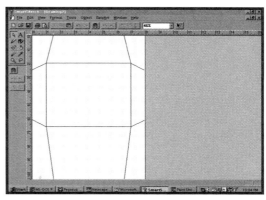

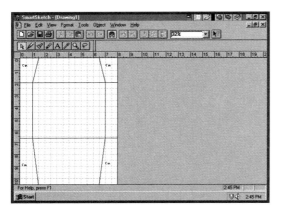

Taper the ends of the lines and add the word "Cut" to make it clear what part of the envelope will be trimmed.

be cut were marked. To add the word *Cut* to the four corners, choose the Text tool (the button with the capital A). Then click and drag where you want the text to appear. Choose a point size from the pulldown menu, and type *Cut*. Copy the word to the Clipboard and then paste it into the other three corners. Save the file.

7. Add a return address to the envelope design by choosing the Text tool and dragging a text box in the upper left corner of the front panel. Match the font, style, and color of the stationery by clicking on the appropriate selections in the pulldown menus on the toolbar. Change the point size, if desired. (We used 14-point Flexure for the font, plain for the style, and blue for the color.)

8. Insert clip art or art elements

that match your stationery by choosing Edit, Insert Object. Click Insert when you've found the image.

9. If your design calls for copies of the clip art, select the art, copy it to the Clipboard, and then paste it onto the page.

FamilyPC Tip: *Do you have a limited type selection? You can buy font packs from computer supply retailers or download fonts as freeware or shareware through online services. Check the "Resource Guide" for more information on Fonts.*

10. Scale the art to the appropriate size. If necessary, drag the clip art to reposition it. Save the file.

Create an additional text frame in the upper left corner so that you can add a return address.

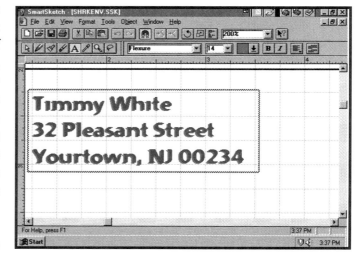

The Write Stuff

Choosing a paper for your stationery is as important as creating a design. To add the right finishing touch, choose a quality paper. For kids' stationery, you'll probably want paper with some personality. Linen and laid-finish papers (20 lb. is a good weight) have more visible lines and light color variations than their woven cousins. And their less formal texture should fit well with your child's design. If you want to get even wilder, take a trip to the stationer's or the copy shop, or peek at a mail-order catalog. You'll find papers that run the gamut from rough and rugged recycled earth tones to chrome-plated colors.

For information on different papers and mail-order paper suppliers, turn to the "Resource Guide" section.

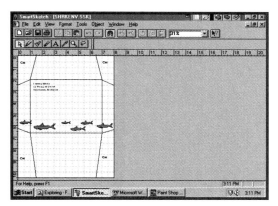

We repositioned the clip art by lining up the sharks along the bottom of the front panel, overlapping them onto the left and right flaps.

11. Check the layout of the page (File, Print Preview) and make any necessary adjustments.

12. Print a test copy of the envelope. Now is the time to make any changes to the location of elements and the overall look. Save the file.

FamilyPC Tip: *In SmartSketch, you can use the Selecting Arrow to grab the end of a line and drag it to the appropriate location. You can also drag the middle portion of a straight line in any direction to make the line curved.*

13. Print the envelope (File, Print), cut, and assemble, folding along the lines and using a glue stick to hold the envelope together.

Products You Can Use

Paint or draw program: *ClarisDraw, CorelDraw, SmartSketch*

Word processing program: *Microsoft Word, WordPerfect*

Works program: *ClarisWorks, Microsoft Works, WordPerfect Works*

Desktop publishing program: *Adobe Paint & Publish, Microsoft Publisher, Turbo Publisher*

Photo-editing program: *Adobe PhotoDeluxe, Paint Shop Pro*

Party Time

Anticipation. For kids, that's half the fun of having a party. Who will they invite? What desserts can they help you bake? What games should they play? What decorations should they make?

Decorations? You can relax. Whether you're hosting a birthday bash or a holiday party, the projects in this section will show you and your kids how to make some special and novel party decorations that are sure to create a festive atmosphere.

You can help your kids choose which decorations to make, or just let them go to town making everything from customized invitations and banners to party poppers and masks. Letting your kids make the decorations is a great way to get them involved in party preparations. Yet, for them, it's like starting the party early!

Board Game

 PREP TIME: 2 HOURS

Materials

Paint or draw program • Clip art (optional) • Color printer •
Paper • Sturdy cardboard • Scissors • Glue •
Bottle caps or buttons (to make into playing pieces)

Roll double sixes, pass your opponent, and you're home free. Roll again and you win! Whether it's Monopoly, The Game of Life, or Chutes and Ladders, board games are ever-popular evening pastimes. They're hours of fun in small packages, but you can't play them forever. Soon everyone is wanting a new game, a new challenge. So here's a challenge: first create your own board game, then play it. You can start simply by paralleling a game you've played for years and progressing to a more complex game. Of course, an advantage to creating your own games is that an updated version or a replacement piece is just a few mouse clicks away.

Before You Begin

This project requires lots of thinking about how your game will look and work before you start. Have your child help you decide on a game you want to mimic. Then think of the different themes you might choose for the game. Next, take time to scan through your clip-art collection, or use the paint tools in a paint or draw program to create art for the board. Remember that you can duplicate one piece of art as many times as necessary. (This is handy for creating du-

plicate images on the board itself.) When your game concept and art are ready, turn to a draw or paint program.

Step-by-Step

Here we'll describe how to create a new version of Chutes and Ladders using palm trees and waterfalls to guide the players through a rain forest board, but you can adapt the concept to your favorite game.

You can use either a paint or draw program. What you choose depends on the

Position the number in each square of the game board.

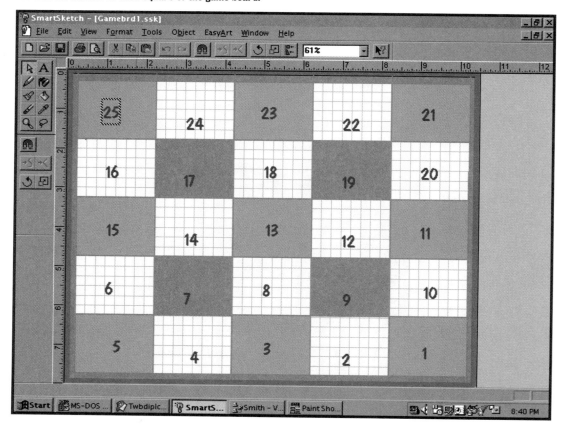

type of game you're creating. For instance, our version of Chutes and Ladders is set up on a simple grid, but certain images must be stretched. Therefore, a draw program is more useful because it lets you stretch and edit objects in a number of ways.

1. Launch SmartSketch (or the program that you plan on using).

2. Set the page in Landscape mode if your game board is wider than it is tall; otherwise use Portrait mode (which is usually the default).

3. If you're using SmartSketch, turn on the grid (in the Format, Document dialog box) to make it easier for you to place items on the screen.

4. Use the Straight Line tool to draw the actual board grid. (In SmartSketch, select the Pencil mode first.) Most games of Chutes and Ladders are played with 100 squares, but you can reduce that number to 25, with 5 squares to a row.

5. Use the Paint Bucket tool to color in the squares and the Text tool to number them. Start numbering in the lower right corner and continue to the left, and then change direction in the next row, creating a path.

6. Save the file.

7. Locate your clip art or saved art and insert it. (Here, we've used clip art from

FamilyPC Tip: *You can edit clip-art images in SmartSketch to suit your needs using the Edit Object command under Object. For instance, you can create a vine from the vinca plant clip art. You'll probably find it's easier to open a new document to work in while creating the vine. Otherwise, the existing lines on the board have a tendency to get tangled up with your new vine.*

Select the vinca clip art, choose Edit Object, and then select the elements that need to be changed. Use the Eraser tool to remove the flower. Then highlight the leaves, choose Edit, Duplicate, and arrange the extra leaves into a vine. When your vine is long enough, select all of it, choose Create Group from the Object menu, and move the vine to the game board.

SmartSketch's EasyArt collection. In this program, you just click and drag the art onto the board.) Use additional clip art to create a border of leaves and jungle flowers. Detailed clip art will slow the operation of SmartSketch, so be patient.

8. Save the file.

9. Next, we'll insert the Chutes and Ladders, or in this case, the waterfalls and palm trees. Start by creating a new file.

10. Draw the palm tree. Use the Paint-brush tool to create a brown trunk and some jagged green leaves. Then select the image, group it, and save it.

11. Next, draw the waterfall. Use the Paintbrush tool to draw a few long blue strokes for the falling water, and use the Pencil tool set on Dotted Line to draw some light gray swirls at the bottom for the spray. With the Arrow tool, drag a square around the waterfall to highlight it, click on Group Objects, and save.

12. Close the drawing window.

13. Return to your grid, and choose Open as EasyArt from the File menu. Your waterfall and palm tree will appear in the EasyArt menu for you to drag into your game board file. If you're using another drawing program, use the Clipboard to import the waterfall and palm tree.

FamilyPC Tip: *To save yourself the frustration of trying to get your original art just right, take advantage of the special features included with many of the SmartSketch drawing tools. To make a monkey's curly tail, for example, just draw a straight line in the Paintbrush or Pencil mode, and then bend it with the Arrow tool. Or to make a feature appear "behind" another, use the Paint Behind feature of the brush as you scribble.*

14. You can create playing pieces from either original art or clip art (such as bananas, oranges, and pineapples from the Fruit and Vegetables section in Smart-Sketch). It's also easy to create original jungle animals using the draw tools. You can create a friendly monkey by using ovals and circles (filled using the Paint Bucket tool) for the body, head, eyes, and ears. Add arms, legs, and a fat tail with the Pencil tool in Smooth mode, set to a larger point size. Then the same elements can be recombined and adjusted to make a black jaguar.

15. When you have finished creating the board and playing pieces, save the file.

16. Print a test copy.

Light and dark blue strokes combine to make water falling into a pool.

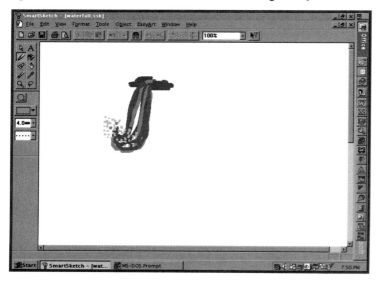

A collection of EasyArt and hand-drawn game pieces.

17. Make any adjustments. Save the file and print again if necessary.

18. Print both the board and playing pieces on standard white paper.

19. Glue the board to a piece of sturdy cardboard.

20. Cut out the playing pieces and stick them on bottle caps or large buttons.

21. Let the glue dry and you're ready to play. Just follow the rules of a regular Chutes and Ladders game.

Products You Can Use

Paint or draw program: *Flying Colors, SmartSketch*
Clip art: *Corel Gallery 2, Task Force Clip Art — Really Big Edition*

Cards and Invitations

Five unforgettable designs

 PREP TIME: 45–60 MINUTES

Materials

Paint or draw program • Clip art (optional) • Printer • Copy shop (optional) • Scanner (optional) • Standard paper • Card stock • Glue • Scissors

You're Invited to... Those are a kid's three favorite words. Today, kids seem to collect invitations as fast as celebrities do. Here's a way to make these occasions special for both your child and the guest of honor: Instead of dashing off to a store to pick up the obligatory card and gift, help your child make

something. Any one of the projects in this book would make a great kid present, topped off with a card from this project. Then the next time you and your child are planning a party, let your party expert design the invitations. After receiving so many invites, he's sure to have some opinions on what makes a good one.

Custom Cutouts

This invitation is designed for a child's birthday party that's themed as a tea party for bears (and their respective owners). The design of the invitation is simple: The cover has several stuffed bears seated and ready for tea. The faces of the bears are cut out, though, so you can insert a photo of the faces of the birthday boy or girl and their friends and have their faces show through.

Before You Begin

Begin by locating a suitable color photo to use inside the card, one in which the faces measure between 1/2 to 1 inch across. Take the snapshot to a local copy shop and have color copies made, one for each invitation. (Copy shops typically offer this service for about $1 per sheet of paper.)

Or, if you have a color printer, you can have the photo scanned and saved on a disk in a format that you can access at home (usually .BMP or .TIF for Windows and PICT for Mac). For more information on digitizing images, see the "Resource Guide."

Step-by-Step

We're using SmartSketch to make the custom cutout invites. Feel free to use your favorite draw or paint program, as long as it has on-screen rulers and lets you rotate objects.

1. Launch SmartSketch or the program you'll be using.

2. Choose Format, Document, and click on Match printer, so that what you see on the screen will match your printed output.

3. The card will be folded into quarters, so divide the page in four quadrants. Click on the Pencil tool and use the Straight Line mode to draw a vertical line at the 4-inch mark on the top ruler to the bottom of the page. Then draw a horizontal rule at the 5 1/4-inch mark on the side ruler to the right side of the page.

4. Save the file.

Divide the card into four equal quadrants to create the lines for folding the card and to serve as guides as you design the card.

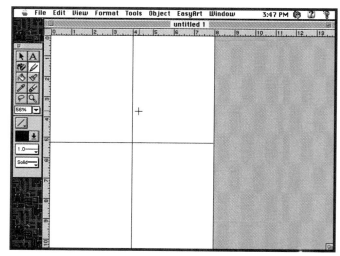

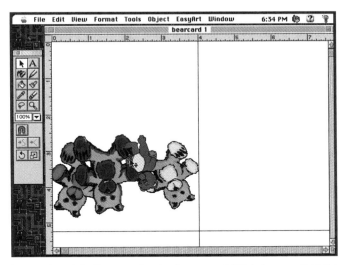

Be sure to rotate the cover image of your card 180 degrees so that the card will be right side up when you fold it.

5. If you have scanned images, import them into your document and place them in the bottom right quadrant. Using the rulers as a guide, note the location of the images within the quadrant.

6. If you'll be gluing a photo in the card, create a mock-up of the card by folding a sheet of paper in fourths. The photo would appear on the inside, right-hand page, which is currently the lower right quadrant of the document. Measure the distances of each face from the edges of the card mock-up, to use in positioning the teddy bears on the cover. (Remember that the faces of the cover bears must end up directly over the faces of your partygoers.)

7. Save the file.

8. Place clip art or your own drawings of teddy bears in the upper left quadrant of the document, which will be the cover of the card.

9. Rotate each bear image 180 degrees, so that it appears upside down. (Rotating the image ensures that it will appear right side up when the card is folded.)

10. Save the file.

11. You want the bears' faces to end up over the faces in your photo. So, measure the distance from the tops of the bears' heads to the horizontal line that bisects the page. Also measure the dimensions from their heads out to the sides of the quadrant.

More Cutouts

You can use the cutout card principle for all sorts of cards, such as:

● A Mount Rushmore birthday card featuring the birthday boy or girl as Lincoln, Roosevelt, or Jefferson

● A VIP card featuring the birthday boy or girl meeting the President

● A Historic Moment card featuring the birthday boy or girl taking the first step on the moon or hitting a home run to win the World Series

● An Open Door card, where the recipient opens the front door on the card cover to read a message

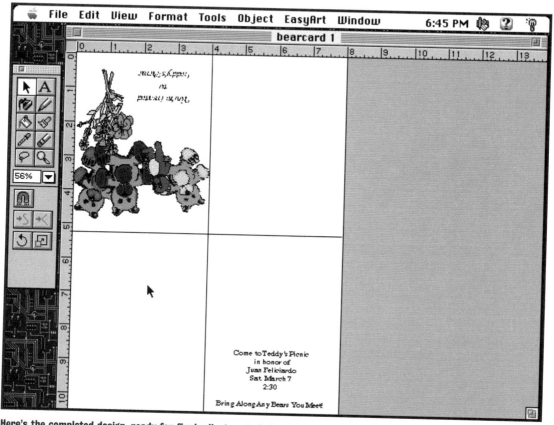

Here's the completed design, ready for final adjustments in bear alignment.

Make sure all these measurements match those for the bottom right quadrant, where your photo will appear. (Be sure to subtract 1/4 inch, or whatever your margins are, because the document displays only the printable surface.)

12. Save the file.

13. Add text to the cover. Choose the Text tool and a scripty font such as Monotype Corsiva, point size 22, bold, aligned center. In the upper left quadrant, type in a fun phrase, such as *You're Invited to Teddy's Picnic.*

14. Rotate the type 180 degrees and place it so that it doesn't cover the bears.

15. Dress up the cover with more clip art, stamps, or drawings. Add a few trees in the background for the picnic setting.

16. Save the file.

17. Now it's time to add the party details

to the bottom right quadrant. Choose the Text tool and a font (we used Times New Roman), aligned center, point size 14 or 16, and black. Type the information just beneath the picture.

FamilyPC Tip: *Clip-art packages such as Corel Gallery 2 let you export images in a variety of formats. This is especially easy to do if you are using a program that's optimized for Windows 95. For instance, with Corel Gallery 2, once you've located the image you want, simply right-click and select an option from the pop-up menu to export the file to your hard drive in a format you can access. You can also right-click and choose Copy, and then paste the image into your document.*

18. Add other elements to the inside pages. Maybe some clip art of trees, birds, or flowers? Rotate and scale the elements as appropriate. (In SmartSketch, you can scale all the elements together by selecting them and choosing Tools, Scale by Percent.)

19. Save the file.

20. Print a test page. Cut out the faces of the teddy bears that are covering your child's face and those of her friends.

21. Hold the paper so that the printed side is facing you, the bears are upside down in the upper left, and the faces

of your child and her friends are in the lower right. Fold the card: crease along the horizontal line, fold the top half backward, and then fold the left half forward and crease it.

22. Check the card to ensure that all the faces peek through the bear cutouts. Also check that the other elements are aligned properly and that there are no errors in the text.

23. Make any final adjustments or additions. (Print another test page if necessary.) Save the file.

24. Print the final version using quality ink-jet paper or card stock. Make sure you print enough for all invitees, plus a few extras.

25. Slip the color copy (if you're not using a scanned image) into place and position it appropriately. Fasten the image with small amounts of paper cement or glue under the corners.

26. Carefully cut out the teddy bear faces entirely or leave just a small bit of each face to act as a hinge. Note that you'll be cutting through two layers of the card (the top layer and the inside left flap of the card).

27. Turn the card over before folding and add a small bit of glue to the entire edge. Smooth with your finger.

28. Fold the card and seal the edges with your finger.

29. Deliver your invitations to the Teddy Bear Picnic.

Try a Tri-Fold

For a unique party invitation, try this tri-fold card. Here, we create one for a young dancer's birthday. The left and right quarters of the card are folded to meet in the middle, creating stage curtains that part to reveal a ballerina en pointe.

Before You Begin

A dancer and a stage are the key design elements in this card, so take the time to locate images in the program you are using or in a separate clip-art package. Or create your own art using the Paint tools includ-

Brainstormer
....

Tri-fold cards featuring a barn door with farm animals (for little folk), a barn door with a square dance (for bigger folk), the back doors of a moving van (Sorry to see you go…), French doors (for an open house)

ed with your software.

Step-by-Step

For this project, we're using SmartSketch, but you can use your favorite paint or draw program.

1. Launch SmartSketch (or the program you plan on using).

2. Set the page to Landscape mode. In SmartSketch, choose File, Print Setup (Page Setup on the Mac), and click on Landscape.

3. To have the screen dimensions match your page layout, choose Format, Document, Match Printer.

4. Divide the sheet in half horizontally with a thin line, which will be your first fold line. Choose the Pencil tool, Straight Line mode, 1-point thickness, and black.

5. Now draw two thin vertical lines that are 2 3/4 inches from the left and right edges. These are the secondary fold lines.

Note: When you fold the card along these lines, the top left and top right panels become the stage curtains, behind which (in the bottom left and right panels) you list the party details. The central bottom panel becomes the stage for the dancer.

6. Save the file.

7. In the center bottom panel, 1 inch from the bottom of the screen, draw the stage floor. Choose the Pencil tool, Straight Line mode, and black.

8. Color the stage floor using the Fill tool and a color. (We used brown.)

9. Save the file.

10. Now it's time to add your ballerina to the stage. Use the Smooth Line tool to draw one, or use clip art of a dancer. (Smart-Sketch's clip art includes faces, human forms, and dresses, all of which can be edited, scaled, and rotated.)

11. Finish the center panel by drawing the outline of a curtain across the top. Use the Pencil tool, Smooth Line mode, and black to draw the outline of the top curtain. Then use the Fill tool to add color. You might try deep purple or red.

FamilyPC Tip: *To give your curtains a three-dimensional look, use the Pencil tool in Smooth Line mode to create a curvy line along all the edges of the curtain. Next, use the Paint Brush tool (set to a small diameter) to add different shades of your original curtain colors in vertical stripes, to bring out the wavy pattern.*

12. Save the file.

13. Now it's time to add the important party details to the bottom left panel. Choose the Text tool and an ornate font such as Aristocrat or Florentine, point size 14, aligned left, black or dark blue. Type the time of the party, the guest of honor, and so on.

14. Now add the directions in the bottom right panel. We suggest that you use the same text style that you used for the party details, but aligned right.

15. Save the file.

Divide the card with fold lines to create stage and curtain areas.

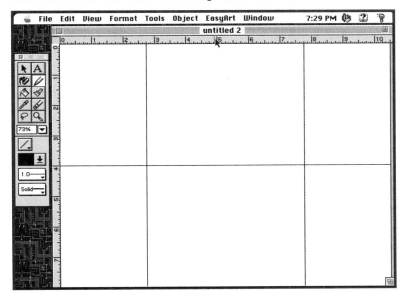

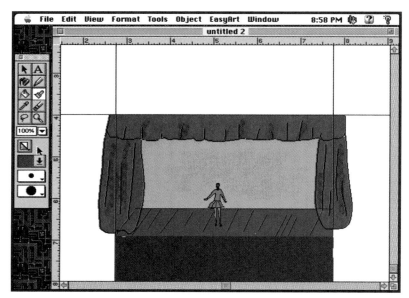

Use the paint tools to add sweeping curtains to the stage.

16. Next, we need stage curtains in the upper right and left panels. Draw one side first (left or right — it doesn't matter) using the same tools you used to draw the center bottom curtain. (These tools were the Pencil tool in Smooth Line mode and the Fill tool.)

17. These curtains are the drapes that the recipient folds back to reveal the inside of the card. You'll be folding back the top half of this card and folding in the sides. Therefore, the curtains must be rotated 180 degrees so that they appear right side up when the card is folded. You do just that in the next steps.

After you've drawn one side of the curtains, select it, group it (choose Object, Create Group), du-

plicate it (choose Edit, Duplicate), and drag the new curtain in place.

18. Rotate each of these two curtains by choosing Tools, Rotation, and grabbing one of the corner handles that appear. Place in the upper corners.

19. Save the file.

20. Include a sign on the stage that reads something like: *The Lynchburg Ballet Presents The Alicia Stark Dance Company,* substituting your child's name in the title. Use the Text tool and a font such as Times New Roman, point size 14, aligned center.

Use one panel for the directions to the party.

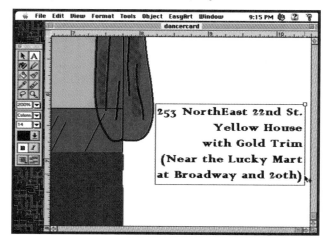

21. Like the curtains that cover the stage, this sign must be created in two sections and then rotated and placed so that it will appear right side up when the card is folded. Therefore, after you type the text for the sign, draw a vertical line through it to bisect it vertically.

22. Rotate each half of the sign (choose Tools, Rotation, and grab a handle). Place each side in the upper left and upper right panels.

23. Save the file.

24. Print a test copy of the card and check the alignment. Also make sure that no vital information is missing or misspelled.

25. Print as many test copies as necessary until you are satisfied with the design.

26. Save the final file.

27. Print the cards on card stock.

28. Flip the printed paper over and run a very thin strip of glue around the edge. Smooth the glue with your finger and wipe away any additional glue.

29. Fold along the lines, first horizontally, so that the ballerina remains in front center. Then fold the curtains in from the sides

The name of the guest of honor appears in the banner, which is upside down until the card is folded.

so that they meet in the center.

30. Let the cards dry, and deliver with a pirouette.

Creating Art from Stamps

Some paint programs, such as Flying Colors, come with clip art in the form of stamps. You can create a variety of objects by combining different stamps or using just a portion of a stamp. For instance, you can build a dance stage for the ballerina invitation by using the table stamp and filling in below the table with the wood paneling stamp.

If you copy a portion of an image to the Clipboard, it too becomes a stamp. For example, make stage curtains by copying just the bottom of the queen's velvet dress. Stamp somewhere in the picture, and then use the Cut/Copy tool with the options set to Rectangle, Copy, and No Canvas to copy the dress from the waist down. Now you have a vel-

vet curtain stamp.

Don't forget that newly created stamps can be resized and rotated as needed. You can use this feature to divide the complete stage in half and rotate each half into position on the outer top panels.

Unfortunately, at press time, Flying Colors works only with the Mac or Windows 3.1 operating system, not with Windows 95.

A Full Page of Fun

This invitation is designed around a Wanted poster that looks like it was snatched straight off the wall of the Tombstone Jail, circa 1880. In the poster, each invitee is featured as the villain, which makes the poster a more valued party favor. However, you could make the project simpler by featuring only the birthday boy or girl as the villain of the day.

Before You Begin

Collect closeups of the invitees (or the birthday boy or girl) before you begin making the invitations. Have the images scanned and saved on a floppy disk in a format you can

access (.TIF is fine for both Windows and Mac platforms). For other alternatives for digitizing your photos, turn to the "Resource Guide." Or you can photocopy the pictures and manually paste them into place.

FamilyPC Tip: *If you are using scanned images that were saved as color images, print them in grayscale for a more authentic look.*

Step-by-Step

Almost any paint or draw program can be used for this project; we used SmartSketch.

1. Launch SmartSketch (or the program you plan on using).

FamilyPC Tip: *If you don't have an appropriate font, download the font you need from the software library of an online service. On America Online for instance, a software search on the words* True Type *fonts yielded hundreds of shareware and freeware fonts. For more information on fonts, turn to the "Resource Guide."*

2. Match the on-screen dimensions to the printable surface by choosing Format, Document, Match Printer.

3. Choose the Text tool and an Old-Western-style font, such as Tombstone or Ghost Town, with a large point size (we used Tombstone, 100 point) and center alignment. Cre-

ate a text box 2 1/4 inches from the top of the page by dragging the cursor across the document. Type the word *WANTED.*

4. Click on the Pencil tool, choose Straight Line, black, and 2-point thickness, and draw a line above and below the word *WANTED.* (To draw a line, hold the mouse button down while moving the mouse.)

5. If you'll be using the birthday child's picture on all the invites, insert the digitized or photocopied villain picture and scale it to size (at least 4 1/4 inches

With the right font, creating a realistic Wanted poster is easy.

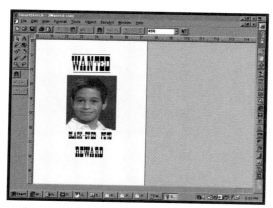

What child wouldn't want to get a personalized invitation like this?

square). If you'll be inserting a different picture for each invitee or gluing a picture instead, leave at least 4 inches of space below the word *WANTED*.

6. Using a Western font with a smaller point size (we used 48) and center alignment, add the villain's name (for example, *Six-Gun Shirley* or *Black-Eyed Pete)* below the picture and 7 inches down the side ruler.

7. Drop down to 8 1/4 inches from the top of the page, and using the same font but a larger point size (such as 12 point), type the word *REWARD*.

8. Use the Line tool to create a 2-point line below the word *REWARD*.

9. Type the party information 8 5/8 inches from the top. Keep the center alignment for the text, but use a smaller point size and a sans serif font (such as 22-point Helvetica).

10. Save the file.

11. Next, we'll want to copy the information for each invitee. Begin by selecting the entire page, choosing Object, Create Group, and copying the page to the Clipboard.

12. Create enough blank pages for the number of children invited to the party, and then paste the original document into each. (To add pages in SmartSketch, choose Format, Add Page.)

13. Customize each invitation with the appropriate picture and name of the vil-

Now that we've added the party information, the first invitation is complete. We'll copy this one and modify it to make the other invitations.

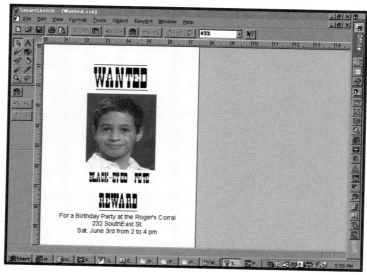

Other Full-Page Ideas

You can use the Full-Page design with a number of themes, including cards or invites designed around:

- A sports page, featuring the birthday girl or boy as the lead story
- A pirate's treasure map leading to the birthday party
- Play money featuring the birthday boy or girl as George Washington

lain. (If you're using the birthday girl or boy as the villain, you can skip this step.)

14. Print the invites on white paper, and then rub the printouts with a used tea bag or coffee grounds for an aged look. Carefully singe the edges using a candle flame or a lighter for the final touch (parents only).

15. Deliver the invitations by posting them on the recipients' front door with tape. Don't forget your deputy's badge.

Classic Pop-up

Pop-up cards are keepers, for sure. Kids like them because of the surprise inside, but also because they're not just cards — they're decorations! Long after the special day has come and gone, kids will keep their pop-up cards displayed on their desk, dresser, or bookshelf.

Before You Begin

What's the special day? Birthday? Holiday? Whatever the occasion, you can make fun pop-up cards with a little clip art or your own original drawings, and a special message. What could be easier? So let's get started...

Step-by-Step

We're using SmartSketch to make these special pop-up cards, but you can use your favorite draw, paint, or word processing program, as long as it has on-screen rulers and lets you rotate and scale images.

1. Launch SmartSketch. Make sure the page orientation is Portrait by choosing File, Page Setup, Portrait.

2. Set the screen to match the printable surface by choosing Format, Document, Match Printer.

3. You'll need rulers for this project, so choose View, Show Page and Rulers.

4. To create fold lines, choose the Pencil tool, Straight Line mode, and a Hairline thickness. Then draw a vertical line at 4 inches to bisect the page vertically and a

FamilyPC Tip: *In SmartSketch you can extend, shorten, or bend any portion of a line by using the Pointer tool and simply dragging the line.*

Drag or insert your child's favorite clip-art image or original artwork onto the page to serve as the pop-up image.

horizontal line at 5 1/2 inches to bisect the page horizontally.

5. In the bottom half of the page, directly over the vertical line, insert the clip art that you want to "pop up." See the "Creative Primer" section for steps on using EasyArt clip art, clip art from another source, or original art.

6. Save the file.

7. Scale the image to the appropriate size.

8. Click in the middle of the image and drag to adjust its placement.

9. Now it's time to add your child's message to the inside of the card. Create a text box in the lower right quadrant of the page. Click on the Text tool, and from the pull-

down menus, choose a light-hearted font, such as Kids, a point size (we used 36), a color (we used purple), and center alignment. Then type your child's message (for example, *Happy Birthday, You Clown*).

10. You can add a second message in the lower left quadrant if you want. We used the same font and center alignment, but changed the color to red and the point size to 20. If you use a smaller point size, you can type in a longer message, such as, *From one fun-lover to another...*

11. Save the file.

12. Now it's time to add text to the cover (the upper left quadrant). Create a text box, and choose a font type, color, size, and center alignment. (We used the same font and purple, but changed the size to 48.) Type your cover message, such as, *On this day, I'd like to say...* Use the Return key to drop words down to the next line.

FamilyPC Tip: *If you want to copy elements from an EasyArt image, click on the overall image and choose Object, Edit Object. Click on all the elements that you want to copy to the Clipboard (each will become highlighted), and select Edit, Copy.*

13. The upper left quadrant will be folded twice to become the front of the card, so everything that appears in this space must be rotated 180 degrees. (That way, it will appear right side up when the card is finished.) Rotate this text by clicking outside the text box and choosing Rotate from the Tools pulldown menu. Use the cursor to grab one of the corner handles and rotate the text counterclockwise.

14. You might want to add to the cover a design element from the inside art. To do so, copy part of the inside image to the Clip-board, and paste it in the upper left quadrant. Rotate it and place it. (We copied just the clown's smile.)

15. Save the file.

16. Print a test copy of the card on a sheet of standard white paper. Make any final adjustment to the placement or size of the elements. Save the file.

17. When you are satisfied with the look of the card, print it on card stock or white paper.

Add text to the inside of the card by using the Text tool and selecting a frivolous font, such as Kids.

18. Make the preliminary folds for the card. Fold the top half back so that the image (the clown in the example) and inside type is facing you. Next, fold the left side forward and to the right so that the image is folded in half inside the card, and the cover type is facing you. Unfold the card.

19. Using a craft knife, carefully cut out most of the image, leaving some points of attachment. (For the clown image, we left 1/2 inch around his hand and elbow.)

20. Refold the card along the original two creases. As you make the second fold, pull the pop-up image gently out toward you, reversing the fold that runs through the center of the image.

21. All that's left is for your child to sign the card and deliver it.

Pull-Tab Card

10-9-8-7-6-5-4-3-2-1... Space exploration is a popular theme for a child's birthday party. So launch your next party with this invitation. It features a rocket

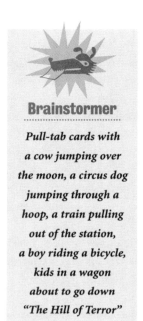

Brainstormer

Pull-tab cards with a cow jumping over the moon, a circus dog jumping through a hoop, a train pulling out of the station, a boy riding a bicycle, kids in a wagon about to go down "The Hill of Terror"

that moves when you pull a tab. The spaceship can be as elaborate as you like, decorated with portholes and mechanical equipment or sleek and unadorned.

Before You Begin

The cover of this card sports a large planet with an assortment of stars, meteors, and galaxies. You can draw these elements in your paint or draw program, or you can use some of the space-theme clip art that's available. If you are using SmartSketch, save each element as a separate SmartSketch file. (That way, you can open each element as an EasyArt element when you create the card.)

The real attraction of the card, howev-

This rocket is ready to be printed and launched.

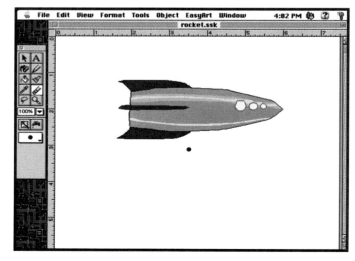

er, is the rocket ready to be launched inside. Draw a simple rocket, about 1 1/2 inches long and 4 inches wide, in your draw or paint program. Or check out your clip-art library for a rock-et and scale it to size. Then print the rocket on card stock.

Step-by-Step

Use a futuristic font to give your card a Star Trek–type look.

We're using Smart-Sketch for the pull-tab card, but you can use your favorite paint or draw program — just make sure it has on-screen rulers and can rotate objects.

1. Launch SmartSketch.

2. Make sure the orientation is in the default Portrait mode.

3. To have what appears on the screen match what you'll be printing, choose For-mat, Document, Match Printer.

4. You need to see rulers for this project, so choose View, Show Page and Ruler.

5. Draw a vertical line at 4 inches (to bi-sect the page vertically) and a horizontal line at 5 1/4 inches (to bisect the page hor-izontally) using the Pencil tool and Straight Line mode. (For a line thickness, select Hair-line.)

6. We'll add text to the cover first. Start by choosing the Text tool and selecting a font (a futuristic font such as CountdownD looks good), a point size (we used 28), a color (we used yellow), and center alignment. (Make your selections from the pulldown menus.)

7. Create a text box by clicking in the upper left panel and dragging right, to just before the vertical line.

8. In the text box, type your message. You might want something like: *Captain's Log: September 6. Starfleet Commander Mark's Birthday.*

FamilyPC Tip: *SmartSketch lets you import digitized images and clip art, but does not always let you rotate the pictures. If you are using SmartSketch and need to rotate an image, use a photo-editing program such as Paint Shop Pro to flip or rotate the photo and then save it. Copy the image to the Clipboard and paste it into your SmartSketch document.*

9. Save the file.

10. Insert your planetary art by selecting Open as EasyArt from the File pulldown menu. If you are not using EasyArt, copy each art element to the Clipboard and paste it in the upper left panel.

11. Scale each element as necessary (Tools, Scale).

12. Move the art elements until they're positioned correctly in the top left panel.

13. When all the elements are the correct size and in the correct place on the page, save the file.

14. Group the elements and the text by clicking on them and choosing Object, Create Group.

15. The upper left panel will be folded twice so that it becomes the cover. Therefore, rotate the elements in that panel 180 degrees (Tools, Rotate) so that they will appear right side up when the card is finished.

16. Save the file.

Use the Create Group command to rotate your cover elements as one, maintaining their spacing and alignment.

17. Repeat the same planetary pattern on the bottom right panel of the invitation. Open the individual pieces of art as EasyArt files and drag the elements onto the page, or copy elements to the Clipboard and paste them onto the page.

18. Save the file.

19. Now it's time to add the party details to

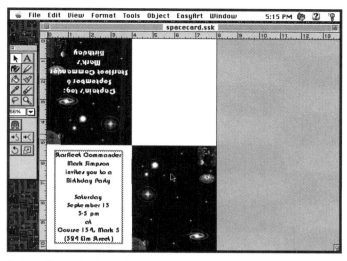

An invitation and a keepsake, all in one.

the lower left side of the page. Choose the Text tool and the same font you used on the cover, black, aligned center. Change the point size to 24.

20. Create a text box in the bottom left panel.

21. In the text box, type the party information.

22. Save the file.

23. Print a test copy of the card.

24. Fold the top half back, and fold the left side forward and to the right.

25. Check the placement of all the elements and make sure the information on the invitation is correct. Make any necessary adjustments.

26. When everything is okay, save the file.

27. Print on card stock, making enough for each invitee (plus a few extras).

28. Fold the finished version the way you folded the test copy.

29. Now it's time to add the rocket and the pull tab to the inside of the card. First, create the pull tab from a strip of heavy paper 4 inches long and 1 1/2 inches wide. Fold it in half lengthwise and glue it together to make a strong strip, 4 inches by 3/4 inch.

30. Cut two more strips of heavy paper 2 inches long and 3/4 inch wide. Fold both ends of the strips (1/2 inch or so from the ends) to create an accordion fold. The profile of each strip will be a Z shape.

31. Flip each Z strip over (making backward Z's), and glue them to the pull tab. One Z should be at the right end of the pull tab and the other should be glued 2 inches from the right end.

This shows a pull tab with the Z's mounted.

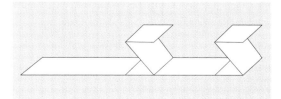

Foil-Face Laser Printing

If you have a laser printer and you want to add a shimmery effect to your rocket pull-tab card, try some foil specialty papers, such as LaserColor (from Paper Direct).

Cut a piece of foil paper and place it over the area of the page to be highlighted. (This assumes that the sheet of paper has been through the printer once already, since the foil will fuse only to the print on the page.)

Secure the foil with the small sticky dots included with the paper. Using the manual-feed tray, run the page through the printer a second time, foil facing up. After the document has passed through the printer, peel off the excess foil. Your laser printer uses its heat and pressure to "iron" colors onto the page.

The result? A shimmery metallic look for your type and images. A 16-sheet package of LaserColor costs $19.95. For more information on specialty papers and suppliers, turn to the "Resource Guide."

32. Unfold the card to make the cuts. On the lower right panel, make three parallel, 3/4-inch cuts. Two of the cuts should be 2 inches apart to allow the Z tabs to stick through the layer. The third should be 1 inch to the left of the leftmost Z. (This slot is where the end of the pull tab appears.)

33. Thread the pull tab and the Z tabs through the appropriate slots and put them into position.

34. Add a small piece of tape to act as a hinge between the tabs and the card, ensuring smooth movement. (The tape goes along one of the slits so that it is fastened to the card and to the part of the Z sticking above the card. The tape prevents the Z from sliding left or right but still lets the Z unfold when you pull the tab.)

35. Glue your rocket to the tabs.

36. For a finishing touch, you can glue some thin metallic curling ribbon to the back of the rocket.

37. Give the card a trial launch by pulling on the tab.

38. Assemble cards for each invitee and deliver.

Products You Can Use

Paint or draw program: *ClarisDraw, CorelDraw, SmartSketch*
Clipart package: *Art Explosion — 40,000 Images, Corel Gallery 2*

Holiday Decorations

Seven festive projects for kids of all ages

 P R E P   T I M E :   2 0 - 3 0   M I N U T E S   E A C H

Materials

Paint or draw program (for nesting Santas and village) • Word processing or desktop publishing program (for ornaments) • Printing utility (optional) • Scanner (for ornaments) • Printer • Standard paper • Specialty paper (transparency, card stock) • Lace (optional) • Glue • Scissors • Thread • Needle

No matter what type of holiday celebration you plan this winter, these festive house decorations will add just the right flair. And they're a perfect way for you and your kids to spend some time together around the holidays. We'll show you how to make several different types of holiday decorations, in-

cluding nesting Santas that are as colorful as their Russian counterparts (and stack up just as neatly!), window transparencies that filter sunlight like stained glass, special ornaments, and even a classic New England village. Making these decorations is sure to put you and your family in a holiday mood.

Nesting Santas

The beauty of nesting dolls is the way they fit together so neatly, one inside the other. Originating in Russia, these figurines were first carved out of wood. In this project, however, getting them to fit inside each other won't be the feat it once was. You'll have a much easier time creating these cone-shaped nesting Santas, which are as colorful as the real thing.

Before You Begin

Have your child help you decide what the key design elements are for your dolls. If

Brainstormer

Make nesting Christmas figures of the Three Wise Men, elves, snowmen, Christmas trees

you're creating Santa, should he have a red suit or a green one (for a "woodland Santa")? A big black belt or a red one? What about his hat? Have your child think through all the details and draw Santa using a paint or draw program, or with crayons or markers. When your child completes the art, use it as a model for the Santa you'll be creating with your computer.

Step-by-Step

Here we'll make the nesting doll model (Santa) in a draw program because its on-screen rulers and tools let you be precise when scaling.

To make a semicircle, you simply draw a very large circle and use the bottom half of it. Then you scale and position it.

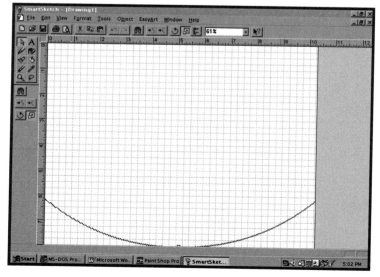

1. Launch SmartSketch or the program you plan on using.

2. Set up the page in Landscape mode by choosing File, Page Setup.

3. In the Document dialog under Format, click on the Match Printer button.

4. Be sure that the grid is turned on (Format, Document, Grid).

5. Set the view to show the entire page (View, Show

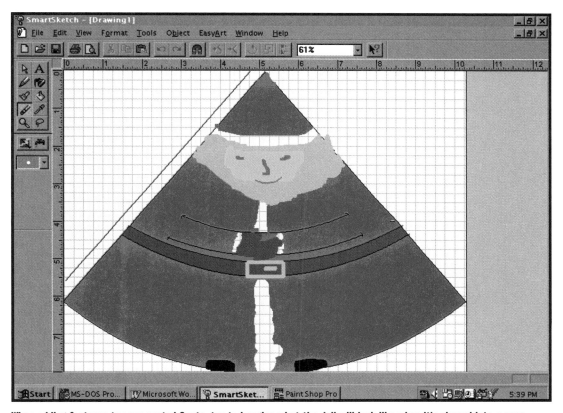

When adding features to your nested Santa, try to imagine what the doll will look like when it's shaped into a cone.

Page) and on-screen rulers (View, Rulers.)

6. Create a semicircle across the top of the page. Start by drawing a circle. In Smart-Sketch, click on the Pencil tool, choose Oval from the Pencil mode pulldown menu, and draw a circle with a diameter of 8 inches. Select and move the circle so it is centered at the top of the page, with the top half of the circle off the page.

7. Scale the circle so that its diameter is 16 inches. In SmartSketch, select the circle, choose Tools, Scale by Percent, and enter 200 percent.

Click on OK. The bottom portion of the circle should be visible at the base of the page and intersect the sides a few inches from the bottom. (You might need to reposition it.)

8. Draw guidelines and cutting lines from the center of the top of the page to the outer edge of the semicircle, to about the 6″ mark on the side ruler. (In SmartSketch, use the Straight Line mode under the Pencil tool.) Add another line parallel to one of the lines you just drew, but 1/2 inch toward the top of the page, to form an overlapping flap for gluing the cone together.

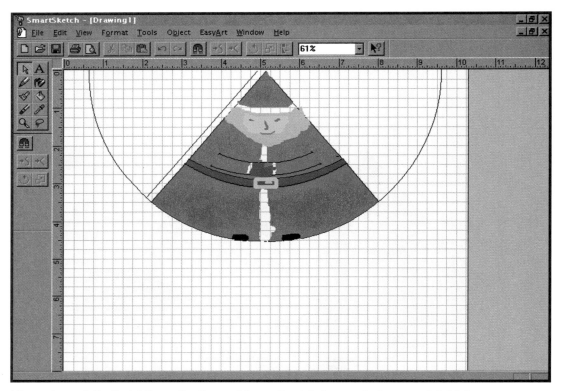

After you've made the first doll, creating the remaining nesting dolls is easy: simply copy and shrink it.

9. Now use the paint tools in your program to draw jolly Saint Nick, including a

FamilyPC Tip: *In addition to stand-alone decorations, the smaller Santas make great tree ornaments. Simply loop a short length of thread through the top of each hat. Or make a long, dangling ornament by running a knotted thread through the tip of each cone, starting with the smallest cone and finishing with the largest. Tie a loop atop the largest (top) doll.*

cone-shaped red hat, a cheery face, and a white beard. For instance, use the Paint Fill tool to create the red material of his jacket. Add a black belt and then a black pair of boots at the bottom edge. To create the belt and boots, just draw smaller arcs that share the same center as your original circle, and fill the areas where the belt and boots would appear with black. To draw arms and mittens, use partial arcs or the Pencil tool in Smooth mode. Use the Rectangle tool with a 8-point line thickness and the color gold to create a gold belt buckle.

10. Save the file.

11. Print a test copy to be sure that all the elements look good when the nesting Santa is folded into a cone. When you are satisfied with the design, save the file again.

12. Select the entire image and group it as one object. (In SmartSketch, choose Object, Create Group.) Copy it to the Clipboard and paste it into a new document. Select the new image, and scale it down 75 percent. (In SmartSketch, choose Tools, Scale by Percent, and enter 75.) Save the new Santa as a separate file.

13. Repeat step 12, using the most recently created Santa as the model, to make as many Santas as you need. (Remember to scale each new Santa to 75 percent the size of the last one.)

14. Print the different Santa files on heavy, white paper.

15. Cut along the outside of the flaps and along the bottom curve.

16. Have your child add finishing touches with glitter, metallic marker pens, and tufts of cotton.

Christmas Village

You can bring to your table's centerpiece the charm of a small New England village on a winter's night. It's a classic holiday image: houses with candles glowing in the windows and wreaths hung on the doors; the big tree in the town square glimmering with hundreds of lights; stained glass windows in churches illuminated during special holiday services; and stores, catering to holiday shoppers, brightly lit and brilliantly dec-

orated for the season.

You and your kids can replicate this type of holiday image or you can capture the special warmth and decorations of your own town or neighborhood during the holiday season.

Before You Begin

Sit down with your child and decide what types of buildings you want to make. Rather than

Brainstormer

What types of structures will your village have?

Blacksmith shop, bakery, stables, church, town hall, general store

making a New England village, you might decide to re-create your neighborhood or the center of your town during the holidays. Or maybe you want to design an imaginary village. If your child is basing her structures on real buildings, give her some assistance getting the details just right by sketching out what they look like on paper. When you have a number of ideas mapped out, turn to your paint program.

In a print program like Flying Colors, choose Full Printed Page to have the picture area fill the screen.

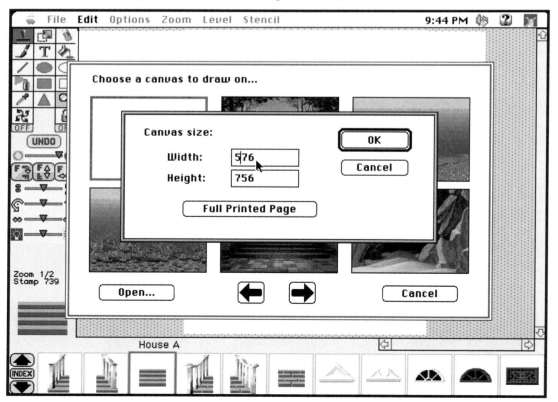

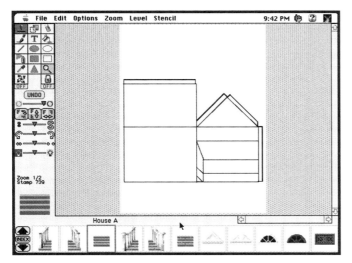

Instead of drawing a building freehand, you can use different geometric shapes that are attached to one another.

Step-by-Step

We used the paint program Flying Colors (available in version 1.05 for the Macintosh and Windows 3.1) to make these buildings because of the wonderful architectural fills and stamps it provides, but feel free to adapt the instructions to the draw or paint program of your

choice. (Note: Flying Colors, as of the publishing of this book, did not work with Windows 95, and we recommend that you use another paint or draw program if you're using that operating system.)

1. Launch Flying Colors (or the paint or draw program that you plan on using).

2. Set up your pages in Portrait or Landscape mode, depending on your building design. In Flying Colors, click on Blank Canvas on the opening screen, and then click on Full Printed Page, Portrait (or Landscape), and OK in the subsequent dialog box.

3. Draw individual buildings using the paint tools in your program.

4. Give the buildings details such as doors, windows, and if possible, siding. You can use

FamilyPC Tip: *One special feature of Flying Colors is that you can edit stamps and then use the part you want. For instance, to create a church bell, select the wine goblet stamp, stamp it on the page (but away from the building), and then use the Copy/move tool to select the top, rounded part. It instantly becomes a stamp that you can rotate and use again and again. You can use the Copy/move tool also to merge stamps.*

paint tools in your program to create the details, or if you're using Flying Colors, you can use the stamps (clip art) that are included.

5. Add tabs (with the Rectangle tool) to your building in areas where you will need to dab on glue, such as along the top of a wall where you'll attach the roof.

6. Print the buildings on the thickest white paper your printer can handle.

7. Cut out the houses, fold, and glue.

Add patterns, and the first building in your Christmas village will begin to take shape. The white tabs are where you'll apply glue.

FamilyPC **Tip:** *The key is to design your buildings so that you minimize the number of individual pieces that you need to glue. For instance, in the case of a small rectangular building, you can create a rectangle in the center of the page, which will be the building's floor, and have all four walls connected to it. The gable-end walls are essentially rectangles with triangles on top; the side walls, rectangles. (In Flying Colors, click on the Rectangle tool to create rectangles; use the Straight Line tool to create triangles.) For larger buildings, skip the base and use one side, one end wall and gable, and half the roof printed on two separate sheets of paper. (A 3-by-4 inch house that will stand 5 inches tall fits easily on two pages.)*

Tree Ornaments

For many families, Christmas tree decorations are something that they gather over the years, adding a few new ornaments each year. It's an assortment of traditional decorations such as Christmas balls, gifts from friends, old-fashioned ornaments from a parent's childhood, and homemade tree hangings fashioned by the kids. This year, have your kids add a year's worth of memories to your Christmas

Brainstormer

Ornament memories of sports awards, scholastic achievements, drawings, poems, vacations, favorite snapshots, birthdays

collection by making this mini-memory booklet, which captures your family's best times over the past year. You and your kids will have as much fun making the ornament as you'll all have decorating the tree.

Before You Begin

The heart of this ornament is your family's memories from the past year — a great topic to discuss over dinner. While one person takes notes, everyone should talk about what they remember most or what made the year special for them. Maybe it was graduating from kindergarten, or being elected to the school board, or being the high scorer on the soccer team. Collect pictures commemorating the events, and then get them scanned and saved to your hard drive in a format you can access with your computer (PICT or TIFF for Macs and .BMP or .TIF for Windows.) See the "Creative Primer" for information on digitizing photos.

Step-by-Step

We'll be describing this project using Microsoft Word 6.0, but you can adapt the directions to any desktop publishing or word processing program. And the secret to making the document miniature is a simple print utility called ClickBook, which automatically formats text and pictures into books of all sizes, even a tiny twelve-page or sixteen-page booklet.

1. Launch Word (or the program you'll be using.)

2. Leave the page orientation in the default Portrait mode.

3. Create the front page of the booklet first. Because the booklet will be printed in minia-ture, all elements need to be large so that they're still readable when reduced. On the cover, insert and center your favorite family picture. (To insert a picture in Word, select Insert, Picture and then find and select the file.)

4. Above the picture, insert your family's

Creating a Christmas Tree

To create a free-standing Christmas tree, use cardboard or foam core. (Essentially, you create two identical trees that are notched in the center, so that when they interlock, they stand on their own.)

Start with a classic Christmas tree design, or locate clip art of a tree. Then you can add birds, decorations, or anything you like to it. On one page, duplicate the tree (or import it twice) and then duplicate it two more times in mirror-image form. You'll now have four

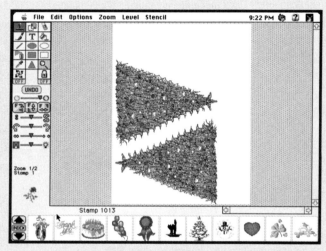

Duplicate and then flip your finished tree to quickly create the mirror image for the back of the cutout.

Christmas trees (two trees per page). Print the page on sticker paper (full-sheet label material). Attach the two printed trees to foam-core craft board or heavy cardboard, and cut them out.

To make the trees interlock, you need to make two cuts

through the foam core. For the first tree, cut a vertical slit down the center, starting at the top and stopping at the middle. Then take the second tree and cut a vertical slit up the center, start-ing at the bot-tom and stop-ping at the middle. Slip the two trees to-gether so they become one and the tree stands on its own. Cover the edges of the foam core with strips cut from an extra printout of the tree, or color in the foam edge using a green marker.

Pictures like these will help you recall the happy times of the past year.

50-point Futura Bk BT), aligned center, type her accomplishments. Include a poem, hand-drawn pictures, anything that tells a story. Create pages for each family member. If you have pages left over, include pictures of your family pets or pictures of big events, such as a vacation to Yosemite.

7. When you've filled 11 or 15 pages, save the file. (By ending on an odd-numbered page, you leave the last page for the back cover.)

name in a large, scripty font such as Lucida Handwriting, using center alignment and a 72- to 100-point size. Below the picture, insert the year using the same font style and size.

5. Add a simple border to give the page a more decorative look. (In Word, select the area that you'll be surrounding with a border, choose Format, Border and Shading, and click on Box.)

6. Create a page spread for each member of the family. Start with the youngest and have pages 2 and 3 focus on her. Include a favorite picture on one page, and in a simple, clear, sans serif font (such as

8. Copy the cover page to the Clipboard and paste it on the final page of the document as a back cover. (That way, when the ornament swings on the tree, the title will

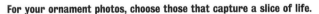

For your ornament photos, choose those that capture a slice of life.

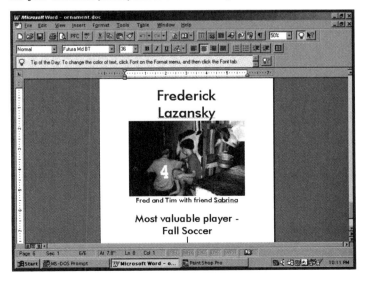

always be visible.)

9. Print the ornament booklet on standard white paper.

If you have ClickBook, select the Click-Book driver first and tell it to print a "tiny book." This format prints up to 32 pages reduced onto one sheet of paper, back to back; a 16-page booklet (roughly 2 by 2 1/2 inches) will take up only one-half sheet of paper. The latest version of ClickBook does not have the "tiny book" predefined, but

Window Transparencies

With transparency plastic and a color ink-jet printer, you can make a variety of fun crafts, including some remarkably beautiful window decorations that filter sunlight like stained glass. The key to making colorful window transparencies is simple, colorful art.

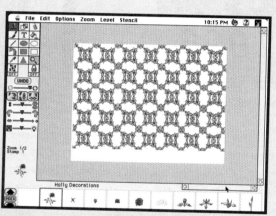

Clip art of holly, repeated in strips, creates a festive window border.

Although you can create your own art in a paint program, some excellent libraries of holiday-theme clip art are also available. Corel Gallery 2, for instance, has doves, stars, snowmen, trees, religious symbols, and wreaths.

Use one or more images per sheet of paper, or create window edging with repeated images printed in strips. (Holly for Christmas or Solstice or African-themed borders for Kwanza look great.) Print the images just as you would on standard paper, but insert only one sheet of plastic at a time into the printer. If the conditions in your house are humid enough, the transparency plastic will stick to the glass on its own. If your house is dry, just dampen the window with a sponge or attach the transparency using little bits of tape.

It is paramount that you make your transparencies water-resistant because ink-jet print-outs will run if they get wet. (The same humidity that helps make transparencies stick to glass can also make the ink on them run.) To make these and other holiday creations water-resistant, use Design Master Super Surface Sealer. Warning: This sealer is a toxic substance and should be used only by adults in well-ventilated areas. When your transparencies are finished, have your kids arrange holiday scenes on all the windows or mirrors they can reach.

More Ornament Ideas

FamilyPC Tip: *To waterproof your booklet ornament, you need to seal the printed surface of your work. Design Master "Super Surface Sealer" clear sealer and satin finish #656, $4.25, works particularly well and is available at most craft stores. Spray the surface before cutting. Warning: This sealer is a toxic substance and should be used only by adults in well-ventilated areas.*

you can define it yourself easily. Just go to the Modify Layout screen and specify a layout with 16 pages (4 x 4) printed on each side of a sheet of paper, in Portrait orientation.

If you don't have Click-Book, take the pages to a copy shop and have the pages reduced by 23.5 percent and copied in color.

10. Cut the pages from the sheet (or sheets) of paper and assemble following the printed Click-Book directions (or by compiling and stapling).

11. Tie the booklet together with a length of lightweight gold cord, leaving a loop at the top for hanging. Be sure to print a few extras as gifts for grandparents.

Before the holiday season is in full swing, take some time to make holiday ornaments with your kids. Some of the best ones are the simplest: things like stars, candles, snowflakes, and Christmas trees. And because they're simple, they're also easy to make. Start by creating outlines of holiday images in a draw or paint program. You can also use clip-art images for your designs.

Next, decorate and fill the image using different colors. Create a mirror image of each picture by copying the picture to the Clipboard, pasting it back into the document,

A Connectix QuickCam works great for capturing images to use in making a photo ornament. The camera works with Windows and Mac platforms.

and flipping it horizontally. Print both images on thick paper. Then cut out the art and glue the pieces back-to-back. Use a piece of paperboard sandwiched between the sides for extra rigidity. Attach some narrow ribbon, and the ornament is ready for hanging.

Another simple — but special — ornament is one with your child's picture. Get a favorite photograph of your child, and have it scanned and saved in a format that you can access with your paint or draw program (PICT for Mac, .BMP for Windows). For more information on scanning images, turn to the "Resource Guide."

Use a photo-editing program, such as Paint Shop Pro or Adobe PhotoDeluxe, to

Christmas Candle Holders

Candlelight festivities are an intrinsic element of many winter holiday celebrations, but so too is hot wax, which can burn your hands. Eliminate some of the danger by creating candlestick holders made of circular discs of heavy paper, with a hole punched through the center and a holiday message printed around the perimeter. A variety of programs let you create circles, but only a few let you print words in circles, including any Microsoft product with WordArt.

This holidayware is pretty — and practical.

Start by drawing a large circle, 6 inches in diameter, on the page. Center a smaller circle in the larger one, with a diameter equal to the size of the candle you will use.

Next, use WordArt to add text in a circle between the two outlines. Use an elaborate font such as Cloister Black, and type in words appropriate to the ceremony you will be attending, such as Shalom, Umoja (unity), Hallelujah, or Peace. Use the size setting Best Fit to automatically size the text.

Print the page on thick paper and cut out the large circle. Cut several slits with a sharp knife extending from the circle's center out to the small circle's edge. (This is where you will push the candle through.) Print a copy for each family member.

erase the background surrounding the subject and scale the image to size. Then print the image on transparency plastic. Cover it with another plain piece of transparency, and seal it with decorative tape or hot glue. Use a paper punch to cut a perfect hole near the top, and add a loop of narrow ribbon for hanging. Finish your photo ornament with bits of ribbon or gathered lace.

Products You Can Use

Paint or draw program: *Dabbler, Flying Colors, Kid Pix, SmartSketch*

Word processing program: *Microsoft Word, WordPerfect*

Works program: *ClarisWorks, Microsoft Works, WordPerfect Works*

Printing utility: *ClickBook*

Partyware

Four favorites that are sure to be a hit

 PREP TIME: 20 - 30 MINUTES EACH

Materials

Draw or paint program (for masks and hats) • **Desktop publishing program (preferred for buttons)** • **Clip art (for masks and hats)** • **Printer** • **Scanner (for buttons)** • **Paper** • **Card stock** • **Markers (if using black-and-white printer** • **Elastic string** • **Stapler** • **Cellophane tape** • **Glue** • **Glitter** • **Gold or silver ribbon**

Streamers strung across the room and a cake covered with candles are an essential part of any party. But to make sure young partygoers really have fun, have plenty of partyware on hand. Partyware? Sure it's easy: a little hardware, a little software, and soon you'll have some terrific partyware. Party hats are one

example — who can eat cake without one? And what's a party without noise? We'll help you out here, too, by showing you how to create some party poppers. Finally, add a bit of mystery and surprise to your party and make masks for your young guests. Now, as long as you have enough to go around, you're ready to have a party.

Masks

Who's who? You and your young guests won't know once they don their party masks. Guessing who's behind each disguise makes a good party game, with a prize going to the person who guesses another's true identity. Or have the partygoers switch masks a few times throughout the party, and keep everyone guessing. And when the party comes to an end, your partygoers will have a memento of their day.

Brainstormer

Create party masks featuring these: bear, cat, mouse, bird, super hero, monster, sports star

Before You Begin

Let your child choose a theme for his party. Then help him select images for masks that will go with your theme. When you've collected an image for each party goer, save the images in a format that you can access with your draw, paint, or word processing program.

Step-by-Step

We're making the party masks with SmartSketch. You can adapt these directions for your favorite paint, draw, or word processing program.

1. Launch SmartSketch (or the program that you plan on using).

2. Alter the page orientation based on the type of mask you'll be making. (Choose File, Print Setup, and either Protrait or Landscape.) If it's a wide mask, change the page layout to Landscape; for tall masks, leave the layout in the default Portrait mode.

3. Change the appearance of the document on the screen so that it will match the printed page by choosing Format, Document, Match Printer. Then choose View, Show Page.

4. Insert the art you'll be using for the mask. If you are using SmartSketch, you can import clip art or original art by clicking and dragging the image onto your page. If you are using another software or clip-art

How about a birthday party filled with teddy bears? Here are two images to get you started making teddy bear masks.

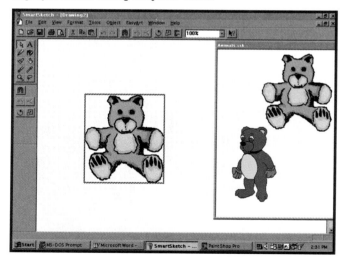

package, insert an image by choosing Import under the File menu.

5. Select a portion of the image (such as the head) and scale it (Tools, Scale) so that it takes up the entire page.

6. Save the file.

7. Print a test copy of the mask in grayscale on standard white paper. See whether the printer has cut off any of the image. If so, make adjustments to the file, such as re-

Papier-Mâché Masks

Making papier-mâché masks can be as much fun as wearing them — and they last longer. So make this activity part of your child's next party.

To start, have your child browse a clip-art package (such as Art Parts from FontHaus) and look at the various images for different features (for example, eyes, ears, nose, eyebrows, warts, and scars) and expressions (for example, a smile, a frown, or a twisted grin). When your child finds the images he wants to use, he can select them and cut and paste them into a file. Alternatively, he can use a paint or draw program to create his own.

After he's collected a bunch (remember, you'll need some

for everyone at the party) in a file, he can scale them to different sizes. Then it's time to save the file and begin printing. Have him color these elements (if necessary) and cut them out so they'll be ready when it comes time to paste them on the masks.

The next step is to make the papier-mâché. The paste is made from flour and water. Start with a cup of water and stir in flour until it becomes

the consistency of thick cream. Soak strips of newspaper in the paste for about 60 seconds. Then apply the strips of papier-mâché in layers to one side of an inflated balloon. Let dry.

Once the papier-mâché dries, remove the balloon and trim the edges with scissors. Apply a coat of latex paint to the surface as the base color. When the paint dries, apply the facial elements with paste or glue.

For final touches, you might want to add yarn, hedge clippings, or shredded newspaper for hair. Silver spray paint and glitter can give a tinman or robot that special twinkle and shine. Finally, cut out eye holes, and attach an elastic cord to keep the mask in place.

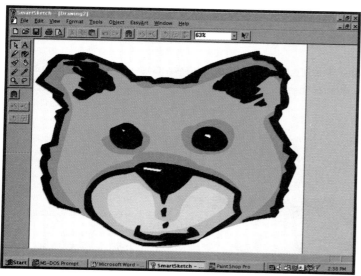

Younger partygoers will love wearing a cuddly bear mask like this! (Some growling allowed.)

If you don't have a color printer, print the image as a line drawing and have your child fill in the colors with markers.

10. Use scissors to cut out the mask. You don't have to follow the outline of the image exactly — just give the mask nice, curving lines.

11. Place the mask up to your child's face and note where the eye holes should go. Remove the mask and use scissors to cut the eye holes.

ducing the margins or the size of the image, and then print a second copy. Repeat your test printings until the mask appears as you want it.

8. Save the file.

9. Print the finished version on card stock.

FamilyPC Tip: *You can edit EasyArt images in SmartSketch by selecting them and then clicking on the Edit Object command under Tools. You can then select and delete colors or lines. Or, to create a mask, select just the head of a character using the Rectangle or Lasso selecting tool, copy it to the Clipboard, and paste it into a new document.*

12. Cut an 8-inch length of elastic cord. Attach the ends of the cord to the sides of the mask. To do so, you can use a stapler, or you can poke a small hole on each side of the mask, slip the elastic cord through it, and knot the end of the cord.

Hats

The point of party hats — well, they're just for the fun of it. (Sorry, bad pun, but we couldn't resist.) Cone-shaped hats are as much a part of birthday tradition as cake and candles. Make them for your child's next party. A nice touch is to customize the hats for each partygoer. By adding the guests' names or pictures, each person will have a special party favor to take home.

Before You Begin

Have your child make a list of all the kids attending his party. Then, next to their names, have him note an image he thinks they'd like to have on their hat. For a friend that loves baseball, for example, he might choose a picture of a bat and a ball. When his list is complete, you and he can fire up a clip-art program and find the appropriate images, or create them yourselves using a paint or draw program.

Step-by-Step

We're using SmartSketch to create the party hats, but you can adapt these directions for your favorite paint or draw program.

1. Launch SmartSketch (or the program that you plan on using).

FamilyPC Tip: *If you are having problems creating an arc using your draw program, you can skip step 5, proceed through the project, and draw an arc on the printed hat. Cut a length of string 8 inches long. Tape one end of the string to the middle of a pencil and the other end to a pushpin. Stick the pin in the center of the top edge of the page. Stretch the string taut and draw a long, sweeping arc along the base of the page.*

2. Change the orientation of the page to Landscape by choosing File, Print Setup (Page Setup for Mac users), and clicking on Landscape.

3. Have the screen appearance match the printed surface by choosing Format, Document, Match Printer.

4. You'll need rulers as a guide for this project, so mark the Show Grid box under Format, Document. Then choose View, Show Page and Rulers.

5. First, you'll create the bottom curve of the hat. Click on the Pencil tool and select Line from the Pencil mode pulldown menu. Place the cursor at the left edge of the document at the 6 1/2-inch

This is what the line for the bottom of the hat should look like.

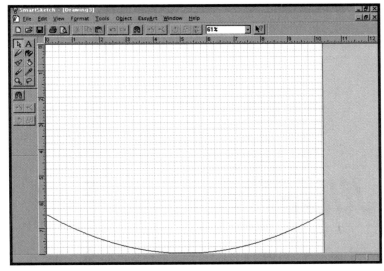

mark on the side ruler, and draw a line that extends straight across to the opposite side of the page. Click on the Arrow tool, grab the middle of the line you just drew (at the 5 1/4-inch mark on the top ruler), and bend the line to the bottom of the document by dragging the cursor down.

6. Add sides to the cone shape. Click on the Pencil tool and choose Line from the Pencil mode pulldown menu. Create two diagonal lines that extend from the 5 1/4-inch mark on the top ruler out to where the bottom arc meets the edge of the document

FamilyPC Tip: *To change the color of EasyArt shapes or images, begin by selecting the item on the page. Click on Edit Object under the Object pulldown menu. Next, choose the appropriate tool for changing the item. For instance, if you have the star shape and you want to make its outline red, click on the Pencil tool, and then click on the Ink Bottle tool. Select red from the color palette, and click on the outline of the star.*

Now that we've added the partygoer's name, the hat could serve as a placeholder at the birthday table, too.

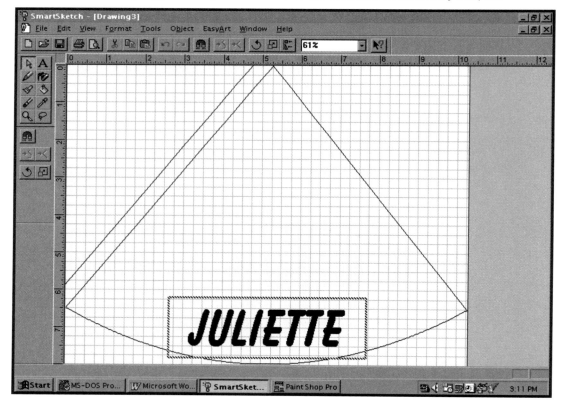

(6 1/2-inch mark on the side ruler).

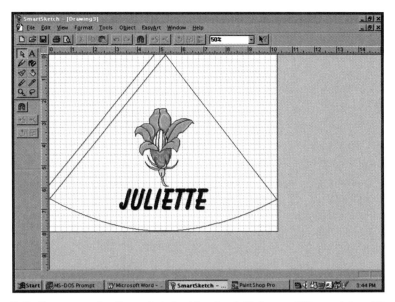

7. To create a gluing flap (a piece of paper that overlaps the other side when folded), draw another line parallel to the left edge line so that its top end aligns with the 4 3/4-inch mark on the top ruler and it intersects the side ruler at the 5 7/8-inch mark.

8. Now it's time to insert the first guest's name. Choose the Type tool, and then choose a font, a point size, and center alignment from the pulldown menus on the toolbar.

To further personalize the party hat, add an image that your child associates with his pal.

9. Create a text box about 5 inches long, just above the arc at the base of the page.

10. Enter the first child's name in the text box.

11. Click outside the text box to deselect it, and then click and drag it so that the name is about an inch above the base of the curve, and centered.

12. Save the file.

13. Add one piece of clip art above the name. (For more information about importing clip-art images, see the "Creative Primer" section.)

14. Scale the art so that it's about 3 inches square, using the on-screen rulers as a guide.

15. Drag the art so that it appears just above the name on the hat, centered on the page.

16. Print a test copy of the page on standard white paper. Make any adjustments to the size and placement of the elements. Continue making test printings until everything on the page is satisfactory.

17. Save the file.

18. Print the final copy on card stock. If you are using a black-and-white printer, have your child color the party hat with markers.

Party Poppers

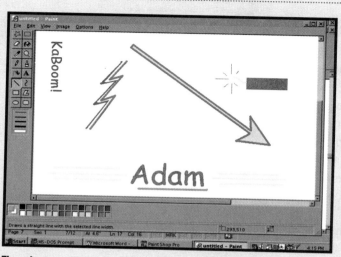

These images will add visual fireworks to your party poppers.

You don't need fireworks to put some pop in your party. These paper crackers provide all the safe, sonic excitement your party needs. These noise-makers, like the party hats, will make great party favors because you can customize each with names as well as clip art, your own art, or even the birthday boy or girl's picture. Once you've created one, just change the name on the popper for each invitee.

Design

The key to this project is the folding pattern, so you can use just about any program to add text and art. Set up your page in Landscape mode and then start adding art elements. Some images you might consider are firecrackers, flames, and bold, jagged explosion lines. If you will be using a dig-itized photo of the birthday boy or girl, insert it and posi-tion it along the bottom edge of the document, centered. (This will allow the picture to pop out when the noisemaker is used.) You can insert a dig-itized image into just about any program, as long as it's saved in a format that you can access (PICT for Macs and .BMP for Windows).

Printing

Print the poppers on standard white paper. For larger pop-pers (and, consequently, loud-er noises), enlarge the pages on a photocopier to 11 by 17 inch-es. (If you try a paper size that's larger than 11 by 17, your poppers probably won't last very long because the paper will be too light-weight, but they will make a rather large pop.)

Folding

Regardless of the size of your paper, folding instructions are the same. Start by orienting your paper as if it were in Portrait mode. Fold the paper in half lengthwise and then unfold it, so that you have a vertical crease down the center. Next, fold one corner of the sheet down so that one edge is flush with the crease and the other is perpendicular. Repeat this fold with the other three corners (fig. 1).

Now fold the sheet in half horizontally so that the top point lies directly over the bot-

continued on the next page

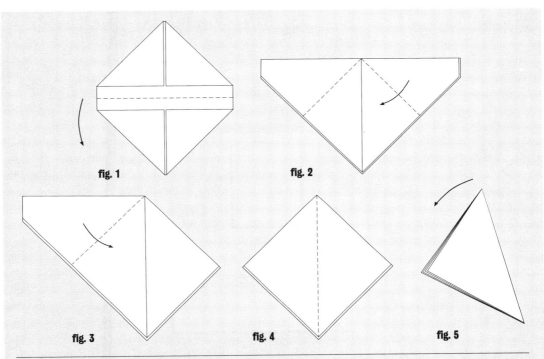

fig. 1

fig. 2

fig. 3

fig. 4

fig. 5

tom point. Fold both top corners down so they meet at the vertical crease (fig. 2). Undo these folds, flip the paper over, repeat the same two folds on this side, and undo them again. For greater popping ease, fold the top two creases back and forth to soften them.

The top edge of your paper now has a fairly pliable crease, which is necessary for the next step. Hold the bottom point of the paper, allow the right side to flare open, and then push on the pliable crease so that it reverses and this sec-tion folds inside itself (fig. 3). Repeat the same process for the left side, and you should be looking at a diamond (fig. 4). Fold the diamond in half from right to left, and your popper is complete (fig. 5).

Proper Popping

To make your popper pop, grip the bottom point firmly be-tween thumb and fingers. Raise your arm, and snap it down with a sharp, swift motion. The corners that were folded inside should pop out with a satisfy-ing *Crack!* To fire the next round, simply refold as be-fore and repeat the process.

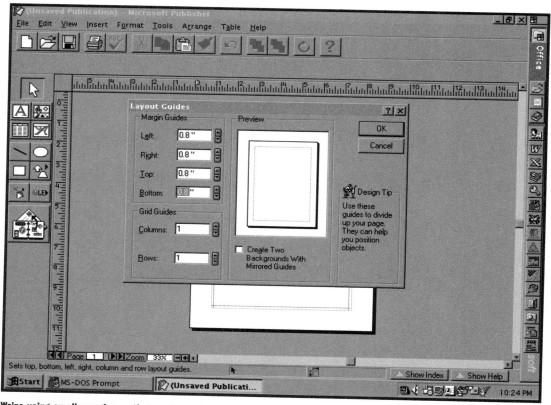

We're using small margins so that we have plenty of room for the buttons.

19. Cut out the hat with scissors. Have your child use glitter and glue to add the finishing touches to the party hat. Finish the hat with a sheaf of shiny, narrow-gauge gift ribbon, poked through the peak of the cap and secured on the inside with a bit of tape.

20. Fold the page into a cone and staple and tape it securely.

21. Make two holes along the bottom edge of the hat, and thread elastic string through them. Then knot the ends of the string to secure it to the hat.

22. Make personalized hats for everyone by calling up the original document and changing the name and the art element to match each guest.

Buttons

A bunch of brightly colored buttons is just the right boost for any birthday bash. The kids will collect 'em, swap 'em, compare 'em, wear 'em — and pin them on things you didn't expect! So you better make a big batch of buttons, because the kids will snap them up. In other words, it's one party favor that's sure to be a hit.

Before You Begin

Have your child choose a favorite picture from the family album. Then have it scanned and saved in a format that you can access with your program. (For Microsoft Publisher for Windows 95, that means save the file as a .TIF or .BMP file at a resolution of at least 72 dpi.) For more information on digitizing images, turn to the "Resource Guide."

Brainstormer

Create buttons for family reunions, neighborhood drives, local government or student council elections, a new baby announcement, sports banquets

Step-by-Step

To create button designs, you can use just about any application. But to create text running in a circle, you'll need a desktop publishing program such as Microsoft Publisher, which lets you shape text as well as crop photos in irregular shapes.

1. Launch Microsoft Publisher or the program you plan on using.

2. Open a new document by clicking on the Blank Page tab.

3. Double-click on the Full Page icon.

4. Leave the page in the default Portrait mode.

5. Choose Arrange, Layout Guides, and change all the margins to .8 inch.

6. Next, you need to make a guide for the shape of the first button. Click on the Box tool and create a 2 1/4-inch square in the upper left corner of the document, using the top and side rulers as measurement guides.

A sheet of button templates, ready for decorating.

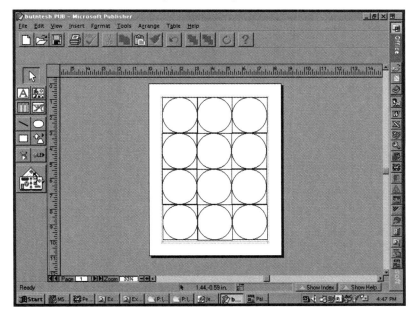

FamilyPC Tip: *When cropping out the background of a photograph, you can fine-tune the process by adding more handles. To add a handle, just hold down the Control key while you click on the wrap line. (To delete a handle, hold down the Control key while clicking on it.)*

7. Click on the Circle tool and create a circle inside the square that is 2 1/4 inches in diameter. (Hold down the Shift key and drag the cursor diagonally from one corner across the space.)

8. Save the file.

9. We'll be making a bunch of buttons, so we should make copies of the one button template we have now. Select both the square and the circle, group them (choose Arrange, Group), copy them to the Clipboard, and paste them in the upper right corner.

10. Paste and place another set in the center of the top of the page.

Add handles around the face so you can crop out the background.

Use Specialty Button-Making Paper

To avoid having to cut out each button, you can use perforated button paper, which is available through paper suppliers such as Paper Direct. This paper lets you print six buttons per page. To use the specialty paper, however,

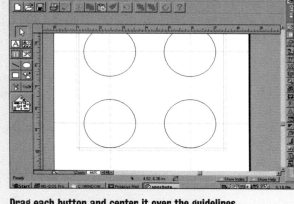

Drag each button and center it over the guidelines.

4. Now hold down the Shift key and drag from the left ruler to place vertical guides at 2 7/16 inch (2.44, 0.00 in.) and 5 15/16 inch (5.94, 0.00 in.).

5. Create a circle that's 2 1/4 inches. (While drawing, hold down the Shift key to make it a circle rather than an oval). Then click and drag the circle into position over one of the guideline intersections. The side handles will fall on the guidelines when the circle is centered. Select, copy, and paste the circle (use Copy Ellipse and Paste Object under the Edit menu) five times. Then drag and position each.

the button designs have to be placed precisely on the page so that they match the cutouts on the perforated paper. So use the following description to set up nonprinting guides on the paper. The center of each button is indicated by the intersection of the guidelines.

1. Under the Tools menu, Snap to Ruler Marks should be checked and Snap to Guides should be unchecked.

2. In the Zoom window, choose 66% so that you can see 16 tick marks per inch on the ruler. (If there are no rulers showing, choose View, Tool-

bars and Rulers, Rulers.) Position the page so that you can see 0 on both the vertical and horizontal rulers.

3. Hold down the Shift key and position the cursor over the ruler at the top of the page until you see the Adjust pointer. Drag a new guide from the ruler down the page to the 2 1/8-inch mark on the vertical ruler, and release the mouse button. (The position window at the bottom of your screen should read 0.00, 2.13 in.) Repeat this process to place horizontal guidelines at 5 7/16 inch (0.00, 5.44 in.) and 8 3/4 inch (0.00, 8.75 in.).

6. Follow the Step-by-Step directions to create your button designs.

7. Print a test copy of your

continued on the next page

continued

buttons on regular paper. Lay the perforated stock over your test printout and hold them up to a window or another light source. (Note: To be consistent, always hold the perforated stock so that the release slots run from the outer edge of each circle toward the top of the page.)

8. Check the alignment of each of the six designs with respect to the perforations, and note where adjustments need to be made.

9. Return to your computer and fine-tune the position of each button as necessary. Repeat the fine-tuning process until you are satisfied with the alignment. (Because of variations in letter shapes, as well as differences in perforations, paper, and printers, it may take several tries to get everything lined up just right.)

10. Print on the specialty paper. Then just pop the buttons out of the paper and into your button frames.

11. Now select the complete row of circles and squares, copy the row to the Clipboard, and paste and position the row on the page. Repeat until the page is full. You should end up with four rows of three, for a total of twelve button templates.

12. Save the file.

13. Fill each circle with a different color. (If you are using a black-and-white printer, you can skip this step.) Click on each circle, choose the Object Color button on the toolbar, and choose a color.

FamilyPC Tip: *Remember that you can always double-click on the text (or any item) to change it. You can also use the Rotation button on the toolbar to rotate your text, which is particularly useful when text appears in the shape of a circle.*

14. Insert a picture of your child in the center of the circle. Choose the Picture tool and create a picture box that is about 1 1/2 inches square. Choose Insert, Picture File, and then locate the saved file of your child's picture using the dialog boxes that appear.

15. Save the file.

16. Crop the background of the photo by clicking on the image and then clicking on the Wrap Text to Picture button on the toolbar. Next, click on the Edit Irregular Wrap button. A series of handles will appear around the image. Drag them so that they silhouette your child's face.

17. Save the file.

18. Now it's time to add text that runs in the shape of a circle. Choose the WordArt tool from the toolbar, and create a text box that's just a little bit smaller than the original square.

19. From the pulldown menu, choose a font that seems to say Party! (such as Arial Rounded MT Bold). Choose Best Fit for the font size. Type a phrase, such as *Kelly Muse turns three!* If the words will appear in a loop, be sure to press the spacebar twice after the last letter or punctuation mark, so that it and the first word don't bunch.

20. To change the position of the text so that it surrounds the picture, select the Circle shape from the pulldown menu.

FamilyPC Tip: *You can vary the buttons after copying them. First, ungroup the elements on any button. Then simply double-click on the specific text and choose a new color from the Shading button on the toolbar.*

21. Change the color of the text to one that contrasts with the background by clicking on the Shading button on the toolbar and choosing a foreground color from the pull-

You can rotate the text by entering an angle amount.

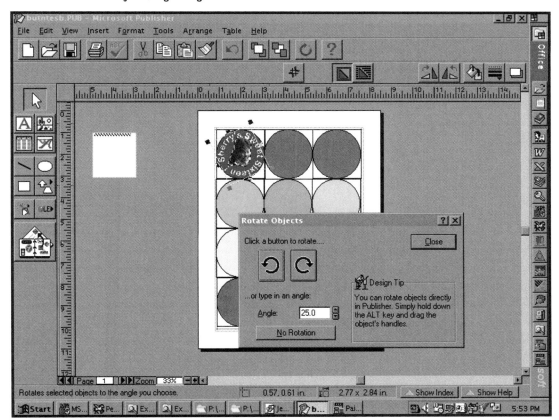

down dialog box. (For instance, you might want to use bright yellow text with a dark green background.)

22. Click in the document to close Word-Art and see how the text looks.

23. Save the file.

24. Adjust the placement of elements as necessary. Select individual items, hold down the Alt key, and tap the directional keys to nudge the item.

25. Print a test page to check the look of just one button. Make any necessary adjustments, and save the file.

26. When you're happy with the look of your button, hold down the Shift key, select the photo and the text, group the elements, and copy and paste them into the different colored circles.

27. Save the file.

FamilyPC Tip: *If you need to change a background color or if the picture or text seems to disappear, click on the image that is immediately visible, and choose Arrange, Send to Back. Repeat with each layer to find what you are looking for.*

A Little or a Lot

To make just one or two buttons, check your local craft store for plastic button frames sold individually. Simply print your design on plain paper and cut out the circle with an art knife.

If you need a larger quantity of buttons, consider metal button-making kits from Badge-A-Minit, Box 800, LaSalle, Illinois 61301, 800-223-4103 or 815-883-9696 (fax).

To have buttons commercially produced from your designs, look in the yellow pages under *Advertising Specialties*.

28. Print a copy of the button designs.

29. Cut out the individual button designs using scissors.

30. Open the button casing and place the button design inside. Snap to close.

Products You Can Use

Paint or draw program: *Paint module in ClarisWorks, CorelDraw, Kid Pix, SmartSketch*

Desktop publishing program: *Adobe Paint & Publish, Microsoft Publisher, Turbo Publisher*

Photo-editing and conversion software: *Graphic Converter, Paint Shop Pro*

Clip art: *Corel Gallery 2, Task Force Clip Art — Really Big Edition*

Posters & Banners

PREP TIME: 60 MINUTES EACH

Materials

**Desktop publishing program or word processing program with tiling capabilities •
Clip art (for the banner) • Scanner (for the poster) • Printer • Adhesive spray,
glue sticks, or rubber cement • Foam core or cardboard (for the poster) •
Craft knife (for the poster) • Cellophane tape • String • Stapler**

Bigger is better when it comes to posters and banners. Here we'll show you how to make larger-than-life-sized posters and wall-to-wall banners. They're great for any number of occasions. For a party, create a life-sized poster of the guest of honor as well as a banner with her name alongside the message, and you're sure

to make her feel special. You and your kids can also create them to announce a school bake sale or a community fundraiser; rouse the team spirit at a sporting event; or notify your neighborhood about a garage sale. In short, whenever you want to send a big wish or spread the word far and wide, these projects are just the right size.

Super-Sized Poster

Kids like to compare their size to their parents' size. What will they look like when they're just as big? What will it be like to have hands and feet so large? Never satisfied with simply pondering the future, however, kids' inquisitiveness usually leads to investigation: They try on our clothes, walk in our shoes (if only they really could!), and hold their head just so to keep our hat from slipping over their eyes. Bring the future a little closer — have some fun showing them what they'll look like when they're big by creating this oversized poster. Of course, who knows how big they'll grow? Do they want to be as tall as Shaquille O'Neil or Michael Jordon? Make a 7-foot poster so they can see themselves as tall — and how much they'd have to grow!

Before You Begin

It's easy to get started making a poster of your child. All you need to do is scan his or her picture, and save it in a format you can access (for example, .TIF or BMP).

Step-by-Step

We describe how to make a poster using the desktop pub-

Brainstormer

Poster picks:

family pet ,

child's teacher,

sports hero,

best friend,

fancy car,

cartoon monster

lishing program Microsoft Publisher for Windows 95. However, feel free to apply the directions to any program that features tiling and the capability to import graphics or scale fonts (such as Microsoft Word, Smart-Sketch, or ClarisWorks).

1. Launch Microsoft Publisher for Windows 95 (or an alternative application).

2. From the four selections (PageWizard, Blank Page, Existing Publication, and Templates), choose Blank Page.

3. In the next dialog box, click on Poster, and then click on OK.

4. Choose File, Page Setup, and enter the dimensions for your poster. For instance, if you are creating a poster that you want to be about the size of a professional basketball player, make your document 83 inches high and 28 inches wide. (With a poster this size, the dimensions will change from inches to feet — 6.92 feet by 2.33 feet.)

5. Next, you'll insert your digitized picture. (In this step, we assume that you have your favorite photo saved on your hard drive in a format that you can access.) Select the Picture tool. Then drag anywhere across the screen to create a picture box. Double-click in the box, and use the dialog boxes that appear to find the file containing the picture.

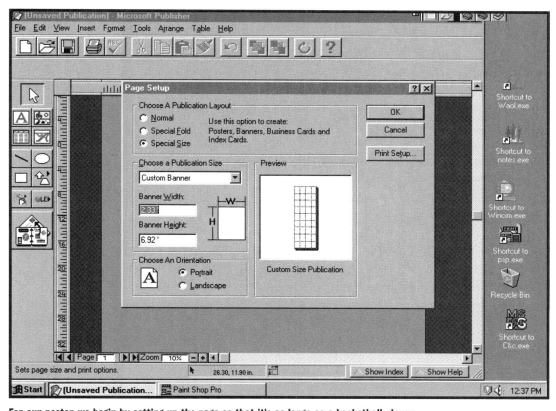

For our poster, we begin by setting up the page so that it's as large as a basketball player.

6. Scale the picture to fit just within the red margin lines.

7. Save the file.

8. You'll be printing the picture on standard-size (8 1/2- by 11- inch) paper, so you need to allow overlap between pages. To set the tile overlap for your document, choose File, Print, Tile Printing Options. Set the overlap to 0.2″, and click on OK.

9. Click on OK in the Print dialog box to print the picture of your child.

10. The poster is assembled row-by-row from the bottom up. Start with the bottom

FamilyPC Tip: *If your photo has extraneous elements that you want to eliminate before sizing it to the poster, click on the Cropping tool, and then position the pointer over a frame handle. When the pointer changes to a pair of scissors, drag the handle to trim the picture on that side. Click on the Cropping tool icon again when you're finished.*

right corner, which is usually the last sheet printed. Place it. Then take the next page to the left (which is usually the second-to-the-last page printed) and trim the right side along the edge of the picture. Align it next to the first sheet. Repeat the process to finish the row.

11. On the next row up, start with the rightmost page, trim the bottom, and place. Take the next sheet to the left, trim the right and bottom edges, and place. Repeat to finish the row. Repeat the trimming process for the remaining rows. (Trimming the side

FamilyPC Tip: *If you don't have a color printer, you can print your poster in grayscale and add color with markers. First, however, use a photo-editing program to enhance the edges, which makes the outline of your image more pronounced. Then insert the image into your document, scale, and print the image in Publisher.*

and bottom edges lets you line up the sheets of paper so that the poster appears seamless.)

We've scaled this photo so it fills the poster but still remains within the margins.

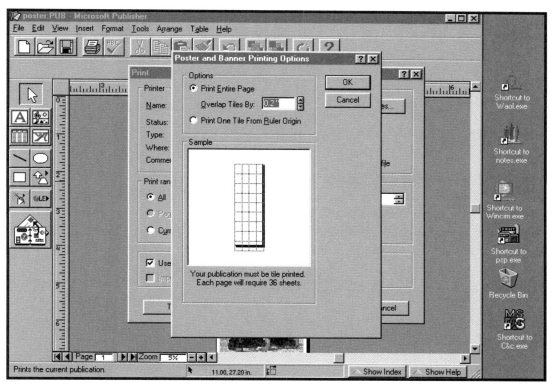

Reduce the tile overlap to maximize the amount of image printed on each page.

12. Starting with the bottom right page and continuing in the same order as step 11, glue the sheets to foam core (you can tape sheets together to make any size you need) or a large piece of cardboard. (Using spray adhesive is the fastest method, though children should not use it unsupervised.)

13. Using a craft knife, carefully cut the silhouette of your child from the foam core or cardboard.

14. Hang the finished poster from a thumbtack or prop it against the wall. You may want to reinforce the poster by taping

FamilyPC Tip: *If you don't have a program that lets you tile an image, you can still use your favorite word processing or draw program to make a banner. Just type one letter on each page, scaling the letter to fill the page. Print each page. Then put the pages face down in reverse order (so that they'll be in the correct order when the banner is flipped), lay a string along the top, and tape the pages to the string, stapling at each corner as the string passes from sheet to sheet.*

a light wooden stick to the back before standing the poster up.

Birthday Banner

A bigger wish for a happy birthday will be hard to come by after you create this 10-foot banner. Even if the party was planned long ago, this super-sized banner will put the surprise back in any birthday celebration.

Before You Begin

This banner features clip art on both ends, so take the time to check out the library in Microsoft Publisher or your own collection and note the location of favorites.

Step-by-Step

We're using Microsoft Publisher for Windows 95 to create the banner. However, you can modify the directions to use any program that allows you to tile and also import graphics or scale fonts (such as Microsoft Word, SmartSketch, or ClarisWorks).

1. Launch Microsoft Publisher for Windows 95 (or the program you plan on using for this project).

2. Click on the Blank Page tab.

3. Select the Banner document template, and click on OK.

4. Change the size of the banner by choosing File, Page Setup and scrolling through the choices under Choose a Publication Size. (We chose 10 feet.) Click on OK.

5. Now it's time to add text to the banner. Create a text box by clicking on the Word-Art button on the toolbar and dragging diagonally across the document.

Microsoft Publisher's poster templates come in all shapes and sizes, so making posters and banners is a breeze.

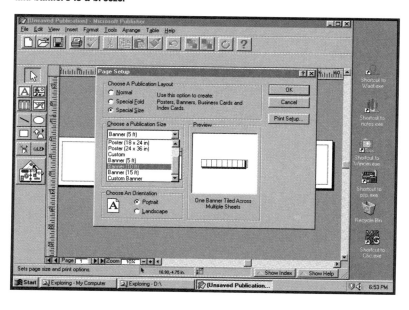

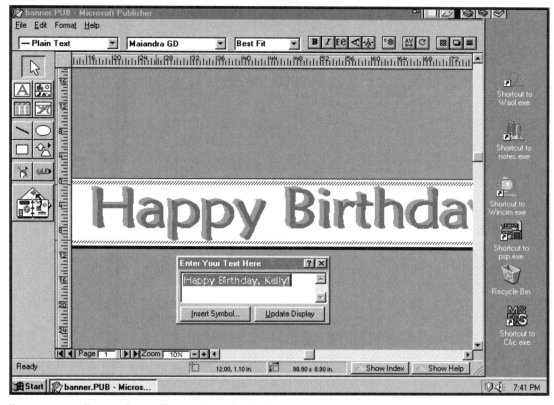

You can create all sorts of type effects, such as the shadow we used here.

6. Choose a festive font from the Font pulldown menu (we used Maiandra GD), and keep the size at the default, Best Fit.

7. Choose a color (we used red) by clicking on the Color tool, which is the third from the right on the toolbar.

8. Give the type a colored shadow (we used orange) by clicking on the Shadow tool, which is the second from the right on the toolbar.

9. In the WordArt text box that says *Enter*

FamilyPC Tip: *If your computer has trouble printing a large WordArt banner, you can simply use regular text for the lettering. (A type size of roughly 500 points will fit nicely on a banner.) You may also want to adjust the tracking to spread out the text. (Tracking is a term that refers to the amount of space between characters.) To adjust the tracking, first select the text. Then choose Format, Spacing between characters. Under Spacing Options, choose Loose or Very Loose.*

Your Text Here, type the text for the banner. (For information on fonts, see the "Resource Guide.")

10. Save the file.

11. Place the finished text in the center of the page by clicking and dragging the text box to the desired location.

12. Scale the text so that it fits within the border.

13. Save the file again.

14. Next, you'll insert clip art on the banner. Begin by creating a picture box — click on the Picture tool and repeat the steps you used to create the WordArt box.

Brainstormer

Banner ideas:

Welcome Home,

Congratulations,

Happy Anniversary,

Merry Christmas,

The Champs,

Bon Voyage,

Happy New Year

15. Then double-click inside the box to access the clip-art library in Publisher. (If you are accessing clip art from another source and the clip art is saved on your hard drive, locate the files using the pulldown menus that appear.)

16. Add a second piece of clip art to the other end of the banner, or copy the current image to your Clipboard and paste it on the other end of the banner.

17. Make any final adjustments to the placement and size of the elements. Be sure that all parts are within the margins.

18. Save the file.

Photo Finish

If you have access to a scanner, you can use the birthday child's picture and fun shapes for design elements instead of clip art. First, you need to have the picture saved in a format that you can access with your computer. (If you're using Publisher, save it as a .TIF or .BMP file.)

Create a picture box for the photo. Then double-click inside the box, and locate the image on your hard drive using the dialog boxes that appear. When the image is on-screen, use the Wrapping tool and the Edit Irregular Wrap tool to crop out the background.

To add colorful shapes, such as a star or a blaze, click on the Shapes tool, choose the shape you want, and then click and drag on the document to create the shape. Fill the shape with color by clicking on the Fill tool and choosing a color. Change the border color by choosing More and then a color from the Border pulldown menu.

Scale the elements to size, place them, and print. Tape the pages together, and staple a length of string along the top of the back of the banner.

Now all that's left for you to do is to hang the banner and join the fun.

19. Print your banner on standard white paper.

20. Compile all the pages.

21. Trim the right edge of each page (except for the extreme right page) up to the printed image.

22. Starting with the right end of the banner, affix all the pages together with a small piece of cellophane tape on the front top and bottom corners. Then flip the banner over and apply a longer strip of tape to the seams on the back side.

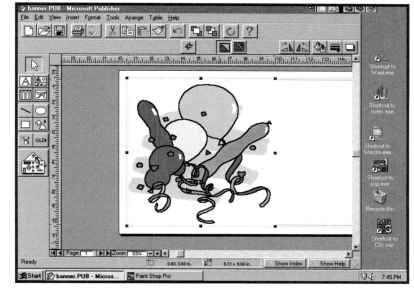

Give your banner added pizzazz by inserting clip art from the clip-art library in Publisher or elsewhere.

Zoom out to look at your entire document to check that all the design elements are balanced.

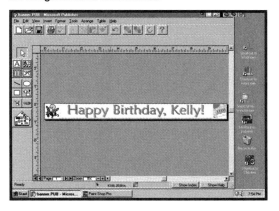

23. Staple a long string along the top edge, making sure to leave enough string at the ends to tie to thumbtacks.

24. Hang the banner in the party room.

Products You Can Use

Paint or draw program: *ClarisDraw, CorelDraw, SmartSketch, TurboDraw*

Desktop publishing program: *Adobe Paint & Publish, Microsoft Publisher, Turbo Publisher*

Works program: *ClarisWorks, Microsoft Works*

Photo-editing program: *Paint Shop Pro, Adobe PhotoDeluxe*

Clip art: *Art Explosion — 40,000 Images, Task Force Clip Art — Really Big Edition*

Pumpkin-Carving Templates

PREP TIME: 60 MINUTES

Materials

Draw, paint, or word processing program • Printer • Paper • Marker • Sharp knife • Long spoon

Did you know that Halloween is second only to Christmas as the most widely celebrated holiday? And that it's just as popular with adults as it is with kids? Perhaps it's because unlike any other holiday, Halloween lets us step out of ourselves and into another role: for a few hours we can pretend to be anyone or anything we want to be. It's a surprise-filled tradition that's hard to resist! So, long before October 31st arrives, the preparations — and fun — begin: Planning and making costumes; stocking up on treats (you don't want to be tricked!); and, of course, carving pumpkins into jack-o'-lanterns that emit an eerie glow.

Before You Begin

You want your jack-o'-lantern to glow this Halloween. And it will if you use a design that spreads across the pumpkin and gives you the opportunity to cut out many smaller holes rather than just the traditional four: two eyes, a nose, and a mouth.

The design we create here is one good example: the image covers a large portion of the pumpkin and it has plenty of areas that you can cut out. By keeping these two things in mind, you'll create a jack-o'-lantern that's radiant and lights your walkway for trick-or-treaters.

Brainstormer

Pumpkin carvings of a skull, witch, cat, bat, vampire, owl, hobgoblin, spider, monster, ghost

Step-by-Step

We used SmartSketch to make the pumpkin template, but you can use your favorite draw, paint, or word processing program.

1. Open a new document in SmartSketch.

2. Set the page orientation to Portrait (under Page Setup on the Mac or Print Setup in Windows).

3. Choose Format, Document, Match Printer so that what appears on the screen will match what will print.

4. You'll need rulers to help draw the lines. Choose Show Grid (which is under Format, Document). Then choose View, Show Rulers and Show Page.

5. Draw a circle, 7 inches in diameter (click on the Pencil tool and select the Oval tool set at a 1-point line thickness). Center the circle using the rulers as a guide.

6. Draw a 1-point horizontal line through

There are lots of lines to draw for the pumpkin-carving template, but you can cut your drawing in half by copying and rotating lines.

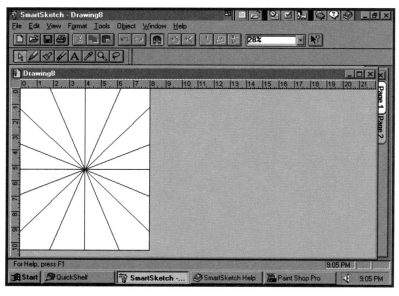

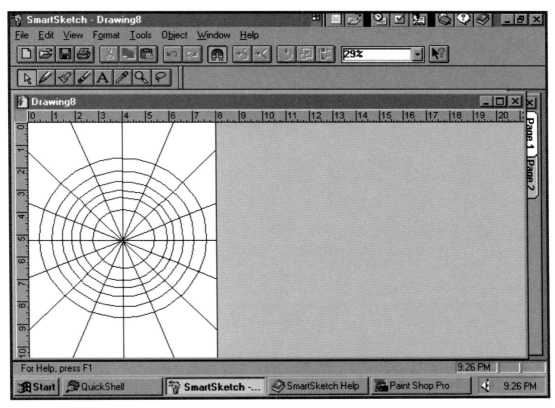

By duplicating and scaling, you can create a number of concentric circles easily. You'll use these as your drawing and cutting guides.

the center of the circle using the Straight Line tool (one of the choices available after clicking on the Pencil tool). Then draw a vertical line though the center of the circle using the same tool. Now draw two more intersecting lines, each running diagonally from just inside the top corners of the page through the center of the circle.

7. Save the file.

8. Select all the straight lines you've just drawn, copy them to the Clipboard, and

paste them back into your document.

9. Move the copied lines until they are directly over the original lines. Click the Rotation button, and rotate the copied lines until they divide the pie-shaped pieces in half. The result should be sixteen equally spaced lines, all intersecting in the center of the circle.

10. We still need more cut lines, so we'll begin by creating an identical copy of the circle. Then, select all the areas of the circle, copy to the Clipboard, and paste them into the document.

11. With the new circle still selected, choose Tools, Scale by Percent, and scale the new circle down to 85 percent.

12. Save the file.

13. Place the new circle centered inside the larger one.

14. Create three more circles that fit one inside the other by repeating steps 10 to 13

FamilyPC Tip: *For a difficult area such as the space between the lips and chin, cut the lips out but carve only halfway through the flesh for the chin. You will get an eerie glow through the chin without the risk of breaking the narrow section between it and the lips.*

three more times, each time using the last circle you created as the basis for the new circle. You should have five concentric circles altogether.

Our design is beginning to take shape.

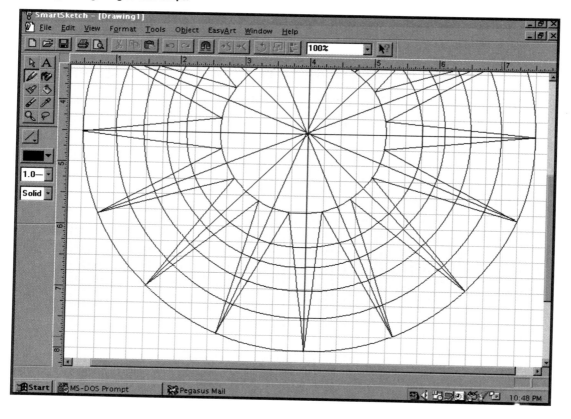

15. Copy and paste the last circle you made, and scale it to 70 percent. Center it. This is the sixth (and last!) circle.

16. Save the file.

17. Next, mark the midpoint of each arc of the innermost circle. Then draw a series of straight lines that extend from the midpoint out to where the lines intersect the outermost circle.

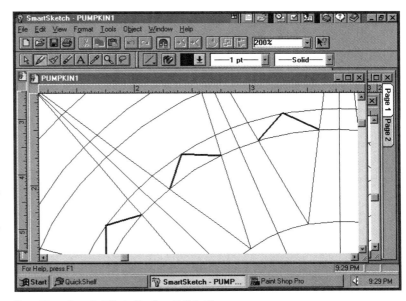

Draw these inverted V's in the fourth "ring."

18. Save the file.

19. Concentrating on the next two circles out from the center, draw a series of upside-down V's in the space between the two circles. The point of each V should be pointing out; the two tips of each V should originate from where the smaller of the two circles intersects the lines from step 17.

20. Save a backup copy of your drawing by selecting File, Save As and renaming your drawing slightly (for example, Pumpkin to Pumpkin2).

21. Delete the lines inside the circle, except the original horizontal, vertical, and bisecting lines that extend from the top corners up to the small V's you just drew. (Just click on each line segment and press the Delete key.) Next, delete all line segments and arcs inside the long points created by the angled lines. Then delete the remainder of the unnecessary lines to match the figure on page 200.

FamilyPC Tip: *If you are having trouble seeing a particular line or understanding what is happening when you draw or select an item, zoom in by either 200 or 400 percent. In addition, remember that most draw programs have an Undo feature, so you can go back several steps and correct anything you don't like. You may also want to turn off the grid (Format, Document in Smart-Sketch) to get a clearer view.*

22. Save the file as Pumpkin3.

23. In the center space, using the Pencil tool in Smooth drawing mode and 2-point thickness, draw the left side of the face, including the eye, an eyebrow, half a nose, half a mouth, and a cheek. As you complete each part, copy it to the Clipboard, paste it, and flip it horizontally (Tools, Flip Horizontal), and then click and drag it to the opposite side of the face.

24. Delete the last of the vertical and horizontal guidelines and clean up any re-

Using Your Pumpkin Template

After you print the design, you and your child can finish the template by cutting out the shapes and face parts. If you make a mistake, don't worry: just print another copy.

Then tape the template to your pumpkin, and trace inside the cutouts with a black marker. Remove the template, and use a sharp knife to cut out the shapes.

Use this figure as a guide to the lines that should be deleted in step 21.

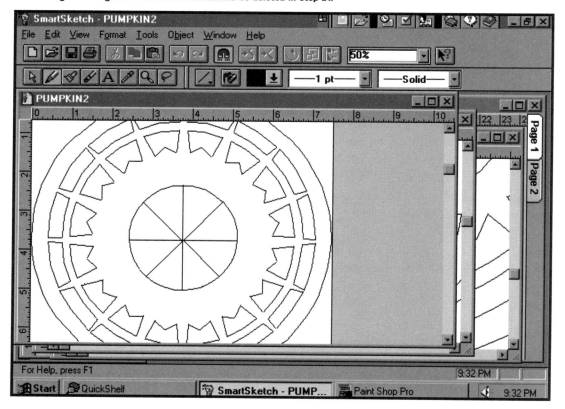

When you are through, you should have a balanced, intricate design for your pumpkin.

gle) and choose Object, Create Group.

26. Scale your design to fit the pumpkin you are carving (Objects, Scale).

27. Save the file one last time.

28. Print the design on one sheet of paper, or use the Scale feature in Print Setup (Windows 3.1) to tile the drawing for larger pumpkins. (The Scale feature is in Page Setup of the Windows 95 version of SmartSketch, and in Print Margins in the Mac version.)

maining lines or glitches. When you're pleased with the design, save the file.

25. You need a template that will be the appropriate size for your pumpkin. Select all (drag from the upper left across the entire design to enclose it in the indicated rectan-

Products You Can Use

Paint or draw program: *Paint module in ClarisWorks, Flying Colors, SmartSketch*

PC Projects, Family Style

Your family's lifestyle is busy. In fact, between jobs, school, sports, lessons, and community interests (just to name a few!), it can be downright hectic. The irony is that all these commitments tend to spawn even more commitments… "Will you coach the soccer team next year?" "Could you bring a dish to the annual cook-off?" This section shows you how

to tackle some of these volunteer projects. If you're the most-loved at bake sales, turn to "Electronic Cookbook." If you're the new coach, check out "Coaching with Your Computer." Who knows? By implementing these projects, you may have some free time to enjoy the other ones in this section: creating a travel guide for your next vacation and tracing the family tree.

Coaching with Your Computer

🦉 PREP TIME: 2 HOURS EACH

Materials
Works package • Clip art (optional) • Printer • Paper

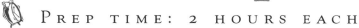

Whatever the season, there's a team that needs top-notch organization. Whether it's baseball or soccer, your roster should include a database and spreadsheet. A database is a good way to keep track of essential information, such as each player's name, address, and phone number. Enter this information at the beginning of the sea-son, and you'll have it readily available when you need to call off an early-morning game or send out special notices. Then, to track each player's statistics (for example, their season batting average), use a spreadsheet. Of interest to every player, this information also comes in handy when you're choosing a pinch-hitter or making last-minute substitutions.

The Database Manager

A database manager helps you organize all that information you normally keep in lists or on scraps of paper. With a database manager, you keep all the important information about your team in one place, and you can list and arrange that information in any way you like. For example, you can generate a list of players' names and phone numbers (perfect for organizing carpools or sending a pregame reminder). Or you can list players by their jersey numbers (handy for creating season programs). And if a new player joins the team in midseason, you can easily update the database and print new phone lists and rosters.

Keep track of all the important information about each player by using a database manager.

Before You Begin

Assemble a list of the important information you'd like to store in your database. Start with last names and first names, and then include everything from parents' telephone numbers and addresses to players' jersey numbers. Try to make the list as comprehensive as possible.

You'll enter these items of information into database *fields*. Although you can add fields while you enter a *record* (that is, the collection of fields for one player), you can save yourself the trouble of reopening existing records and filling in new information if you compile a complete list of the fields before you start entering data.

Step-by-Step

1. Launch ClarisWorks (or the program you plan to use).

2. In the New Document dialog box, choose Create a database.

3. In the dialog box that appears, create text fields for the various categories that you plan to include in your database. To create a field, enter the name of the field in the Field Name box, leave the Field Type as a text field, and click on the Create button.

Here are some fields you might want to include:

- First name
- Last name
- Parents' names
- Address
- Telephone number
- Caretaker's name
- Caretaker's phone number
- Jersey number
- Position(s)
- Innings played
- Batting average
- Batting spot
- Errors
- Notes

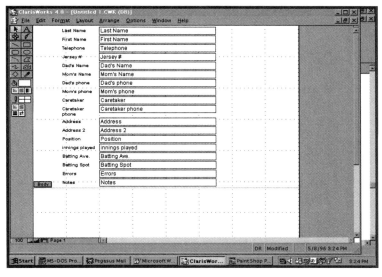

Create separate fields in your database to store the various pieces of information about each player.

All the fields can be text fields, though you can use numbers where appropriate. (The Caretaker field is for the name of someone who may be taking care of the kids in the afternoon — such as a grandparent, relative, or friend.)

FamilyPC Tip: *You can add other fields later — for example, one showing whether people have donated their money for the pizza pep rally — by using the Define Fields command in the Layout menu.*

4. After you've defined all the fields in your database, click on Done to move on to the Layout screen, where you arrange the fields on a page.

5. Arrange the fields to create a clear, logical layout. First, change the page orientation to landscape. In ClarisWorks, choose the Page Setup or the Print Setup command.

6. Next, alter the physical dimensions of the fields by choosing the Layout command from the Layout menu. ClarisWorks displays a builder's view of the database; the boxes around the fields all have corner handles for resizing and reshaping. Just grab a handle and drag it in to shrink the box or out to enlarge it.

7. To move a field, just click and drag it anywhere on the screen. Don't forget to move the field's label at the same time, though you should feel free to modify the label in any way that will make the screen easier to understand.

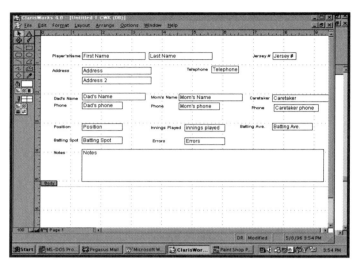

In ClarisWorks, arrange the fields in your database by using the Layout mode.

box so that the entire name appears on one line.

11. Change the alignment of the text to centered by choosing the menu commands Format, Alignment, Center.

12. To insert a team logo into the header, use clip art or your own drawing. Copy the artwork from the clip-art collection or your paint program to the Clipboard, and then paste it into the header.

8. You can also select all your fields and align them by choosing Arrange and then either Align to Grid or Align. The Align command gives you options for aligning fields from top to bottom or from left to right. Our advice: Keep fields aligned to the left, evenly spaced.

9. Save the file.

10. Add your team's name so that it appears at the top of each record. In Claris-Works, insert the name and a team logo in the header area of the layout by choosing Insert Part from the Layout menu. Click on Header, and then use the Text tool to enter your team's name. You may need to resize the text

13. Now, adjust the size of the layout by clicking and dragging the bottom line of the body to just beneath the field boxes. (This eliminate excess white space at the bottom of each record when you display

Add your team's name and logo to the header, so that they appear on each record you print.

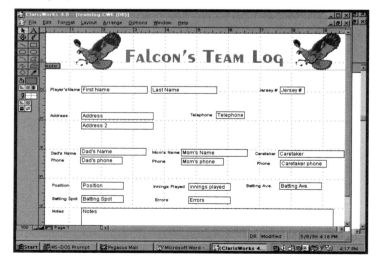

Using Your Database

You can use your database to generate phone lists (for car-pooling parents), mailing lists (for off-the-field events), batting orders, or a summary list of players and playing time for end-of-the-year reviews. (Some leagues require that all players get at least a certain amount of playing time.)

To create a phone list (you must be in Browse mode to do this), choose Layout, New Layout, and select Columnar in the dialog box that ClarisWorks displays. Select Last Name and click on Move. Do the same for First Name, Home Phone, Parent's Name, and Work Phone. Click on OK. To save the new file as Phone List, choose File, Save As, and then type *Phone List* in the dialog box that appears.

You can use your original information again and again,

by creating new layouts, selecting criteria to list, and then saving each file under a new name. For example, to create a batting lineup, choose Sort

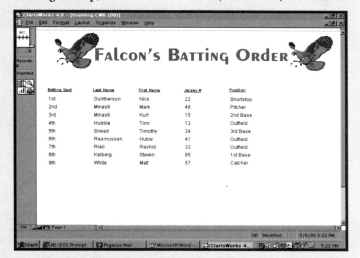

Move. Choose Layout, New Layout, call it *Batting Order,* and click on Columnar. Click and Move Batting Spot, Last Name, First Name, and Position

You can use your database in various ways — for example, to generate lists such as batting orders.

Records from the Organize menu (or press Ctrl + J). Select the Batting Spot field as the sorting criterion, and click on

as the fields to be shown in your new layout. Click on OK. Save the new file as *Batting Lineup* and print.

and print the records.)

14. Save the file.

15. As you create your layout, periodically check the appearance of your data-

base screen. In ClarisWorks, choose the Browse command from the Layout menu. Enter dummy information to see how the fields look. If a field box is too small to hold a name, switch back to the Layout view and resize the field.

Enter each player's information as a separate record.

16. When you finish the layout, delete the record containing your dummy information (or any other record). To do this in Claris-Works, switch to Browse mode, select the record, and choose Edit, Delete Record.

17. Save the file.

FamilyPC Tip: *Although you can freely add new fields later, if you change the type or the name of an existing field in your database, you lose all the information that field contained. Be sure to make the design of your database as complete as possible before you start inputting information.*

18. Enter all your players' data in Browse view by typing the information in the appropriate fields. Create a new record for each player by choosing the commands Edit, New Record.

19. After entering all the information, print copies of your database, pass them out to the players on the team, and ask the players to check for errors. Because you stored the list on the computer, you can easily make the necessary corrections.

The Spreadsheet Manager

Young ballplayers are very interested in keeping track of their stats. As a coach, you can use these numbers to help you determine the batting order or plan your defensive strategy (based on fielding percentages). You can keep track of all those numbers by using the spreadsheet capability of your Works package. After you set up your spreadsheet, just tally the numbers from your team's most recent game, enter them into the spreadsheet, and let the software automatically calculate the totals, the percentages, and the averages for you.

Before You Begin

Determine which statistics are important to your team. Here's the bottom line: The more numbers you want to generate, the more time you'll spend entering information after each game. For

now, stick with batting averages, playing time, fielding percentages, and earned-run averages. If you're really into statistics, though, go nuts!

Step-by-Step

1. Launch ClarisWorks (or the Works or spreadsheet program you'll be using).

2. In the opening dialog box, choose Create a new spreadsheet.

3. Insert the team name in the header. In ClarisWorks, choose the Insert Header command from the Format menu, and enter the team's name.

4. Select the text you just entered, and choose a font from the Font menu (we used

By using a spreadsheet, a baseball manager can easily keep track of all the players' statistics.

Haettenscheiler), aligned center (choose Format, Paragraph, Center), with a point size of 36 (click on 36 in the Size menu).

5. Save the file.

6. Click on cell A2 and type *Players*.

Using Your Team Spreadsheet

Print your statistics spreadsheet before each game. That way, you can show your players how they're doing as well tally statistics during the game you're about to play. (You can use your notes to update the spreadsheet after the game.) You can also take data — for example, batting average and innings played — from the spreadsheet and enter it into your database. Finally, remember that you can copy any part of the spreadsheet to the Clipboard and then paste it into a new spreadsheet. Good luck and have a great season!

Print updated statistics after each game to pass out to players.

7. In the cells below A2 (A3, A4, A5, and so on) type each player's last name and first initial. After entering a name, press the Return key to jump down to the next cell.

8. After you enter all the names, save the file.

9. To alphabetize the list, click and drag from cell A3 down to the last name, choose the Sort command from the Calculate menu, and click on OK.

10. For each player, insert eight rows for entering the statistics — number of hits, at bats, fielding attempts, and so on. In ClarisWorks, click in the cell that contains the second name in the list (cell A4), and choose Calculate, Insert Cells. In the dialog box that's displayed, select Shift cells down and click on OK. Use the Insert Cells command to insert eight rows of cells for each player on the roster.

11. Next, in column B, enter the following abbreviations to identify the various statistics:

Abbreviation	Description
AB	At bats
H	Hits
TB	Total bases
AVG	Batting average
SLG PCT	Slugging percentage
FA	Fielding attempts
FS	Fielded successfully
E	Errors
FLD PCT	Fielding percentage

Baseball Spreadsheet Calculations

In step 16, you enter the formulas for the baseball statistics. Here are the calculations to use. Be sure to save the file regularly.

The first calculation is batting average (AVG). The formula is simple: the number of hits divided by the number of times at bat (walks and batters hit by pitches don't count as times at bat). For the first player and the first game in our spreadsheet, we used the formula in cell C6:

=(C4/C3)

Select the field for the calculation, and then type =(C4/C3). Notice that the cell displays the error message "#DIV/0!", meaning "division by zero," until you enter a value in cell C3. To format the number so it looks like a baseball average, select cell C6 again, and choose Format, Number. In the dialog box that's displayed, choose Fixed format with Precision set to 3, and then click on OK.

To calculate the slugging

Enter the appropriate formula for each field throughout the season.

percentage (SLG PCT), you divide the total number of bases a player reached on hits by the number of times at bat. For example, if your son had a home run and a double in two at-bats, his slugging percentage would be 3.000. In spreadsheet language, you use the formula =(Bases/At Bats). For the first player on your roster and the first game of the year, enter the following formula in cell C7:

=(C5/C3)

Format the slugging percentage in the same way as the batting average, by choosing Format, Number, and choosing Fixed and a precision of 3. Click on OK.

To determine the fielding

percentage (FLD PCT), you divide the number of balls that were successfully fielded by the number of fielding attempts, or =(FS/FA). To enter the first player's fielding calculation for the first game, select cell C11 and enter =(C9/C8). Again, format the number as Fixed, with a precision of 3.

Next, input formulas for the Team Totals fields. For example, the following formula calculates total at-bats for the first game:

=SUM(C3+C12+C21...)

Enter this formula in the Team Totals AB cell for the first game (column C).

To calculate the team's batting average for the first game, add all the batting averages and divide the total by the number of players — that is, =SUM(C6+C15+C24...)/*the number of players who batted.* Remember to format the result of this calculation in the

continued on the next page

continued

same manner as the other averages.

Use a similar calculation for the team slugging percentage (SLG PCT), dividing the total number of bases by the total number of at-bats. (For fielding percentage, use the

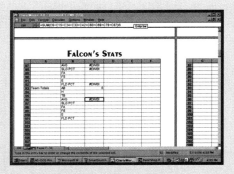

same model, but divide the total by the number of fielders who had at least one opportunity to field a ball. In other words, exclude any players who didn't make plays in the field.) Use the same models to complete the calculation totals for each player in the final column.

Enter formulas for tabulating team and player totals.

12. If you're feeling ambitious, include additional lines and fields for singles, doubles, triples, home runs, strikeouts, walks, stolen bases, innings played, and putouts. For pitchers, put in additional rows for total pitches, walks, strikes, balks, innings pitched, earned runs, earned-run average, and hit batters.

FamilyPC Tip: *To input formulas into a spreadsheet quickly, copy a formula from one cell to the Clipboard. Then move to another cell that uses the same basic formula, paste the formula from the Clipboard into that cell, and change the column or row numbers as required.*

13. At the bottom of the spreadsheet, enter the label *Team Totals* and include the same fields as listed for each player (AB, H, and so on).

14. Starting with column C in row 2, list each team on your schedule (for example, enter *vs. Red Sox* in C2, for the first team on the schedule; *vs. Mets* in D2, for the second team; and so on). After entering a team name, press the Tab key to move to the next cell to the right.

15. In the last column, you should enter the label *Totals*.

Insert rows for each player, covering at-bats, hits, and other relevant information.

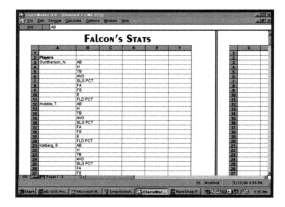

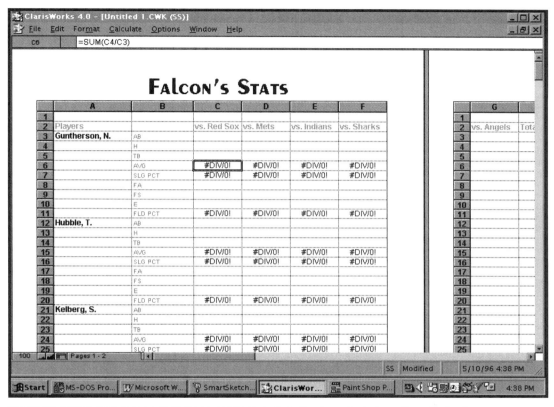

Change the format of various parts of the spreadsheet, such as the players' names, so they stand out.

16. Insert formulas to calculate statistics, where appropriate. For a list of the formulas we used, see "Baseball Spreadsheet Calculations."

FamilyPC Tip: *To alter the size of columns or rows, you can open the Format menu and click on Column Width or Row Height, or you can use the mouse to grab dividers in the row and column headings and drag them to the desired location.*

17. Change the format of various sections in the spreadsheet by selecting specific cells, and then opening the Font menu and changing the text's font, size, or color. For example, change the color of all totals to red and display the names of the fields in blue, 9-point text. Change the style of the players' names to Bold.

Products You Can Use

Works program: *ClarisWorks, Microsoft Works, WordPerfect Works*

Clip art: *Corel Gallery 2, Task Force Clip Art — Really Big Edition*

Electronic Cookbook

 PREP TIME: 30 MINUTES

Materials
Database program • Printer • Paper

The joy of cooking (and eating) — if only you could find that recipe! Inevitably, just when you have a hankering for your mother's stew or Aunt Sally's deep-dish apple pie, you can't find the recipe. No doubt it's carefully tucked away under the cover of your favorite cookbook — along with a hundred other recipes handwritten on scraps of paper and clipped from magazines. If you can never seem to find the recipe you're looking for, it's time to bring your cookbook into the electronic age! Using a database, you can not only store your recipes, but then search by ingredient, ethnicity, or preparation time. You can also easily update your collection instantly, print recipes for friends, or make a family cookbook heirloom. You'll quickly see that an electronic cookbook truly puts your recipes at your fingertips.

Before You Begin

Databases are composed of records that contain related information. For our project, each record is a recipe, and each recipe has related information (ingredients, directions, and so on) that are entered into sections called *fields*. To make your database useful, first you need to decide how you might use it, and then you need to create the appropriate fields to make the database fulfill your needs. For example, our electronic cookbook was set up with fields based on the ways we might want to search and sort recipes: by title, ingredients, instructions, ethnicity, total preparation and cooking time, source of recipe, food category, and a section for notes. We've also added a "key words" field for even faster searches.

Decide what fields you want to include by looking at your favorite recipes, figuring out how you want to organize the information, and then testing your setup against a random sampling of recipes. That way, you'll be sure that all types of food will have a place in your database.

Step-by-Step

We used the database manager in Claris-Works to create our electronic cookbook, but you can adapt these directions to just about any database program.

1. Launch your database manager.

2. Entering field names and types. Begin creating your cookbook by entering the names of each field and assigning a field type — for example, text or number. Because we want to be able to enter at least some text in each field, we entered Text for all field types.

Make fields for the following:
- Name of the recipe (title)
- Prep time
- Ingredients
- Instructions
- Category (entrée, dessert, and so on)
- Ethnicity
- Source of the recipe
- Key words
- Notes

All the fields should be text fields except those titled Category and Ethnicity, which are pop-up menus. (In ClarisWorks 4.0, you can also choose pop-up menus or radio buttons as the field type.) For these, you'll need to define the choices of the menu.

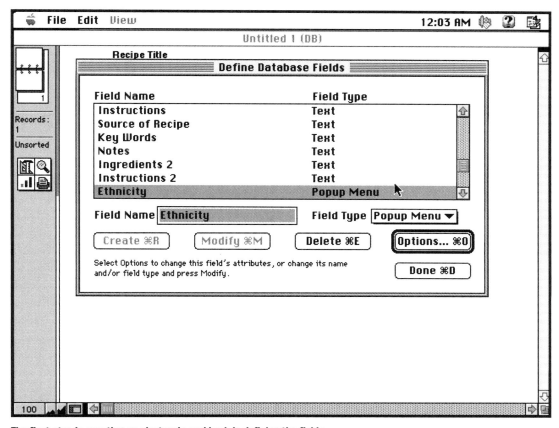

The first step in creating an electronic cookbook is defining the fields.

For instance, for Ethnicity, include Italian, Mexican, and Chinese. Choose one element to be the default choice. The Category menu

FamilyPC Tip: *Both ClarisWorks and Microsoft Works limit the number of characters allowed in any field. To have room for any extra details for the ingredients and instructions, simply create an additional, "overflow" field for each of these two.*

choices might include Main course, Dessert, Side dish, and Other.

3. Creating a new record for each recipe. After you've defined the fields, you must create a new record for each new recipe that you enter. (In ClarisWorks, create a new record by choosing Layout, Browse, Edit, New Record.) Then select a field and enter the information. Save the data after.

4. Making changes to records. You can easily edit your records at any time by

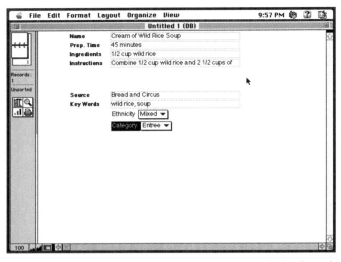

To enter recipes in ClarisWorks, switch to Browse mode (under Layout), and create new records (Edit, New Record.)

switching to Layout mode (in Claris-Works, choose Layout, Layout) and clicking on individual fields. You can change the appearance or function (change from text to pop-up menus) of any field, or you can add or delete fields.

One warning about altering a database layout after you've entered records: If you change the type of the field, the field name, or an item in a pop-up menu, you lose all the information that was previously in the field in each saved record. So take the time to plan your database; if you need to make changes down the road, think before you do so.

5. Tailoring your cookbook. Unlike changing the type of a

certain field, you can customize the appearance of your cookbook at any time without jeopardizing any information. The latest versions of both Claris-Works and Microsoft Works let you give your database a more personalized look by changing the position of any field, modifying the text appearance with different fonts, sizes, and styles, and adding background color, patterns, or borders. (To make changes, you must be in Layout mode in ClarisWorks and Design View in Microsoft Works.)

To reformat our recipe file, we positioned the recipe classifications (e.g., Category and Ethnicity) and the Notes section in a group

Customize the look of your cookbook by adding shaded areas to the background, altering the location, size, and alignment of fields, and changing the font and font size of particular fields.

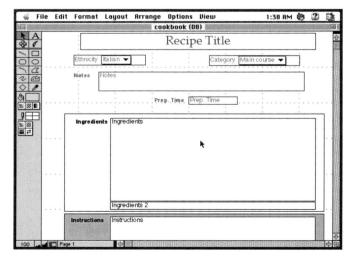

Cookbook Publisher

If you think you'll be printing your cookbook often, consider purchasing the print utility ClickBook. A simple program to use, it lets you print your database in a variety of book formats. (ClickBook works with any software program that supports printing, and is activated from your Page or Print Setup menu.) When you have the recipes ready to print, follow the nor-

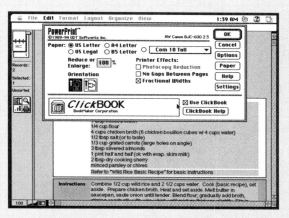

Use a print utility such as ClickBook to publish a booklet from your database.

mal steps in your software to print the document. After you click on the Print button, the ClickBook dialog box pops up

on your screen, listing a choice of layout styles for your booklet.

A special version of ClickBook, available through PaperDirect (800-APAPERS), includes printing layouts customized for PaperDirect's preprinted papers. The mail-order company also sells accessory products, such as binding staples, tassels, and specialized booklet covers.

above Ingredients and Instructions. To add emphasis, we changed the font and size of the recipe title. To add a more professional look, we placed two different-sized rectangular boxes on the recipe layout, and then shaded each box before moving them to the background. (On the Macintosh, if you choose a shading option, you need to change your print options from the default black-and-white to color/grayscale. Otherwise, shaded boxes will print over your text.)

6. Using your cookbook. Normally, a database is organized in the order records

are entered. If you prefer, you can sort one or more fields in ascending or descending alphabetical order. You can even view your entire database alphabetically by recipe name, in the format of a list. (In Claris-Works, choose Layout, List.)

But the biggest benefit of using a database manager is being able to sort recipes based on a variety of criteria. For instance, you can use the Find function to search for recipes by ingredient, ethnicity, or any other criterion (or combination of criteria) as listed in your fields. Just be sure to use the exact spelling of words.

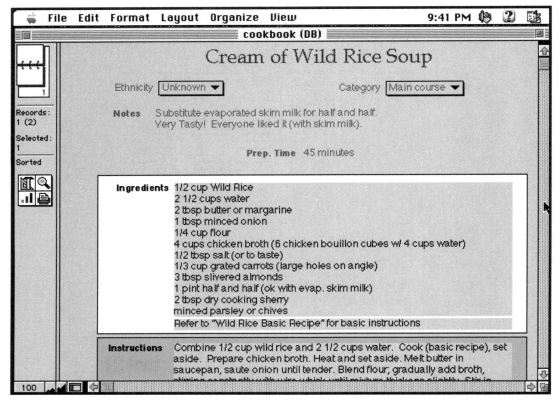

You can use Find to locate all your soup recipes.

7. Printing your cookbook. You can print a single record (mark Current Record in the Print dialog box), which is handy when a friend requests a copy. You can also print the entire database (the print default), which is ideal when you want to share all the family favorites with siblings. Printed cookbooks make great gifts and are perfect fund-raising items for schools and other nonprofit organizations. Bon appetit!

Products You Can Use

Works program: *ClarisWorks, Microsoft Works, WordPerfect Works*

Family History Map

PREP TIME: 60 MINUTES

Materials

Paint or draw program • Digitized map (from a clip-art collection, CD-ROM encyclopedia, CD-ROM atlas, or scanned image) • Printer • Paper

Stories about the past are interesting, but history becomes compelling when you put your own family into the mix. Creating a family history map is an intriguing way for you and your kids to explore your past. It will also prove as enlightening for you as it will be for your kids. As you map out your family history, you'll realize there are gaps in your stories, you'll remember things you haven't thought about in years (and may have forgotten to tell your kids), and you'll see connections between past events you never saw before. Here, you'll start tracing your roots by imposing your stories (text) and photos on a map of the United States. But tracking your past need not stop here; in fact, it's a terrific on-going family project.

Before You Begin

Find a map you can use as the foundation for your family history presentation. If your family has lived in the same area for several generations, you can use a state or regional map, though a plain outline map of the entire country works fine, too. You can get these images from a CD-ROM encyclopedia — for example, Grolier's, Compton's, or Microsoft Encarta — or an atlas, such as Software Toolworks or 3-D Atlas. The Corel Gallery and Gallery 2 clip-art collections also have excellent maps. Most programs allow you to copy the map to the Clipboard by selecting the image and then choosing Edit, Copy.

Next, collect several old family photos and images that show places where your family has history. (You could add these to your map by scanning them in. Turn to the "Creative Primer" for more information.) Compile a list of locations and write short descriptions telling how each place fits into your family's history.

Step-by-Step

We created this family history map by using the draw program SmartSketch, but you can adapt these steps to any paint or draw program that lets you insert images and add text.

1. Launch SmartSketch (or the paint, draw, or Works program

you'll be using for this project).

2. Begin a new document.

3. Change the orientation of the page to Landscape, so the map will fill the page. In most programs, you make this change in the Page Setup or Print Setup dialog box, which you open from the File menu.

4. Open the program (atlas or reference) that contains the map you plan to use. Find the image, select it, and copy it to the Clipboard. Close the program.

5. In your draw program, copy the map from the Clipboard to your new document by choosing Edit, Paste.

6. Resize the map to fill the page. (In SmartSketch, select the map, choose Scale

---

Insert a map from another source as the foundation for your family history map.

A Multimedia Family Map

To create an interactive family history map, you can use a multimedia authoring program such as Media Wrangler for Windows ($99). Media Wrangler lets you easily link family pictures to other photos, text descriptions, sound clips, and even video clips. Imagine clicking on a daguerreotype of an ancestor who fought in the Civil War and then hearing an audio clip in which your grandmother tells a story about that person.

Media Wrangler is simple to use. You create links between various files (text, scanned photos, audio, and video) by dragging and dropping. Of course, before you can assemble your presentation, you need to record sound files and digitize your photos and video in a format that you can access. Scan your collection of images and save them in a format that you can

access with the paint or draw program you'll be using (usually PICT for Macs and .BMP for Windows). The images will be small on the map, so

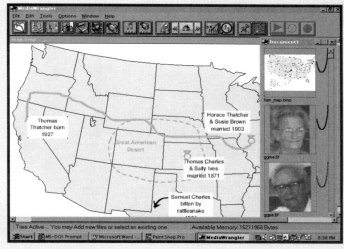

To create an interactive, multimedia family history, use a multimedia authoring program such as Media Wrangler.

you can scan them at 100 dpi. (For more information on scanning, turn to the "Creative Primer" section of this book.)

When the presentation is complete, the user simply clicks

on objects on the screen to hear audio, see video and scanned images, read about a particular person or place, or view another picture that's linked to

the currently displayed image. You can even save your presentation in a stand-alone format that lets others see your family history presentation on their computer, without having Media Wrangler loaded.

from the Tools menu, and just click and drag a corner handle to the new dimensions.)

7. Save the file. Now you're ready for the next step — adding descriptions to your family map.

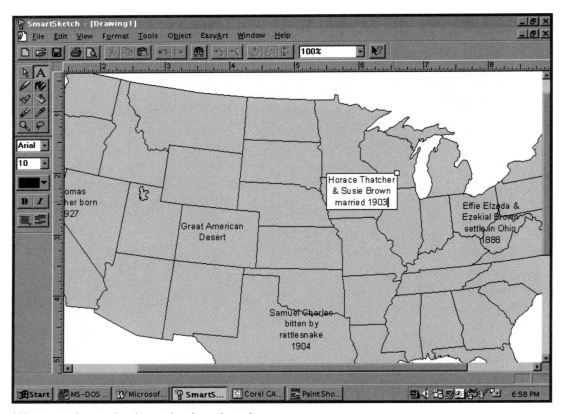

Add text notations to show how regions have changed.

8. For each location on your list, create a text notation near that site on the map. For example, if your great-great-grandmother was born in Boston but settled on the frontier in Ohio, add labels showing the dates and locations for both events. Add details such as the story of great-uncle Samuel's rattlesnake bite near El Paso, Texas. Use the Text tool to create these labels, and choose a plain, sans serif font such as 10-point Helvetica.

9. For historical accuracy (and more fun), add notations for regions of the country that have changed names over the years. Perhaps your great-great-grandmother married a man from Maine when most of it was still part of Massachusetts. Or maybe a distant relative moved to Montana while it was still part of the Louisiana Territories. Your kids will gain a better understanding of history when they see The Great American Desert (Kansas) on the map.

10. Save the file.

11. Depending on the capabilities of your draw program, you may be able to dress up

Family History Map and Tree

If you're looking for software that lets you record and show your family history, check out Family Atlas for Windows and Family Origin, both from Parsons Technology.

Family Atlas is a specialized mapping program that lets you input pictures and information and create links to genealogical information. The program includes drawing and text tools and various useful symbols that you can insert to create a visually interesting map of your family's history. The program also has a database of information on more than 700 locations across the country. You can easily create links between your own map and the database, making this information available at the click of a mouse. You can add your own text about family members and their anecdotes, and then link that text to map locations; you can also add hypertext links between text elements — for example, linking the description of the original Horowitz family homestead with text files describing each

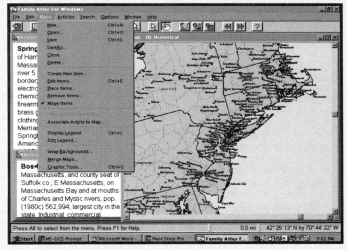

Family Atlas from Parsons Technology provides all the tools you need for creating a detailed family history map.

son and daughter and their travels across the country.

Family Atlas also lets you import standard GEDCOM (Genealogical Data Communication) files from other genealogy software, such as

Family Origin for Windows. Family Origin is a specialized program for creating family trees and collecting and recording your family's roots

to create your own database. You can then use your database records to produce charts and reports. Together or alone, these two programs can help you record your family's history.

each label by enclosing it with a box and adding arrows pointing to specific locations. (In SmartSketch, use the Rectangle

tool to create boxes and use EasyArt shapes for arrows.) If your map is cluttered with background colors and topographic features, use solid background colors for your text boxes.

12. Use colored or distinctive lines to mark any paths your ancestors followed. For example, many California residents trace their ancestry to people who traveled the Oregon or Santa Fe Trail. Others may have come from Cuba. A family from the New Orleans region might add a line representing a boat trip from Nova Scotia. Anything that helps people understand your family history is fair game.

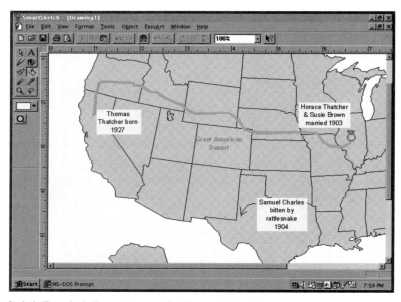

Include lines depicting routes your family traveled, such as a trek on the Oregon Trail.

13. When you're satisfied with your map, save the file and print it. Don't worry if it's not complete; you can update your family history at any time, because you stored it on your computer.

Products You Can Use

Paint or draw program: *SmartSketch, Windows Draw, CorelDraw*

Clipart package: *Art Explosion — 40,000 Images, Corel Gallery 2, Task Force Clip Art — Really Big Edition*

FamilyPC Tip: *Create and use small icons to represent various events — for example, a baby to depict birthplaces or a wedding ring to show wedding locations and dates. You can create these icons by using clip art or original art, or you can let your child draw them after you print your family map.*

Holiday Greetings Postcard

 PREP TIME: 30 MINUTES

Materials

Paint, draw, or word processing program • Printer • Heavy paper •
Full-sheet label paper (for the postcard labels) • Scissors

A personal, handmade wish from your family will brighten up the holidays for everyone on your list this season. It's a wonderful way to let them know that the folks in your house are thinking of them. Nothing says "From all of us" better than the holiday postcard

in this project. With a picture of the whole family, this postcard will make your wishes more meaningful and truly special. It will surely make friends and family feel close to your family during the holidays, whether they live across town or halfway around the world.

Before You Begin

The most important element of the holiday greetings postcard is a great photograph of your family. Take the time to shoot a special holiday photo or find a favorite family picture from the past year. If you have a scanner, scan the picture in either color or grayscale (100 dpi) and save it in a format you can access (usually PICT or TIFF for Macs and .BMP or .PCX for Windows). For other scanning options, turn to the "Resource Guide." For tips on scanning, refer to the "Creative Primer."

Step-by-Step

We used the draw program SmartSketch to create our card, but you can adapt the instructions to almost any program, including the draw program in your Works package.

1. Launch SmartSketch (or the program you plan to use).

2. Set up your page in Landscape mode.

3. Make sure the on-screen rulers are displayed and turn on the background grid, if your program has this feature. In SmartSketch, choose Format, Document, and then click on the grid option. The rulers and the grid help you arrange items in your design.

4. Change the view so that you can see the entire document on the screen.

5. Divide the page into four quadrants, one for each postcard, by creating straight lines that bisect your page vertically and horizontally. For example, if your printable area is 10 1/2 by 8 inches, draw a vertical line at the 5 1/4-inch mark on the top ruler and a horizontal line at the 4-inch mark on the side ruler. These lines mark the postcard edges and will be your cutting lines.

6. Create two versions of the file: one for the front of the cards and one for the back. To do this, first save the file as Front, and then choose the Save as command and save the drawing a second time as Back.

7. Return to the Front file.

8. Insert a copy of your family's photo in

Outline your cards by using the Pencil tool in Straight Line mode.

A Multimedia Christmas Greeting

For a '90s-style holiday greeting, create a brief computer video postcard of your family that you can send to friends and relatives on a floppy disk or via e-mail. To view your message, the recipient just needs the same computer platform as yours (Mac or Windows). The tools that make this possible (and easy) are the Connectix QuickCam, an inexpensive (about $100) black-and-white video camera that plugs into your computer, and shareware utility programs available online.

Create a video greeting for family and friends by using the Connectix QuickCam.

Like a postcard, your message must be brief, because digitized video consumes lots of disk space and memory. To make sure your video fits on a floppy disk, restrict your message to 10 seconds or less. Take quick shots of each family member saying something and then the entire family wishing the recipient happy holidays, in unison. You can use the Connectix camera to record the entire scene, including sound. (Windows users need to have a microphone set up; Mac users can use the built-in mike, but for better sound quality, we recommend using a separate microphone.)

For all but the shortest greeting, compress the video clip in a self-extracting format by using a program such as Stuffit (Macintosh) or PKZip (Windows). These compression programs allow you to pack a large amount of video into the smallest possible space. Macintosh users also need to include a Quick-Time movie viewer such as Peter's Player (shareware by Peter Lee, also available from the online services) on the floppy so the recipient doesn't have to hunt around for a way to view your video clip. Finally, be sure to include brief written instructions for uncompressing the file and starting the playback.

Note: Now you can record your holiday greetings in color. At press time, Connectix announced the release of a color version of the QuickCam.

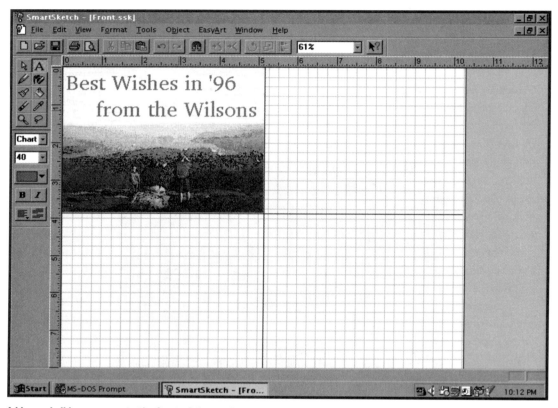

Add your holiday message to the front of the card.

the upper left quadrant. To insert a scanned photo in SmartSketch, choose Edit, Insert Object, Create from File, and then locate the file on your hard drive.

9. If necessary, scale the photo to fit just within the cutting lines. In SmartSketch, open the Tools menu, choose Scale, and then resize the image by clicking and dragging a corner handle.

10. Save the file.

11. Using the Text tool and a large, clear,

serif font such as 40-point, center-aligned Charter BT, insert a few words of holiday cheer (for example, *Best Wishes from the Wilsons*) on the front of the card.

12. Try to position the type over a solid background such as the sky, and don't obscure any faces. The color you choose for the type should contrast with the background — for example, dark blue lettering on a cloudy sky.

13. When you're satisfied with the art on the front of your card (you can check the re-

Wish You Were Here...

No matter where your family spends its vacation this year, you'll probably be able to find racks stocked with postcards showing off beautiful scenery and historic landmarks. However, if you've seen one postcard, you've seen them all, and no store-bought postcard can tell the story of your family's vacation as compellingly as your own snapshots can.

So before you go on your next vacation, create postcard labels that you can bring with you. Then, after you shoot a roll of film, get your photos developed at a one-hour developing service, apply a postcard label to a favorite snapshot, write a note, address your custom postcard, and mail it.

You can easily create these labels by using a draw, paint, desktop publishing, or word processing program (similar to the way you created the back of the holiday greetings postcard). This assumes you have 4-by-6 photographs. If you have 3-by-5 prints, change the dimensions of your page to reflect the smaller size: use a 10-by-6 printable surface. Divide the page into two quadrants (for 4-by-6 photos) or four quadrants (for 3-by-5), and then divide each card into a left and a right side, using two vertical lines.

ements, group them, and duplicate the group to fill the remaining postcard backs on the same page. (If your program does not let you duplicate, use the Copy and Paste commands instead.)

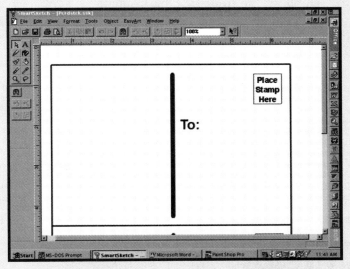

For instant postcards, create postcard labels, print them on label paper, and apply them to favorite snapshots.

Working now on one card, leave the left side of the postcard back blank for writing, and mimic the right side of the holiday card, including the stamp box and the address area. When you've completed one postcard back, select all its el-

Print a test copy on standard white paper. Make any necessary changes, and print a bunch of copies on full-sheet label paper. Use scissors to cut out the labels, and then be sure to pack them before you leave home.

sults by printing a test copy on standard paper), save the file.

14. Group the elements you placed in the upper left quadrant. To group these objects, just click on the photo and the text to select them, and then choose Create Group from the Object menu. Grouping the elements lets you treat the artwork as a single object to copy into the other three quadrants.

15. Duplicate the group (in SmartSketch, choose Edit, Duplicate), and place the copy in one of the empty quadrants. Repeat this process to fill the remaining two quadrants.

16. Save the file.

17. Open the file named Back.

18. Divide each quadrant (that is, the back

of each postcard) into a left half and a right half. Do this by using the Pencil tool in Straight Line mode to draw vertical lines that bisect the cards. (Use the top ruler as a guide. If your printable area is 10 1/2 by 8 inches, draw lines at 2 5/8 inches and 7 7/8 inches.)

FamilyPC Tip: *In SmartSketch, make slight adjustments to the placement of an object by selecting it and using the direction keys to nudge it one way or another.*

19. Use the Text tool to create a holiday message in the left half of the top-left card. To give the note a more personal appearance, use a handwriting font or, better yet, the Personal Fonts (see the "Resource Guide"), which is based on your own handwriting. Fonts such as Freedom Script, Scripty, and Freehand produce a similar effect.

20. Use the Rectangle tool to draw a small box in the upper right corner of the card, to mark the spot for affixing postage stamps.

21. About halfway down the right section of the card, type *To:* (aligned to the left), to indicate the space for the address.

22. Make any necessary changes to the style of the text and the lo-

You'll use the left side of each card for your holiday message and the right side for addressing the postcard.

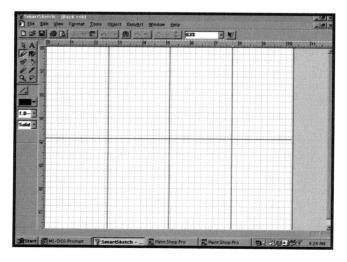

cation of the elements. When you're pleased with the design, save the file.

23. Select the elements in both the left and the right sides of the card and group them (Object, Create Group.)

24. Duplicate the group (Edit, Duplicate), and drag the copies to fill the remaining three quadrants on the page.

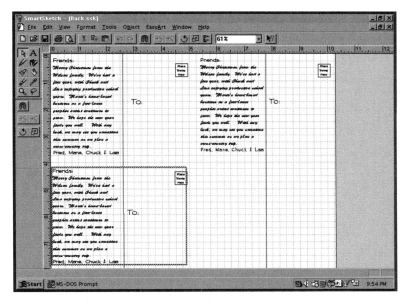

25. Save the file.

You can easily duplicate and place several items at once by using your program's grouping capability.

26. Print a test sample of the cards on standard paper. Print one side,

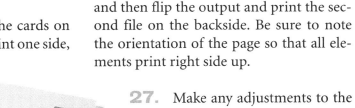

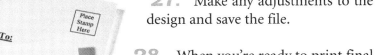

and then flip the output and print the second file on the backside. Be sure to note the orientation of the page so that all elements print right side up.

27. Make any adjustments to the design and save the file.

28. When you're ready to print final copies, load your heavy paper and print.

29. Finally, cut, address, and post the cards.

Products You Can Use

Paint or draw program: *ClarisDraw, CorelDraw, SmartSketch*

Works programs: *ClarisWorks*

Desktop publishing program: *Microsoft Publisher*

Newsletter

 PREP TIME: 40 MINUTES

Materials

**Desktop publishing or word processing program • Scanner •
Printer (preferably color) • Paper**

Did you volunteer to keep the community informed on the status of special projects? Do you want to make sure that upcoming school performances are sold out? Or maybe your child wants to tell fellow computer-gamers about how-to-win strategy secrets, or create a publication that's written by kids, for kids. For these and more, a newsletter can be the ideal vehicle for getting the informa-

tion out. Its multicolumn format lets you pack a lot into a small space. And it's easy to include photos, text — even drawings — to get your message across. The key, though, is creating a newsletter template. If you do this at the outset, you'll find it relatively quick and easy to publish subsequent editions. Print on regular paper and your costs for producing and circulating your newsletter will be minimal.

Before You Begin

You and your child can get ideas for developing your newsletter design by looking at other newsletters. In addition to choosing features that appeal to you, keep the following basic rules in mind when creating a design:

● Leave white, or open, space around text and art.

● For a simple, consistent look, use only one or two font families. For the body text, most newsletters use a common serif font such as Times Roman. A sans serif font such as Helvetica works well for bold headlines and small amounts of body text or captions.

● Break text into multiple columns (many newsletters use a three-column layout). The shorter line length

of a multicolumn layout makes this format easier on the eyes than a one-column design.

● To break up the text, include one or two photos or pieces of art per page. Think of photos and art elements (for example, headlines and drop caps) as having weight. You want the layout to appear balanced, avoiding too much weight on the left or right side of each page.

Take the time to brainstorm the right name for your newsletter, and encourage your child to do the same. This step can be difficult because you need to choose a name that not only catches the reader's eye, but also reflects your newsletter's content.

The key to a great newsletter is high-quality information. Whatever the topic of your newsletter, get an early start on collecting your news. Get more than you need, and find as much art as possible. In the end, you want to choose from a lot of information, condensing it to bite-size pieces.

While using your word processing program to assemble the text for your newsletter, choose your lead story — the one you want to emphasize — and insert an appropriate headline at the beginning of that story. At this point in the process, focus on collecting information and writing the text; don't bother formatting the text yet.

Finally, if you plan to include any images, scan them or have them scanned and saved in a format your desktop publishing program accepts. (For more information on digitizing images, turn to the "Resources Guide.")

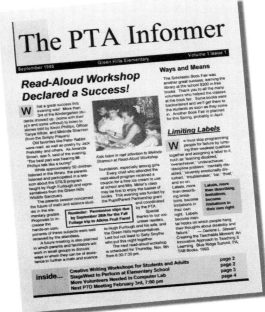

Step-by-Step

We used Microsoft Publisher for Windows 95 for the newsletter project. However, you can adapt these steps to the word processing or desktop publishing program of your choice.

1. Launch your word processing or desktop publishing program.

2. Create a blank page. In Publisher, click on the Blank Page tab, choose Full page, and click on OK.

FamilyPC Tip: *If you don't want to custom-format your page and are more concerned with just getting the newsletter out quickly, you can use Microsoft Publisher's PageWizard design assistant. It prompts you with simple questions, and uses your answers to automatically create a completed format — headlines, columns, picture boxes, and all.*

3. Leave the page in the default Portrait mode.

Be sure your newsletter title grabs the reader's attention and reflects the content of the publication.

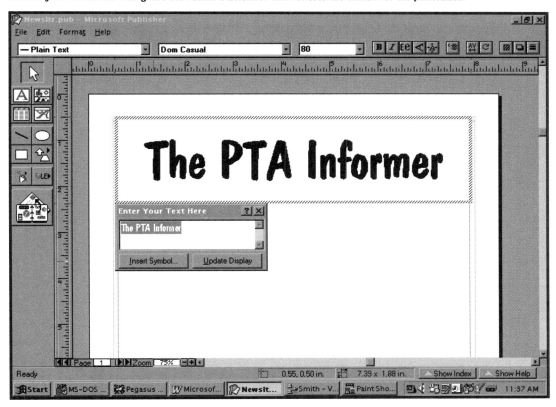

4. For the largest possible print area, set all four margins (top, bottom, left, right) to 1/2 inch. To change the margins in Publisher, open the View menu and choose Go to Background. Hold down the Shift key and click and drag the margins to 1/2 inch. (Use the on-screen rulers as guides.)

5. Put the newsletter's title at the top of the page, using a distinctive font such as Dom Ca-

Brainstormer

Produce a newsletter for community groups, kids, school, parents, hobbies, clubs, sports league, neighborhood activities

sual. To insert the title in Publisher, choose the WordArt tool and create a text frame at the top of the page by clicking and dragging out a rectangle.

6. Choose the font you want to use. The title should be aligned center, and the font size should be large (approximately 72 point) although the size depends on the length of your newsletter title. For the title in our example, we used a font size of 80 point.

Use text frames to insert the date and the name of your organization, just below the title.

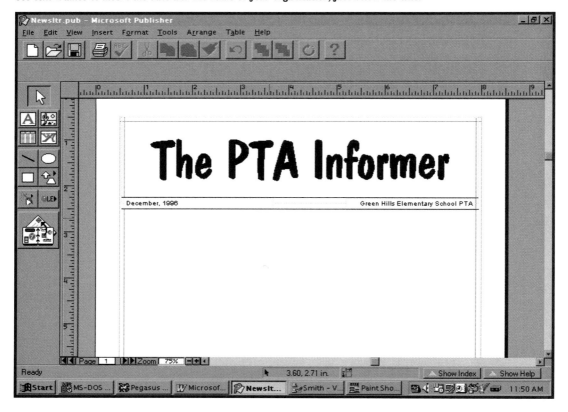

Place your digitized photos or art on the pasteboard next to the document and size them there before adding them to your newsletter.

7. Just below the title, insert two hairline-thin, horizontal lines, 1/4 inch apart and extending to the width of the page. To create lines in Publisher, choose the Line tool,

FamilyPC Tip: *If you're creating a multipage newsletter in Publisher and you want to use the same layout for all the pages, duplicate the entire first page by choosing Insert, New Page and checking off Duplicate all items on Page 1.*

set the thickness to Hairline, and drag the lines on the document. Use the on-screen rulers as guides.

8. Insert the date and the name of your organization between these lines. You do this in Publisher by using the Text tool to create two text frames. (Individual text frames make it easier to place text.) Choose a small point size, such as 10 point, for this text. The date and the name of your organization should be left- and right-aligned, respectively.

FamilyPC Tip: *If you create a multipage newsletter and you want to continue a story from the front page to another page, use the Linking tool (in Publisher, the button that appears at the base of a text box) to link two text frames. As you pour text into one text frame, the overflow runs into the second frame.*

9. The body of our newsletter consists of several columns of text (perhaps three to four stories) broken up by one or two photos. First, define the columns by inserting column guides on the page. To do this in Publisher, open the Arrange menu, choose Ruler Guides, and then click on Add Vertical Guide.

10. Hold down the Shift key and drag the column guide to the 3-inch mark on the top ruler. Create a second column guide and drag it to the 5 1/2-inch mark. Your page now has three columns.

11. You should place your photos in the newsletter before you add your text. Im-

Pour your text into the newsletter by creating text boxes and then inserting the text files.

port the images and click and drag each one to the pasteboard area (the blank space beside the newsletter).

12. Size (scale) each image so that it fits either one or two columns in width. (To determine the right size for each image, you have to consider how clearly you can see the image and how well it fits the page.)

13. Drag the photos onto the page and place them so they visually balance the weight of the newsletter title.

14. If you plan to add photo captions, remember that readers tend to look at photos and captions before the main text on a page. With this in mind, make sure your captions grab the reader's interest. Insert

FamilyPC Tip: *Don't be afraid to experiment with different styles. For example, you can insert a drop cap — a large capital letter — at the beginning of a story to make it more visually interesting. You create this effect in most page-layout programs by creating a separate frame for your drop cap. Enlarge the first letter in the first word of a story to two or three times the size of your body text characters, and position the drop cap so that the top of this character is even with the other characters in the first line, forcing the remaining text to wrap around the drop cap. In Publisher, select the letter, and then choose Format, Fancy First Letter.*

Making Text Fit

If your story doesn't quite fit the space you've created, cut or add text as necessary. If the text still doesn't fit after all your editing, you can adjust the leading (spacing between lines) and the tracking (spacing between characters and words). But for aesthetics' sake, use these capabilities sparingly and as a last resort.

Another solution for text that is too short is to create a pull quote — an interesting quote from the text that you copy and enlarge for more effect and to fill the leftover space. Simply create a frame in your body text, and copy and paste the selected quotation into that frame. To make the pull quote stand out, make it bold or italic, or enlarge the type.

Many programs let you wrap text around an image. Publisher takes text wrapping another step, letting you wrap words around the contours of an irregularly shaped object. For example, you can wrap text around the silhouette of a statue, flowing the text along the outer lines of the artwork. Just select the image around which you want the text to wrap and click on the Wrap Text to Picture button. To edit the wrap shape, click on the Edit Wrap button.

FamilyPC Tip: *If you plan to mail the newsletter, lay out the last page with one-third of the page left for an address block. Include your return address and a spot for a stamp or your bulk mailing permit. After printing the newsletter, fold it in thirds, so the mailing address appears on the outside. If you'll be sending many copies of the newsletter — say, more than 10 — you might want to take the master printout to a copy shop and get as many copies as you need.*

the captions in text frames or boxes (use the Text tool in Publisher). Use a font such as 12-point Helvetica Italic for your captions.

15. Next, you need to add the body text (the stories for your newsletter) and the headlines. Create text boxes in each column, position the cursor in one of the boxes, and import the text. (In Publisher, import stories by choosing Insert, Text files.) The body text of a newsletter is usually printed in an 11- or 12-point font.

16. Insert a headline for each story, using

To give your newsletter a more professional look, insert a drop cap at the beginning of each news item.

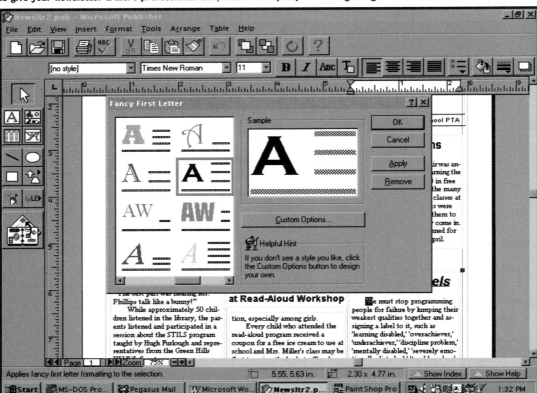

Mail Merge Mania

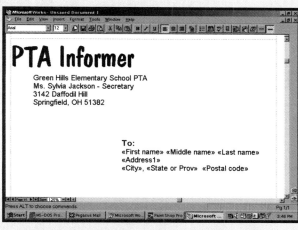

PTA Informer

Green Hills Elementary School PTA
Ms. Sylvia Jackson - Secretary
3142 Daffodil Hill
Springfield, OH 51382

To:
«First name» «Middle name» «Last name»
«Address1»
«City», «State or Prov» «Postal code»

For help with addressing your newsletters, use the mail merge capabilities of a Works program.

Desktop publishing programs cannot merge mailing addresses into the layout as they print. For that, you need to use a word processing program and a database program. A Works package includes both of these modules, usually with special facilities that make it easy to perform a mail merge. Call up the Help system in your program and search for mail merge for additional help. Or you can simply print from your address database directly onto labels, and stick them on the newsletters before mailing.

If you use Microsoft Works or ClarisWorks, however, you can create a database of addresses and use the database manager's mail merge capability to automate the process of addressing your newsletters. To add merge fields to your newsletter address page, choose the form letter or mail merge option. Highlight the name of the database that contains your addresses; then at the next screen, select each field needed for the addressee's box, and click Insert Field. (You'll need fields such as First Name, Last Name, Address, City, State, and Postal Code.) Be sure to add commas and to put the fields into the address box in the correct order and format. In Microsoft Works, this requires going to the Advanced dialog box and choosing Edit.

To print the database of recipients, load the back pages of all your newsletters and choose Print.

the Text tool to create text boxes. Your lead story — the one you think is most important — will usually fill two adjacent columns, so the headline for the lead story requires a frame that spans two columns. Use a bold, sans serif font, such as 20-point Helvetica Bold, for the headlines.

17. Add visual effects such as rules (lines) to separate the columns and boxes around pictures or entire stories.

18. As you create your newsletter, regularly view your work as full pages, even if the text is too small to read, so you can see whether

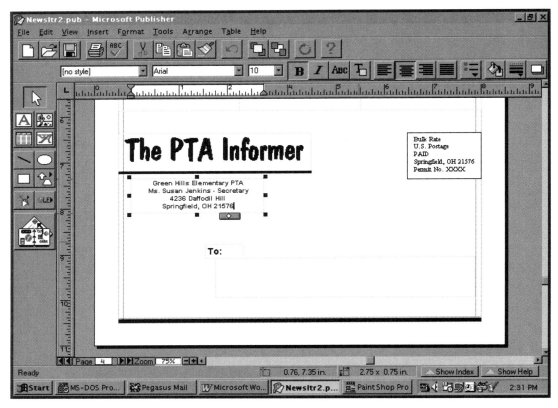

For easy mailing, add an address area to the back of your newsletter.

the layout has balance. Don't try to get everything perfect with your first edition of the newsletter. As you get more comfortable with your software, you can add new features such as drop caps and pull quotes.

19. When you're satisfied with the look of your newsletter, save the file.

20. Print the newsletter on standard paper (or a slightly heavier paper).

Products You Can Use

Desktop publishing program: *Adobe Paint & Publish, Classroom Publisher, Microsoft Publisher*
Word processing program: *Microsoft Word, WordPerfect,*
Works program: *ClarisWorks, Microsoft Works*

Travel Booklet

Materials

**Desktop publishing or word processing program • Print utility (optional) •
Reference CD–ROM (optional) • Printer • Paper • Scissors • Stapler**

A vacation becomes more meaningful and cherished when kids do some prep work before they go. Whether you're planning a trip to the Grand Canyon, the Grand Caymans, or Grand Rapids, your kids' curiosity will be piqued when you create this special travel booklet together. In the guide, you and your kids can plan your family's itinerary for every day of  vacation. Make sure to include a list of all the things you want to do, pictures of the sights you want to see, information about the place (or places) where you're going to stay, and maps showing how to get to all these destinations. If you want your kids to enjoy vacations now and remember them in the years to come, creating a travel guide is a good place to start.

Before You Begin

The first step in creating your travel booklet is to collect information about the place you plan to visit as well as photos of the sights you want to see. You can do this research by using travel magazines from your library, but a reference CD-ROM such as Microsoft Encarta can provide the basics — for example, historical information about Philadelphia, a photograph of the Liberty Bell, and a portrait of perhaps the most famous Philadelphian, Ben Franklin. Noting the main historical facts is important because you use this information for some of the trip activities that appear in the guide. So take the time to do a little research, remembering whose interest the guide is supposed to pique.

You also need the following elements for your travel booklet:

- A map showing your route

- A detailed map of the city you plan to visit

- Your itinerary

- Descriptions of the places you plan to visit

- Information about the place where you plan to stay (perhaps a hotel brochure)

When you have the basic ingredients, you can start assembling your booklet.

Step-by-Step

We used Microsoft Publisher to create this booklet, but you can adapt the instructions to your word processing or desktop publishing program.

1. Launch Publisher (or the program you plan to use).

2. Create a 12-page document. To create a document in Publisher, choose Blank Page, then Full Page, and click on OK. This creates a new, one-page document. To add the remaining eleven pages, open the Insert menu, choose Page, and enter 11 for the number of pages.

3. Save the document.

4. Make a title page for the booklet, featuring a catchy title, your family's

name, and some fun art or clip art. Add text by using text frames, and insert clip art by using the Insert command. After you import the art, fine-tune its placement and scale it to the appropriate size.

5. On pages two and three, insert a map showing the route to your destination, as well as printed directions, so your child can check off legs of the journey, keep track of travel time, and trace progress directly on the map. Here are three ways to include a map in your booklet:

Create a title page for the travel booklet by combining text and clip art.

• Create a map by using a mapping program such as TripMaker. Then insert the map —

FamilyPC Tip: *The Publisher CD features 1000 pieces of clip art, including FAM3.CGM (a family), CAR.CGM (a car), and CITYPLAN.CGM (a city skyline) — all perfect for the cover of your travel booklet. To access these images in Publisher, just create a picture box where you want it, double-click inside the box, and locate and select the files in the library dialog box that appears.*

including the directions this travel program generates — in your Publisher document.

• Scan a road map and insert the scanned image in your Publisher document as a picture. Type the directions and the approximate travel time for each leg of your journey. When you have the information in place, size the elements as necessary.

• Make a photocopy of a road map and glue it into the final copy of your travel guide.

6. Save the file.

7. Reserve pages four and five for on-the-road activities. For each game or activity, create a separate box and include directions

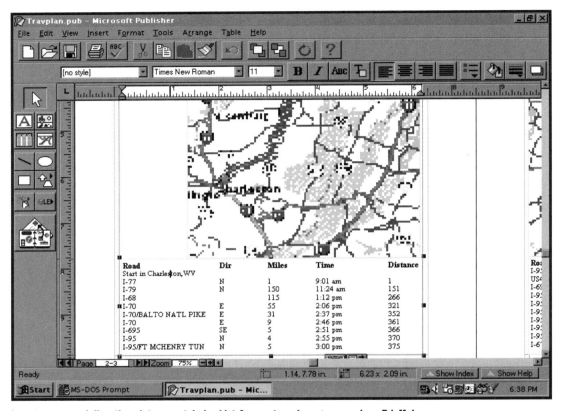

Insert a map and directions into your trip booklet from a travel program such as TripMaker.

where necessary. (In Publisher, use the standard Text tool to create a text frame, and

enter the instructions using a font such as 12-point Times New Roman, aligned left.)

FamilyPC Tip: *To insert information from TripMaker into Publisher, select the information in TripMaker, copy it to the Clipboard, and then paste it into your Publisher document. To insert directions, create a table in your Publisher document and then copy the information from TripMaker and paste it into the table.*

8. When you have all the elements on pages four and five, make final adjustments to their size and placement, and then save the file.

9. On page six, type your itinerary for the entire trip, so your child can see where you plan to go and what you plan to do every day. Keep the descriptions clear and concise and organize them by days. (You might want to leave extra space next to each description so your child can check off each stop as the vacation progresses.) To type the text in Publisher, create a large text box by using the standard Text tool, and enter the information using a font such as 14-point Times New Roman.

10. Insert pictures (from Encarta or other sources) to highlight points of interest in your itinerary. To wrap text around the outline of an art element — for example, a statue — insert the picture, select it, and click on the Wrap Text to Picture button. Then, click on the Edit Irregular Wrap button and click and drag the wrapping line, to make

it hug the picture more closely.

11. Save the file.

12. On page seven, insert a city map (just as you did with the road map in step 5). Number the locations of important places, such as the hotel where you will be staying, landmarks (the waterfront), and points of interest (for example, Philadelphia's Independence Hall).

13. Save the file.

14. Use pages eight and nine to provide

Road Trip Activities

Road trips can be long unless you plan in advance to have fun along the way. So remember to include a few activities in your travel guide. Here are our favorites:

● The lyrics for a multi-verse, sing-along song ("She'll be coming 'round the mountain"), with space to write in a new verse or two

● A word scramble or a crossword puzzle of important people

● A matching game of pictures and facts about the places you are visiting

● A fun poem for memorizing and reciting

● Games such as License Plate Lookout (in which your kids try to spot and record as many different states as possible) and How Many Minivans Can You Count? (We guarantee that you'll see more than 100 by the time you reach your destination.)

You can include the words for a poem or a song in your booklet by typing them (aligned center) or by scanning the verses as an art element.

You can add a crossword

puzzle or a word scramble (based on facts about the city you're visiting) by creating the game as a graphics file in a paint or draw program. Or you can create a customized game by using a specialized game program such as Puzzle Power. Simply copy the game from Puzzle Power to the Clipboard, and paste it into the Publisher document.

If you include the counting games, remember to leave plenty of space for recording how many license plates or minivans your kids spot.

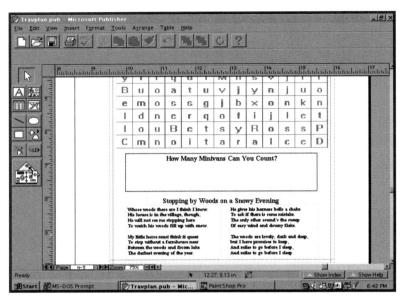

ture. As in the itinerary, keep the descriptions brief. We used 14-point Times New Roman text, aligned left. Any pictures should be small, but still large enough or cropped so that you can clearly see the subject. (Encarta includes numerous pictures of popular spots in various cities.)

15. Save the file.

16. Your child can use the remaining three pages for making journal entries, collecting autographs, and drawing pictures of the things he or she sees. For example, for the first of these pages, create the heading *My Trip to Philadelphia,* using a bold, sans serif

The activities pages are an important part of the booklet, so be sure to include games (such as word scrambles) that your child will enjoy.

information about the attractions in the city you are visiting. For Philadelphia, you could include pictures and brief descriptions of the Liberty Bell, Ben Franklin, Independence Hall, even Rocky Balboa's sculp-

pages for making journal entries, collecting autographs, and drawing pictures of the things he or she sees. For example, for the first of these pages, create the heading *My Trip to Philadelphia,* using a bold, sans serif

Creating Text Frames in Publisher

To create eye-catching text frames in Publisher — perfect for headlines or titles — choose the WordArt tool and create a text box at the top of the page. Choose a thick, sans serif font such as Britannic Bold, and also choose Best Fit.

Select "Your Text Here" in

the dialog box that appears and type something like *Roadtrip.* Create a second WordArt text box below the first one and, using the same font, type your destination — for example, *Philadelphia or bust!* Add a third box at the bottom of the page that says *Travels with the*

(your name) family. Stretch the letters to the extremes of the text box by clicking on the Stretch button in the tool palette.

To add art, you must either create it first in a paint or draw program and then insert it, or choose from a clip-art library.

FamilyPC Tip: *For more precise wrapping in Publisher, you can add more control points. Hold down the Control key while you click the mouse over the wrapping line, wherever you'd like to add another point.*

font such as Britannic Bold. Set up the pages like a journal, with sections for each day of the trip. Add evenly spaced lines (using the Line tool) where your child can write his or her observations, and create small picture boxes (using the Rectangle tool) for illustrations.

17. Review your travel guide and add design elements as necessary; just don't clutter pages, and keep type large and clear enough so that your child can easily read it.

18. Save the file.

19. Print a test copy of the pages. Carefully review each page and make any necessary changes in your Publisher document (for example, adjusting the size of text boxes

---

Use the wrapping tool in Publisher to wrap your words around irregular shapes.

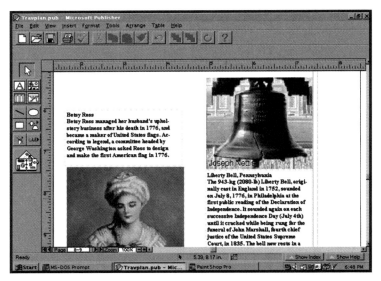

Include fun facts about the city, with accompanying pictures.

Enhancing Your Map

You can make your map more meaningful and interesting to follow by enhancing it with various map elements. For example, designate the places you plan to visit with small white triangles. To do this in Publisher, simply use the Shape tool. Then use the WordArt tool to add a number to each triangle. Using the standard Text tool, create a list at the bottom of the page to identify the numbered locations.

or the location of clip art). If you use the ClickBook print utility to print your pages, view each page before printing by using the Print Preview option. This lets you ensure that all elements appear as you want them to.

20. When you are satisfied with the look, save the file one last time, and then print the finished pages in color or black and white. ClickBook lets you create a book with pages printed on the front and the back. To do this without ClickBook, create separate files for the odd and even pages, and print the file containing odd pages on one side of the paper and the file containing even pages on the other.

21. To complete your book, bind it with staples or yarn.

Products You Can Use

Desktop publishing program: *Adobe Paint & Publish, Microsoft Publisher*
Word processing program: *MacWrite, Microsoft Word, WordPerfect*
Printing utility: *ClickBook*

Creative Primer

Tips and Techniques for Making PC Projects

f you're relatively new to computers, or at least to the programs we rely on in this book, you might find some instructions unfamiliar or confusing. In this section, we've gathered pointers and hints to make using the most common software a little easier. We'll start with some basic information and definitions, and then move quickly to tips on using particular programs. You don't need to read this entire section, though; the organization is designed to provide quick reference when you need help. One thing to keep in mind is that there is usually more than one way to accomplish something. We try to use the easiest, most common methods, but you'll undoubtedly discover your own techniques.

In This Section

Working with Kids

Children as young as two or three can assist you with many of the computer tasks in the projects in this book. To put in your child's name, for example, point to the keyboard keys and let your child press the key and see the result. Here are a few other tips that we've found useful.

• What if your child is too young to draw a straight line on the PC? That's fine — you can do the drawing on the more rigorous parts of the project. The paper football project, for example, has been completed with children as young as two by creating a template and then letting them decide how to decorate it before printing. Very young children can choose the colors for the fills by pointing at the screen. You position the Paint Bucket took and then let them click.

• Children can also choose their own clip art from the SmartSketch EasyArt collection. Then you can drag it onto the drawing, but they give the final mouse click to place it. Size the EasyArt window appropriately before you let them choose, and the art won't even need much resizing after they've placed it. But do let them tell you how big they want the image. This technique works great for other projects, too, such as creating your own envelope designs and decorating pinwheels.

• If cutting out envelopes and other projects is too difficult for little fingers, go ahead and help out. Let them hold the paper while you cut. Or have them cut off the large white excess areas; you "touch up" by cutting on the lines.

• They can help with the folding, too, especially if you do one at the same time, side by side, so they can copy your moves. Or have them apply the glue stick, then you fold, then they press into place.

• Some projects require that holes be punched or needles threaded through artwork. If your child will be helping, place the artwork on a clean, dry cellulose sponge. Then your child can push a push pin or needle through, and pull it from the sponge. This prevents pricked fingers and "wadded up" crafts.

• Although a small child can certainly help out at the mouse or keyboard while you hold her in your lap, she will benefit from a properly designed workstation just as you do. Consider putting the computer on a low table, where kids can sit on kid-sized furniture to operate it, or using an adjustable office chair that raises the child up to an adequate height. Yes, you'll have to make sure the floppy and CD-ROM drives don't become repositories for leftover peanut-butter sandwiches, but even the youngest children can quickly grasp this basic rule. Our observation is that putting the computer within easy reach is the single most important factor in encouraging children to use it.

• Kids younger than about three will have some trouble operating a mouse because they don't understand the concept of relative motion that the mouse relies on. When the mouse goes off the pad, for example, they can't understand that picking up the mouse and setting it back doesn't make the mouse pointer move on the screen. But give them a digitizing tablet like the Wacom ArtPad (about $150), and you've given them a tool they intuitively understand. The cordless pen operates like a crayon on a piece of paper: the top left corner of the pad is the same as the top left corner of the screen. Drawing a house on the screen is as simple as drawing with a pencil.

You'll appreciate it, too, because it's also a lot easier for adults to draw with a pen than with a mouse. You can also use a digitizing pad also to trace existing drawings such as house plans into the computer. The newest Wacom pads are pressure sensitive (pressing harder with the stylus makes bolder lines) and have a built-in electronic eraser.

Working with Programs

To create the craft projects in this book, you'll need some basic computing skills. Knowing how to start and stop programs, finding data files on your hard disk, and naming new files are all important prerequisites to using the computer as a craft tool. In addition, you'll often find it valuable to run more than one program at a time. You might use one program to draw a picture and another to place that picture in a newsletter, for instance. In those cases, you'll want a way to quickly switch between those two programs. In this section, we'll briefly cover all these topics.

Finding Files

Knowing how to locate programs and data files on your hard disk is fundamental. Fortunately, the techniques are straightforward and you'll pick them up quickly.

There are different interfaces (ways of interacting) with your PC's operating system. The Macintosh uses the Finder, Windows 3.1 has the File Manager, and Windows 95 uses Explorer and My Computer. All three, however, have many similarities. In each, you will find programs and data files organized in a hierarchical arrangement of folders (also called directories). Opening a folder by double-clicking on it reveals its contents, which might be computer files or more folders. Often, the contents of your computer's hard disk are displayed like an outline, with the contents of a folder indented under the name of that folder.

If you're looking for a file and don't know where it is on your hard drive, use the facilities provided by the system. Macintosh users will usually see Find File on their Apple menu or Find on the File menu. Windows 95 users have Find on their Start button. Windows 3.1 users have no Find command, but they can scan directories using File Manager. Similar procedures will work to search for a file on a floppy disk or CD-ROM.

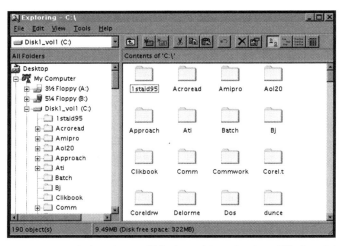

The Macintosh Finder, Windows 95 Explorer (shown here), and Windows 3.1 File Manager have similar functions.

Naming Files

Both the Macintosh and Windows 95 let you name computer files (both programs and data files) with long filenames, using both uppercase and lowercase. Windows 3.1, however, will let you use only eight characters for the file name and three more for the extension. In addition, all the characters are converted to uppercase. Both Windows 3.1 and Windows 95 use the file extension to identify the type of file: .EXE for executable programs, .SSK for Smart-Sketch data files, and .WPS for Microsoft Works word processing data files, for example. The file extension doesn't exist just to let you know what type of file it is, however. It also tells the system what programs can work on it. The Macintosh uses hidden information, called the creator bytes, for this same purpose.

Starting Programs

Starting a program is usually referred to as launching the program. A program can be launched by double-clicking on its name or icon in the Finder (on the Mac), File Manager or Program Manager (in Windows 3.1), or Explorer (in Windows 95). A double-click is simply clicking twice in rapid succession while holding the mouse pointer over a word or object. Windows 95 users can launch programs by clicking on the Start button and navigating through a series of folders to the program name. For example, the Paint program is found by clicking on Start, then pointing to Programs, then pointing to Accessories.

Another way to start a program is by double-clicking on the name or icon of a data file that, in turn, launches a program. For example, if you draw a picture with SmartSketch and save it under the name MyHouse, double-clicking on MyHouse will start SmartSketch and simultaneously tell it to read in the MyHouse file for you to work with.

Switching Programs

Depending on how much active memory (RAM, or random access memory) your computer has, you can probably run more than one program at a time. This is handy when you want to use one program to edit a picture and another program to use the picture in your project. In Windows 95, you can switch between programs that are running by clicking on a section of the taskbar at the bottom of the screen. In addition, all Windows users can press Alt+Tab (hold the Alt key and press Tab) to toggle between active, running programs. As long as you hold the Alt key, each press of the Tab will bring up another program; when you've found the one you want, release the Alt key. On the Mac, use the mouse to click on the Finder icon at the top right of the screen (it looks like a small computer) and, holding down the mouse button, select the program you would like to use.

Quitting Programs

To quit a program in Windows 95, simply click on the X icon in the upper right corner of the window. Windows 3.1 users can double-click on the File Cabinet icon in the upper left corner. Macintosh users should click on the File menu and choose Quit. (On the Mac, the File Close box doesn't exit completely from the program; it closes only the data file, not the program itself.)

Using Your PC Efficiently

Your time at the computer will be more enjoyable if you use time- and energy-saving tricks to increase your efficiency. This section describes a few techniques.

Naming Files Logically

As you work through a project, you are periodically prompted to save your work. Sometimes you need to use a saved file a number of times throughout the project. For instance, you might save a party invitation template that will be customized for each recipient. In this case, use filenames that help to recall the step. The long filenames allowed on the Macintosh and in Windows 95 make this easy to accomplish — you can save the file as Party Invite Before Customizing. The task is more complicated in Windows 3.1, however, because you have only eight characters to work with. Consider using numbers to indicate the step you are working on (for example, INVITE04.SSK). Another option is to use a code such as TEM for template (for example, INVTEM01.SSK).

It's also a good idea to create a new folder (directory) to contain all the files you'll create in a project. Go to the folder in which you want to create this new folder. (We call this main folder Projects.) Then, on the Mac, go to the File menu and select New Folder. A new folder will appear with the default name selected, ready for you to type in your own. Under Windows 95, go to the File menu and select New. On the submenu that appears, select Folder. Again, replace the default name with your own title. Windows 3.1 users can move to the directory in the File Manager, and then go to the File menu, select Create Directory, and type in a name for the new project. Directory names under

Windows 3.1 are also limited to eight characters.

Moving Dialog Boxes

While you are working with menus, dialog boxes will often pop up to ask you further questions. Sometimes the dialog box is covering information on the screen that you need to see in order to answer the dialog box. You can move many dialog boxes around the screen by simply clicking on the title bar and dragging.

Maximizing and Minimizing Windows

Under Windows, you can minimize a program window (close the window temporarily to free up the screen) using the icons in the upper right corner of the window. In Windows 95, click on the icon that looks like an underline. In Windows 3.1, use the down-pointing arrow. Macintosh users who have WindowShade (a utility included with System 7.5 and later) installed can double-click on the title bar to roll up the window.

When a program is minimized in Windows, you can maximize it (bring it back to its original size) by switching to that pro-

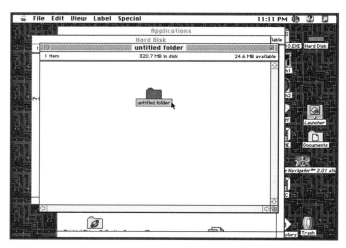

Creating a new folder or directory is similar on Windows computers and the Macintosh (shown here).

gram. In Windows 95, you can use the taskbar. In both Windows 3.1 and Windows 95, you can use the Alt+Tab keyboard shortcut. Mac users repeat the action of double-clicking on the title bar, thereby unrolling the window.

Managing Memory

Graphics programs (ones that work with images in addition to text) can require a great deal of the computer's memory. If you have only 4 or 8 megabytes of RAM, you'll need to be careful how you work on some projects. Most important, don't try to keep more than one program open at a time. Remember that the Clipboard can retain anything copied to it when the program ends, so you can use it to copy an image from one program to another (see "Using the Clipboard" for more info).

Similarly, each open window on your

computer uses some memory, so close unnecessary windows when you are through with them. The number of colors visible on the screen, or sent to the printer, also affects the amount of memory used by a program. If your system is short on memory, use no more than 256 colors (also called 8-bit color mode) in your projects. Not all programs can vary the maximum number of colors, but photo-editing programs such as Paint Shop Pro for Windows have this capability. Macintosh users can select 256-color mode from the Monitors control panel (on the Apple menu). Windows 95 users can choose Setting, Control Panel, and Display.

Using Two Windows

A handy trick when creating complicated artwork in programs such as SmartSketch is to open a temporary file to work in while you keep the main drawing open. This gives you a new, blank canvas, unencumbered by lines and objects in your main window, where you can experiment freely.

Before you start, save your main drawing "just in case." Then go to the File menu and choose New to open a fresh window in which you can express your creativity without fear of messing up your main drawing. You can even have both windows shown

at once — use the choices on the Window menu to split the screen.

When you are finished, select the image (click on the top left of the object and drag down and to the right to create a square that encompasses it) and make it into one object (usually Object, Group). Copy the object to the Clipboard (Edit, Copy), switch back to the main window (the windows are listed in the pulldown Window menu), and paste in your creation (Edit, Paste).

Right-Clicking in Windows 95

To right-click, you point at an object with the mouse cursor and then click and hold down the right mouse button. When you right-click in Windows 95, a properties menu pops up, listing the actions you can take with the object, such as copying it to

You can open another window in SmartSketch to work on a portion of your drawing.

the Clipboard, printing it, and changing its formatting. Most properties menus contain shortcuts; experiment with each object to see what you can find.

Drawing 101

Although every draw and paint program is different, they all share some similarities. Here we'll discuss the commonalities among draw and paint programs and touch on the basics of SmartSketch in particular.

What distinguishes a draw program from a paint program? Paint programs are analogous to using a paint brush or a box of crayons. Color is applied to the page in one layer, like little dots of paint on a canvas. When you draw a tree in front of a house, for example, the tree and the house become merged and cannot be separated. You can't erase one object (such as the tree); you can erase only the dots of paint. However, paint programs are intuitive, so they are commonly used as children's creative software. Examples include Flying Colors, Kid Pix, Paint, and Dabbler.

Draw programs, including CorelDraw, Adobe Illustrator, and Windows Draw, represent things as objects. The tree in front of a house, for example, is a separate object (as if it were on a separate, transparent sheet). Removing the tree reveals the portion of the house that had been hidden. In fact, the tree can be selected as an object and moved to a new location in the drawing without affecting any other objects in the drawing.

Using the Drawing Tools

Paint and draw programs share many of the same tools. Most can create straight lines, freeform lines, and certain primitive shapes such as ovals and rectangles. You start by choosing the color of your line.

Freeform lines are usually drawn by first clicking on the Pencil tool (in the toolbar or the toolbox). Then you hold the mouse button down, to turn on the "ink," and move the mouse to draw the line. Similarly, you create *straight lines* by choosing a Line tool. Then you select one endpoint by clicking at that location. Some paint and draw programs then require you to drag the cursor to the other endpoint and then release; with other programs you release the mouse button and simply click on the second endpoint.

To create an *oval,* you select the Circle tool, and then click in the top left area, drag down and to the right, and then release the mouse button. Holding down the Shift key often forces the oval to form a *circle.* A few programs (Flying Colors and CorelDraw, for example) form circles from the center point out — you drag a radius to define them. *Rectangles* are made the same way, but using the Rectangle tool. In addition, these shapes can be hollow or filled with color or patterns.

SmartSketch is slightly different in that straight lines, curved lines, and the basic shapes are all different *modes* available using the *Pencil* tool. After selecting the Pencil tool, an icon showing the current mode is visible. Clicking on the icon displays a dropdown menu of other icons for each of the drawing modes. Holding the Shift key doesn't force an oval into a circle, but it does reveal a little circle near the mouse pointer that changes size when you are at certain pre-determined points, including symmetric shapes.

In addition to the Pencil tool, most programs use Paintbrush tools to create larger freeform lines and curves. You select a brush shape and size appropriate to your drawing. The SmartSketch Paintbrush lets you paint freely. Changing the brush mode can constrain the paint to flow only inside an object or behind existing lines.

Filling Shapes

In paint programs, shapes are filled in with color or pattern using the Paint Bucket. You choose a color from the available palette, click on the Paint Bucket tool, and then click where you want to "pour" the color. If the shape is not completely closed, however, the paint will flow out of the shape and fill other portions of your drawing. Remember, most programs have an Undo command (check the Edit menu) for just such occasions.

Most draw programs do not have Paint Bucket tools, because an object is colored as a unique individual object. Click on the object to select it, and then click on the color palette to turn the object a chosen color. Usually, clicking the right mouse button changes the color of the interior of the object, and clicking the left mouse button

changes the border color (or vice versa). SmartSketch, a draw program, uses the Paint Bucket from paint programs, plus adds a twist. You can not only fill an object, but also specify how large a gap will let paint out of the shape and into other areas.

Selecting Objects

In paint programs, the only way to select a piece of a painting for moving or deleting is to mark the area. This is usually accomplished with a Pointer tool (for rectangular areas) or a Lasso tool (for random shapes). Moving or deleting an area of the painting leaves a "hole" with no color.

In draw programs, you can select a complete object with a Pointer tool. Holding the Shift key lets you select multiple objects. (In SmartSketch, you can click on the objects without holding the Shift key.) In addition, you can create a box around objects by clicking and dragging to select every object within the region. These selected objects

You can select an entire area of a drawing by dragging a box around it with the Pointer tool.

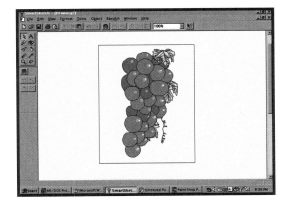

can then be moved, deleted, or resized.

In draw programs, individual selected objects can be grouped into a single object and moved or resized together. So, after drawing all the parts of a bicycle, for example, you can group the parts together into one bicycle. Select each portion and choose Object, Group. If you need to edit the object later, choose Object, Ungroup. Grouping the bicycle lets you move it or duplicate it without repositioning each wheel and spoke separately.

Moving, Resizing, and Reshaping Objects

To move an object in a draw program such as SmartSketch, select the object (you'll see a four-way arrow icon) and drag it to another location. To resize the object, select it and drag the corner handles in or out. These resizing handles don't appear in Smart-Sketch until you either click on the Scale icon on the toolbar or choose Scale from the Tools menu. Using the corner handles will scale the object proportionally; using the handles in the middle of the sides will stretch or squash the object in the direction you drag.

SmartSketch adds a feature to the resizing of objects, allowing you to reshape objects, too.

While a line is not selected, you can click anywhere along it and drag that point to distort the line smoothly. For instance, you can grab the middle of a straight line and pull it to create a semicircle stretched between two points.

Page Orientation

Most draw and paint programs default to a Portrait page orientation, with the long edge of the page running vertically. Changing the orientation (usually with Page Setup or Print Setup on the File menu) to Landscape orientation will make the long edge run horizontally. Many programs also let you set page margins in the same dialog box.

SmartSketch requires one more step to match the on-screen display to the printer setup. Choose Document from the Format menu, and then click on the Match to Printer button in the dialog box.

Click on Match to Printer in the Format, Document dialog box.

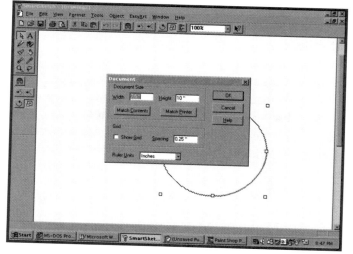

Working with Fonts

Choosing the right font will help give your projects a professional look. We're usually not aware of type fonts when we read, but they help set the mood, make the text flow easily, and draw our attention to certain parts of the page. As you look at others' work, pay attention to the subtle ways fonts are used to enhance a project. See the "Resource Guide" for more information on fonts.

Font Families, Metrics, and Names

Fonts are arranged in font "families" consisting of different sizes, weights (for example, regular and bold), and styles (such as italics) of the same font. Font sizes are measured in points, where one point is equal to 1/72 inch. The size of the font is measured for a typical character, but there is no absolute standard, so you will see large variations in the size of a 14-point character among different font families.

Font names can be copyrighted, but the actual shapes of the fonts cannot. This has led to much confusion surrounding the naming of fonts. When we call for a particular named font in a project, you may have that font on your system but under a different name. When you install a new printer driver or a piece of software, you often will be installing more fonts at the same time,

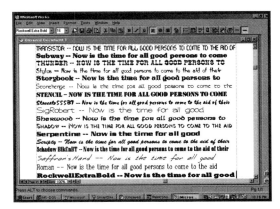

Create your own font catalog to use when choosing a font.

or even installing more copies of the same fonts but under different names.

We recommend that you go for the "feel" of the font, rather than looking for a font by name. If we've used a font reminiscent of calligraphy and you want to reproduce that, look through your own font collection for something similar. Many fonts are available on the Internet or through online services.

Utility programs such as the shareware Fonter will let you print a font catalog of your own system, which is quite handy when you need to choose a font. You can create your own font catalog by simply reproducing and printing the same short sentence in each font, and then printing.

Symbol Fonts

Some fonts include nothing but symbols. The Wingdings font is a good example. After you choose this font, each character (such as lowercase *a*) prints as a different symbol. To figure out the mapping of keyboard characters to symbols, you'll need to use a utility such as Character Map for Windows or Key Caps (under the Apple menu) on the Mac. Character Map is found in Windows 95 by clicking on Start and choosing Programs, Accessories, Character Map. In Windows 3.1, it is in the Accessories program group.

Click on a character to see the keystroke required to produce it. If the character map applet shows the keystroke as Alt+number (for example, Alt+041), the character is produced by holding down the Alt key while entering the digits 0, 4, and 1 on the numeric keypad — not the numbers at the top of the keyboard. When you release the Alt key, the character is displayed.

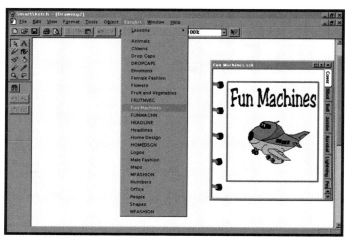

Using clip art is simple with SmartSketch's EasyArt.

Working with Art, Text, and Photos

Drawing realistic images with computer tools can be laborious. (Not everyone is an artist!) To get around this, you can use other people's work in the form of clip art and photos, but you need to know a few fundamentals about working with images and text. Turn to the "Resource Guide" for more information on clip-art packages for Windows, Windows 95 and the Mac.

Clip Art

Easy Art is the collection of clip art included in the SmartSketch package. In the Windows 3.1 version of SmartSketch, the EasyArt Finder is on the Help menu; the other versions of SmartSketch include EasyArt as a main menu choice.

EasyArt includes a submenu of artwork in a variety of categories. Choosing a category such as Clowns opens a "book" with tabbed pages, with each page containing one or more clip-art images. You click on the labeled tabs to flip through the book looking for artwork you can use. Then simply click on the image and drag it to the page for editing.

Clip art is great because you can modify, or edit, it to suit your needs. When you want to edit your EasyArt selection, go to the Object menu and choose Edit Object. Without this step, the object is protected from changes — it will look like you are moving a line or filling in with a color, but the changes go away when you pause.

SmartSketch lets you quickly turn clip art into *line art* (outlines). Click on the Color button located above or below your clip-art image in the corner of the EasyArt catalog. The image will turn into a black-and-white clip-art image. Click on the image again to turn it back into a color image.

Clip-art collections such as Corel Gallery 2 include a printed catalog that you can refer to when choosing images from the disc. Like artwork, clip art varies greatly in style. There are realistic drawings, cartoons, period pieces, and more. Most of the time, you'll want to be consistent, so that you aren't mixing cartoon-style drawings with near-photo-quality art.

Clip-art collections usually come with a utility for searching for particular artwork and copying it. In Corel Gallery, you can copy an image to the Clipboard and paste it directly into your project. Under Windows, Corel Gallery supports context-sensitive menus to help select and copy clip art with a right mouse click.

If you need more than one image, try to keep both Corel Gallery and your main project software open at the same time. The Clipboard can hold only one image at a time, so you'll spend a lot of time opening and closing programs otherwise. (See "Using the Clipboard" for more tips on this process.) In addition, when inserting large or complex objects, you may encounter problems with available memory (see "Dealing with Memory Limitations"). If this occurs, export the image and save it as a file on your hard disk. (The Export option is usually on the context menu or under the File menu.) Then import the file into your other program. See the tips in "Export, Import, and File Formats" in this section for more information.

Note that even simple-looking clip art from programs such as Corel Gallery can be made of many complex pieces of smaller art. This may cause your computer to slow down substantially as you work with these images. You may even think the program has crashed, even though the computer is still working hard to paint the image on the screen or send it to the printer. If you're working with a complex image, be patient.

Use the Corel Gallery 2 browser to choose from a large clip-art selection.

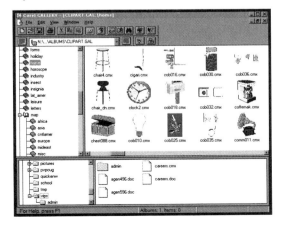

Original Art

SmartSketch and many other programs will let you open your own saved artwork like the built-in EasyArt collection. Before you save the art, make sure you group each entire drawing as an object. First select everything in the drawing by choosing Edit, Select All or drawing a selection box around everything. Then choose Object, Group. Save the file.

When you want to import your saved drawing, choose Open as EasyArt from the File menu. Select your saved file in the dialog box to open an EasyArt-like "book" with your artwork on the page. Click on your artwork and drag it to your page. Like other EasyArt objects, you can resize it or ungroup it for more editing.

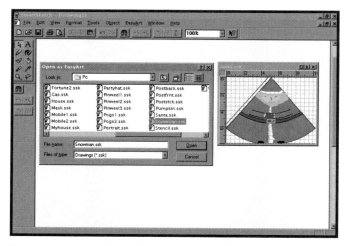

You can open a saved SmartSketch drawing as if it were EasyArt.

Of course, you can use any other paint or draw program to create artwork, too. If you need to import the art into another program, either use the Clipboard or make sure you save the art in a compatible format. The most common format for Windows machines is the .BMP (or bitmap) format; Macs use the PICT (or Picture) format.

Text Frames

In Microsoft Publisher, as well as many word processing programs, you can create a text frame, or text box. This element lets you place a block of text anywhere on the page. In most programs, you do this by choosing Insert (usually on the Object menu), and then specifying Frame. In Publisher, click on the Text tool (the icon with the letter A) and drag diagonally across the screen, creating a box outline where you want the frame to appear. You can type into the box as if it were a small document standing alone. The text frame can be resized or moved. First click on the frame so that handles appear at the corners. To then move the frame, click in the middle or on the edge until a four-pointed arrow appears, and drag. To resize the frame, click on a handle and drag in or out.

Like other programs, in SmartSketch you drag the frame horizontally to change its width. But the text frame's length changes automatically as needed when you type in more text.

When you're working with text, there's one more thing you should be aware of. If a block of text is selected (that is, highlighted, either from clicking and dragging over it or by a shortcut specific to your software), that text will be replaced by the next thing you type. This is handy for quickly replacing the words *My daughter, who knows all the elements in the periodic table by heart* with *My daughter, the genius.* But it can come as quite a shock when the paragraph you have struggled over for half an hour gets replaced by a randomly hit space bar. Use Undo right away.

Using Photos

Many of our projects involve photos that you must get into digital (computer-readable) form. You can find a service to digitize your photos or undertake the process yourself. After you have your photos in the computer, you might want to touch up and modify the pictures to suit your projects. In this section, we've gathered tips on this entire process.

Scanners and Digital Cameras

If you'll be working with photos on a regular basis, you may want to get your own scanner or a digital camera. Scanners come in a variety of shapes and sizes, including handheld, flatbed, roller style (shaped like a roll of waxed paper), and ones specifically designed for scanning snapshots. Prices range from a hundred dollars to well over a thousand. We recommend either an inexpensive flatbed scanner ($300 to $500) or a small snapshot scanner such as the Easy-Photo Reader (about $250).

A digital camera is the quickest and easiest way to get images into your computer. Plug it into the serial port and your PC will suck in the photos, saving them as separate files on your hard disk. Prices now range from $500 up, but are coming down quickly.

Digitizing Images

Unless you have your own scanner, you'll need help getting photos into your comput-er so that you can use them in your projects. To ensure that you have current photos of your children ready for use, consider getting their school photos digitized each year using one of the methods we mention here.

Your first option is to have the photos scanned at a service bureau such as Kinko's, but the price is significant (up to $10 per image). They return your digitized image on a floppy disk ready for use. If you have a Windows machine, get the image stored as a .BMP file or as a .TIFF file. Mac users should have the image stored as a PICT file or, again, as a TIFF file.

If you have an entire roll of film to digitize, you can send it to Seattle Film Works (see the "Resource Guide" for the phone number) or drop it off with a local retailer such as a CVS drugstore for processing by Konica. You will receive regular prints of your photos, along with a floppy disk containing digitized versions of the images. You'll also get a utility program that can read the proprietary file format and save the images in standard formats such as .TIFF. PictureWeb (again, see the "Resource Guide") takes an individual print or set of prints and place the scanned file on its World Wide Web server for you to download.

Photo-Editing and Retouching

Photo-editing programs such as Paint Shop Pro, Adobe PhotoDeluxe, or PhotoStudio are essentially paint programs that have tool sets customized for working with photos. These programs can resize an image, crop the background from a photo, add special effects, reduce the "color depth" of a picture, and change its saturation, brightness, or darkness.

If your computer is running low on memory while you're working with photos, consider reducing the color depth to ease the load on your PC. Photo-realistic images are usually rendered in 24-bit color, which means there are more than 16 million possible colors in the palette. Allowing for the possibility of this many colors requires substantial amounts of memory to represent the image. Most photos can be accurately represented using no more than 65,000 possible colors, reducing the required memory capacity by one-third. And although 256 colors may not produce a smoothly rendered image, the required memory is reduced by another third. Another way to reduce the amount of memory you need to work on an image is to reduce the size or complexity of the image.

Use the Airbrush tool in Paint Shop Pro to remove distractions in the background.

Another handy tool in photo-editing software is the Airbrush tool. This is an excellent way to remove distracting portions of a photo background. You can use this tool also to fade out the background, resulting in a soft, cloudlike feeling in the setting.

Export, Import, and File Formats

Many programs store their files in a proprietary (company-specific) file format. The file format is indicated by the file extension. For example, SUE.TIF, SUE.BMP, and SUE.PICT are all the same picture saved in different file formats. SmartSketch, for example, stores drawings in its own .SSK format.

However, other formats are more widely used, especially for storing paint and photo images. On the Macintosh, the PICT format is common. On Windows PCs, the BMP format is the most common. Other formats such as TIFF (Tagged Image File Format), GIF, and JPEG are common to both platforms, Windows and Macs.

Why is this important? Sometimes you will want to take a file created by one program and use it in a project that you're working on in another program. In this case, you are looking for a file format that the two programs have in common. You can then *export* the file from one program (save it to disk in a known format) and *import* it into the other (read it back in from disk). Many programs have an Insert command to carry out the import process.

A *utility* (a specialized, small program) is handy for converting graphics images between varying file formats. Fortunately, two of the best, Paint Shop Pro for Windows and GraphicConverter for the Macintosh, are available as shareware. This means you can try them out before you buy them. If you don't find them useful and you don't want to keep them, you don't have to pay for them. Both are available from the online services and over the Internet.

OLE versus Drag and Drop

As mentioned in the last section, the Insert command can import a saved file into the current project. In addition, many Windows programs use Insert to directly link to the output from another program, without saving an intermediate file. This is known as *OLE*, or Object Linking and Embedding. While working on a newsletter in Microsoft Publisher, for instance, you might want to embed a drawing created with SmartSketch. You would choose Object from the Insert menu, and then choose SmartSketch from the list of programs that support OLE on your computer. Double-clicking on the embedded SmartSketch drawing in the newsletter being laid out in Publisher will cause the menus and toolbar to temporarily

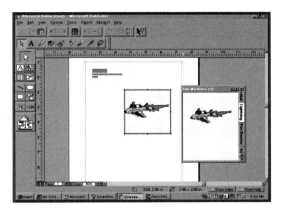

You can edit a SmartSketch file embedded in a Publisher document.

change to SmartSketch tools, so you can make changes in the drawing.

Programs that support OLE usually also support drag and drop. With this technique, you can copy a drawing into another document by opening both programs next to each other on the screen (do this by sizing the windows so that each occupies only half the screen), clicking on the drawing, and dragging it into the other document.

Using the Clipboard

The most reliable method for copying an object from one program to another is to use the Clipboard. The Clipboard is a temporary holding place in your computer. Copying images to the Clipboard works for both Macs and Windows PCs and for most (though not all) programs. When copying with the Clipboard, the operating system knows the types of formats each program supports and mediates between them. Only one object can be held on the Clpboard at a time, but that one object can be text, a drawing, a photo, or an entire document.

To copy an object to the Cipboard, select it using the tools in the current program. To select text, highlight it (click and drag over it). To select an object in a draw program, click on the object or use the Arrow tool. In a paint program, select the object with the Arrow tool or the Lasso tool, depending on the object's shape. In any case, you then choose Edit, Copy or the keyboard shortcut Control+C (or Command+C on the Mac).

If you want to delete the object from its present location while copying it to the Clipboard, use Edit, Cut (Control+X under Windows or Command+X on the Mac). By the way, the Mac Command key is the one with the little apple icon on it.

Next, switch to the program where you want to insert the object. If this requires exiting from the current program and launching the new one, go ahead. The Clipboard will continue to hold your object unless you turn off the machine or copy something else to the Clipboard and overwrite its contents. Position the cursor where you want the object inserted, and choose Edit, Paste (or Control+V under Windows or Command+V on the Mac).

The same technique works within a program. To duplicate an object, copy it to the Clipboard and paste it. (You can paste the object more than once, if you want more than one copy.) And to move an object, "cut" it to the Clipboard and paste it.

Manipulating Your Artwork

We've talked about the basic operations in a draw program, but they are capable of much more. Still just skimming the surface, in this section we describe rotating, duplicating, scaling, and building complex images from simpler clip art. We wrap up with a discussion of the powerful WordArt modules in Microsoft programs such as Publisher and Word.

Rotating

Often you will want to rotate objects or clip art in your drawings. In SmartSketch, rotating EasyArt is quite painless. Click on the Rotation icon to display a special set of handles for rotating images. Then click on a handle and pull the image around to rotate it. If you're working with a non-Smart-Sketch image, especially under Windows, the results are less predictable.

Rotate an object in SmartSketch by selecting it, clicking on the Rotation tool, and then dragging a handle.

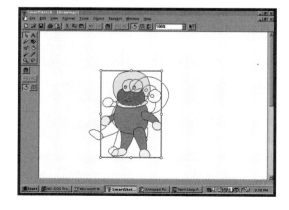

Some imported artwork will rotate like SmartSketch drawings or EasyArt, but other imports — even different images from the same commercial clip-art package — do not. When you drag on their rotation handle, it looks like the screen image is rotating; but when you release the mouse button, the image snaps back to its original orientation, though its size might change slightly.

To overcome this problem, you may want to use a different program to perform the rotation. On Windows machines, Paint Shop Pro can perform this task admirably. Corel-Draw and others work as well. After the image is rotated, it can be exported in a common file format, such as .BMP (see "Export, Import, and File Formats") or copied to the Clipboard (see "Using the Clipboard") for pasting back into SmartSketch.

Duplicating

As detailed earlier, you can create multiple copies of an object by copying it to the Clipboard and repeatedly pasting it wherever it is needed. SmartSketch, as well as many other programs, lets you accomplish the same thing with the Duplicate command. Select the object, go to the Object menu, and choose Duplicate to make a copy of the object. The Duplicate command leaves the new copy selected, ready for moving into position by simply clicking on it and dragging.

Scaling

SmartSketch offers two ways to scale a selected object to the appropriate size. You can scale by dragging handles around an object, or you can work with a more exact

"percentage" menu.

In the first method, you begin by clicking on the Scale icon or choosing Object, Scale. Either of these will display resizing handles on the object. Click on a handle and drag inward to scale the object down or outward to scale it up. Note that you can scale in the horizontal and vertical directions by different amounts if you use the middle handle on any side. To constrain the scaling so that it's equivalent in both directions, use the corner handles. Most other draw programs work similarly, though in some you hold down the Shift key for proportional resizing.

The second option for scaling a selected object in SmartSketch is to choose Object, Scale by Percent. A dialog box will appear in which you type the scale factor. Objects are scaled in both the horizontal and vertical directions, either larger for percentages over 100% or smaller for percentages under that amount. Use your Help menu to see whether you have this option in other programs.

Words as Art

Words arranged on the page in unusual fonts or colors can be more compelling than a chunk of simple text. In this way, words become an art element in a layout, like the graphics they accompany or replace. The ultimate example of this is the use of WordArt in Microsoft programs such as Publisher and Word. Using the WordArt module, you can shape words into circles, banners, wavy lines, or many other configurations. The text can also have shadows and appear in different colors. Adobe's Type

Twister (available for both the Macintosh and Windows) can perform many of the same actions.

In Windows, WordArt is a separate miniprogram, activated by using the OLE facility. This means your regular menus and toolbars will be temporarily replaced or enhanced by the WordArt tools. All text entry and editing is performed in an entry window, which opens with the default text, Enter Text Here. Your text will replace these words. To see how changes made in this box will be displayed, click on the Update Display button periodically as you make changes.

To change the size of the box in which the formatted WordArt is presented, click somewhere in your document outside the WordArt area. This will cause WordArt to exit, but it will leave your formatted text as a frame on the page, complete with resizing handles. Click on a handle and drag in or out to re-size the box. If you need to make more changes in the text or formatting of the WordArt, double-click in the box to reopen the WordArt module.

The toolbar in WordArt is a little confusing, so we'll go through the features, from left to right. First is a drop-down text box for the shape of the text. Then there's another drop-down text box for choosing a font, followed by one for font size. The default font size is Best Fit, which means the font size will adjust to the size of the box in which it is enclosed.

Next is a series of buttons, starting with five that control the formatting of the text — Bold, Italic, Large Lowercase (lowercase letters are enlarged to the size of uppercase), Vertical Text (the text is arrayed vertically, reading from top to bottom), and Stretch to Fit (the text font is stretched in both directions to fill the enclosing box).

A text alignment button is alone in the next group. Clicking on this button drops down to a selection including centered text, left aligned, and right aligned. Two text arrangement buttons are next, each of which displays a dialog box. First is one for adjusting the spacing (also called tracking) between characters, followed by one to define an arbitrary rotation of the text, in degrees.

Finally, there are three buttons that display dialog boxes for text features — text color, shadow effects, and border color and size.

Type your text into the entry box, and then click on Update Display to see how it looks.

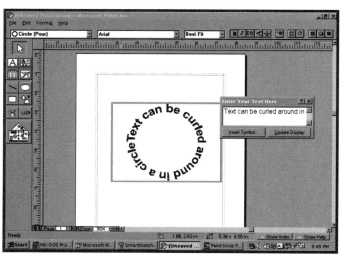

Getting Projects on Paper

Most of the projects in this book require printing on regular paper or special material such as transparency plastic or sticker paper. In addition to choosing the type of paper, other concerns that arise include the many printing options (such as printing on both sides of the page or printing an image that is larger than a single sheet of paper) and using print utilities such as ClickBook to create different-sized booklets.

Card Stock

Many projects use card stock, which we define as the heaviest paper your printer can print without difficulty. Many printers can use 67-pound "cover" stock, designed to be used as the cover and backing sheets for reports. If your printer can use 100-pound paper, all the better. You may have to feed the sheets individually, especially for printers with a convoluted paper path (the route the paper takes through the printer). Many laser printers have a switch or lever to change to a more direct paper path when printing on envelopes or special paper.

Transparencies

Transparency plastic, for overhead projectors, works quite well in printers. Make sure you get the appropriate type for your printer, either laser or ink-jet. Regular write-on transparencies will melt in a laser printer and will not hold ink-jet-style ink.

Two brands of ink-jet transparency film are Avery #5277 and Highland #707 (made by 3M). You will probably need to feed each sheet individually into your printer. Leave the backing sheet attached as you print. And don't forget to allow about 15 minutes for the ink to dry before handling the page extensively.

Label Paper

Laser and ink-jet labels are available in a variety of sizes. For many projects, the most versatile is Avery #5165 laser label. These are full-sheet labels, 8 1/2 by 11 inches, that work well in either a laser or an ink-jet printer. Again, you will probably need to feed each sheet individually into your printer. After printing, you can cut the sheet into any size or shape you need. If the label will get much handling, you may want to waterproof and smudgeproof it — see the waterproofing section in "Finishing Touches." Avery has also begun a special line of labels expressly for kids.

Printable Area and Margins

Almost all printers have a maximum printable area that is smaller than the size of the paper. For most, this means a 1/4-inch margin on the right and left edges is mandatory. Top and bottom margins vary from printer to printer, but 1/2 inch is common.

Often, one of these two margins is larger to accommodate the paperfeed mechanism in the printer. It's a good idea to know the maximum printable area of your printer so you can work around the limitation. If you produce a birthday card with a blue background, for example, you may need to trim the finished card to remove the unprinted area. Remember also that a page printed in Landscape mode (in which the long edge of the paper is horizontal) will move these unprintable margins, too. Now the 1/4-inch side margins will become limitations on the top and bottom of the page.

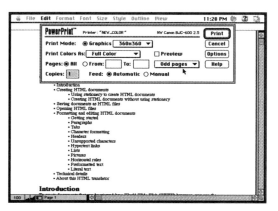

You can elect either Print Odd Pages or Print Even Pages in the Macintosh Print dialog box.

Two-Sided Printing

Almost all printers can print on both sides of the page, though you need to reverse the pages manually. Depending on your printer, you may also need to flip the pages end to end before feeding them back in. Experiment with your own printer to find out. Sheets that are fed back in for printing on the reverse side tend to stick together due to static electricity. For that reason, many printers require hand-feeding of each sheet when the second side is printed. If you are printing large areas (as in the pinwheels project), allow the first side to dry fully before reinserting; otherwise, wet ink will come off on the inside of your printer and smear other sheets.

Odd/Even Printing

If you are printing a booklet with pages printed both front and back, you may want to print all the fronts followed by all the backs, rather than feeding each sheet one by one, both front and back. This requires printing all the odd-numbered pages on the fronts and all the even-numbered on the backs (or vice versa). Only a few Windows programs, such as Microsoft Word, have that capability.

In Word, select the required option in the Print dialog box. In other Windows programs, the easiest way to do this is to use the ClickBook utility (described later in this section). Mac users can simply go to the Print dialog box and select Print Even Pages or Print Odd Pages, rather than the default Print Every Page.

Tiling

Sometimes you might want to print an image larger than a single sheet of paper, perhaps to make a poster. Many programs, including Microsoft Publisher and SmartSketch, have this capability, which is called tiling because you piece together the printed sheets like pieces of tile. In Microsoft Publisher, you select this option when you first create a new document. After that, you can change the height and width of the expanded page using the Page Setup dialog box in the File menu. Finer adjustments, such as the amount of overlap to allow between tiles, are available in the Print dialog box. Simply click on the Tile Printing Options button.

SmartSketch uses a different approach. You produce your entire drawing using the regular limitations of one sheet of paper. Then choose File, Page Setup and set a scaling factor. For instance, 200% scaling will enlarge the image by a factor of two in both the horizontal and vertical dimensions, resulting in a drawing that will take four sheets of paper to print. There is no control over page overlap; in fact, there is no overlap. Trim off the unprintable area and tape the sheets together.

ClickBook

The ClickBook print utility (available for Windows, Windows 95, and the Macintosh) lets you transform any multipage document into a complete booklet. This is perfect for creating all booklet-type projects. Booklet formats range from the simple (a 5 1/2- by 8 1/2-inch booklet in which each sheet of paper contains four complete pages of print) to the complex (a small top-fold booklet in which one sheet of paper contains 16 pages of print).

You simply create regular pages in the program you are using, and then ClickBook takes over the print process and prints the

pages, complete with cutting, folding, and stapling instructions. It's a good idea to create your content (text fonts and graphics) somewhat larger than usual, because it will be scaled down to fit on smaller "pages."

On Windows machines, choose a printer driver that begins with CB, indicating a ClickBook printer driver. Macintosh users can click in the Use ClickBook selection box in their Page Setup dialog box. Then print as usual. In the ClickBook dialog box that appears, choose one of the predefined layout options or invent your own. You can click on Preview to see how the pages of your document will print. If adjustments are necessary, click on Cancel to return to editing. If you're happy with the layout, click on the Print button to continue.

When ClickBook has finished printing one side of each sheet of paper, follow the directions that appear for printing on the backs. The directions will specify whether pages should be rotated or flipped, faceup or facedown. Click on Continue Printing, and then follow the instructions for cut-

With ClickBook, you can print custom booklets as easily as you can print on regular paper.

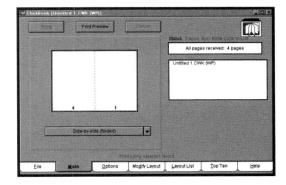

ting, folding, and stacking the pages. Staple through the middle if you want.

You can easily create your own "tiny book" layout, which is perfect for mementos or Christmas tree decorations. This booklet is only 2 1/8 by 2 3/4 inches, squeezing 32 pages onto one sheet of paper (16 on the front and 16 more on the back). Create your pages as usual, but make sure you use a large font such as 24 point and don't try to squeeze too much onto each page. Print to ClickBook, and then select the Modify Layout tab in the ClickBook dialog box. Define a new layout of 4 pages across and 4 pages down, printed Back-to-Back, in a Folded Book style. Give the new layout a name such as Tiny Book and click on Save. Return to the main ClickBook dialog box and continue printing. This format is perfect for booklets from 4 to 32 pages long. It even makes a great little phone book to pop into your wallet or purse.

Finishing Touches

We've included a few miscellaneous tips for adding a professional touch to the computer crafts you create. We've also included tips on file compression, so you can squeeze larger files on your floppy disks.

In addition to reading these tips, though, spend some time wandering around craft and office supply stores to find out what's available to make your life easier. Supply companies are constantly introducing new products such as glitter pens and fancy deckle-cutting scissors.

Waterproofing and Smudgeproofing

Printer inks will run quite badly if they get damp. If your project is at all likely to be exposed to moisture or wet hands, consider protecting the surface with a spray sealer. There are many available from craft stores; we have had varying success with them. One that has consistently stood out is Craft Master's Super Surface Sealer #656. This spray product creates a wonderfully water-resistant seal, but it is somewhat noxious. Make sure you spray it outside or in a well-ventilated area. Mist lightly from a distance of 16 to 18 inches. Allow the coat to dry, and then repeat for a more complete seal. If your pieces are small, such as little finger puppets, spray the printed sheets before you cut them out. To do several sheets at a time, place them on an old plastic tablecloth and spray.

Craft Knives and Paper Cutters

When it comes time to cut out a delicate piece, such as a pop-up clown for an invitation, scissors are too bulky. Craft knives like the X-Acto are the perfect tool for this job. Use a scrap of wood or an old catalog to cut on so you don't ruin the kitchen table. If you're going to be making a lot of cards or cut notepads, you may want to consider purchasing or borrowing a paper cutter for beautifully straight edges.

Foam Board

Foam board, also called foam core, is a lightweight, easily cut material available at most craft stores and many office supply stores. It is essentially a sandwich of slick-surfaced paper with a layer of foam in between. The standard thickness is 1/4 inch, and it also comes as thicker sheets. Cut it with a sharp craft knife. The thicker sheets can be cut the same way, but a sharp knife becomes even more critical.

Making Notepads

Padding glue for making your own notepads and memo pads is available from mail-order suppliers. They also sell specialized presses to hold the pads while gluing, but a press isn't necessary for everyday home use. Line up the sheets of paper and sandwich your pad between two scraps of wood, using common C-clamps to hold them together. Stout rubber bands can even be used if C-clamps aren't available. Then paint the glue along the top edge of the paper and allow to dry. You can stack several pads to glue and "tear" them apart after drying.

Compression

If you want to mail a large file or files on a floppy disk, but there isn't room to shoehorn it all on, you need a file compression utility. Especially handy with space-hogging multimedia files, compression programs squeeze the "air" out of the file without losing any content. When the floppy disk arrives, recipients can uncompress the file back to its original size on their own hard disks. The two most common compression utilities are Phil Katz's PKZip for Windows-based machines and Aladdin Software's StuffIt for the Macintosh. Both are shareware, available through online services and over the Internet. In addition, many other free or shareware utilities use the same compressed file formats. Because PKZip was originally written for DOS rather than Windows, the shareware WinZip utility has become the most popular Windows-specific version.

WinZip lets you compress files from Windows or Windows 95.

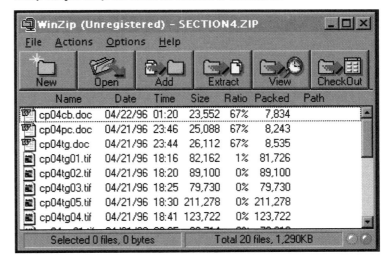

Resource Guide

For any good craftsman, having the right tools for a job is very important — whether you're building a house or starting a computer project. Using the right tools can help you accomplish your task in a timely fashion and with a great deal of satisfaction. Using the wrong tools can cause endless delays and a great deal of frustration.

This resource guide will help you locate the products we used in this book as well as provide ideas for product substitutions. You'll find important information such as company name, phone, platform, and price. This guide also features specialty paper providers — the ones that make your projects distinctive with their numerous offerings, and specialty software titles — programs that shine at doing one particular thing well.

Paint and Draw Programs

SOFTWARE	DESCRIPTION
ADOBE ART EXPLORER DELUXE CD-ROM	This program has basic paint functions along with blending, textures, glaze, dye, and tinting tools; spatter, smudge, and kaleidoscope effects; fun stamps and more. *Adobe, 800-888-6293, Mac CD, about $30.*
CORELDRAW 3	Includes four programs in one: CorelChart, Corel PhotoPaint (for photo editing), CorelShow, and CorelDraw, with 14,000 pieces of art and 250 fonts. *Corel, 800-772-6735, Windows CD, about $100.*
CRAYOLA ART STUDIO II	Includes animated stickers, coloring books, mazes, connect-the-dots, along with simple paint and drawing tools with patterns, watercolors, and splattering effects. *Micrografx, 800-676-3110, Mac and Windows CD, about $40.*
DABBLER 2	Realism is the key to Dabbler's appeal; its tools act like the real thing: markers bleed, charcoal smudges, etc. This latest version includes flipbook animation and tracing-paper tools. *Fractal Design, 800-297-2665, Mac and Windows CD, about $45.*
FLYING COLORS	Cool stamps and animations accompany this paint and draw program that's fun for kids and adults. Unfortunately, the stamps are not resizeable, and the program is not compatible with Windows 95. *Davidson & Associates, 800-545-7677, Mac and Windows disk and CD, about $35.*
KID PIX STUDIO	Besides the basic paint and draw tools, Kid Pix offers animated Moopies, Digital Puppets, and stamps, plus a slide show for displaying created art. Terrific creative fun for kids and adults. *Brøderbund, 800-521-6263, Mac and Windows CD, about $50.*

continues

Paint and Draw Programs

SOFTWARE	DESCRIPTION
MICROSOFT PAINT	Included with Windows 95, Microsoft Paint offers basic paint and draw tools along with some manipulation features like flip, rotate, and stretch. *Microsoft, 800-426-9400, included with Windows 95.*
SMARTSKETCH	Simple draw tools with over 500 fully editable drag-and-drop images, which can be painted, stretched, erased, or filled. Includes eight how-to tutorials. *FutureWave Software, 800-619-6193, Mac disk, about $50, Windows disk, about $60.*
TURBODRAW	A simple, easy program similar to CorelDraw 3. It includes templates and layout assistants to get you started, 50 levels of Undo, 1,200 clip-art images, and 100 fonts (same as TurboPublisher). It also includes PhotoCD, a clip-art browser, a font organizer, and Autotrace tools. *IMSI, 800-833-4674, Windows CD, about $30.*
WINDOWS DRAW 4.0	Three programs in one: Windows Draw, Photo Magic (for scanning/editing photos), and ABC Media Manager (a clip-art browser). Includes more than 150 templates, 15,000 clip-art images, 250 TrueType fonts, and 30 freehand drawing tools. *Micrografx, 800-733-3729, Windows 95 CD, about $50.*

Photo-Editing and Conversion Software

TITLES	DESCRIPTION
GRAPHIC CONVERTER 2.31	This shareware converts over 70 graphic file formats to Macintosh or Windows formats. Also features an image slide show and batch conversion. *LemkeSoft, available for downloading from http://www.shareware.com, Mac, about $35.*
PAINT SHOP PRO 3.12	This shareware includes ample image-editing and filtering tools, handles several file transfer formats, and supports TWAIN scanners. Also offers a handy thumbnail image viewer. *JASC, 800-622-2793, Windows and Windows 95 disk, about $70.*
PHOTODELUXE	Specifically designed to work with digital cameras and scanners, this is a scaled-down version of Adobe Photoshop with a more family-friendly interface offering tools like red-eye reduction and color correction. *Adobe, 800-888-6293, Mac and Windows CD, about $90.*
PHOTOFINISH	One of the least expensive image editors available, it includes automatic color and contrast adjustment, special-effects filters, and an image preview function. *Softkey, 800-227-5609, Windows, about $50.*

Desktop Publishing Software

TITLES	DESCRIPTION
ADOBE PAINT & PUBLISH, OR PAINT & PUBLISH DELUXE	Adobe HomePublisher and SuperPaint in one program. Home-Publisher has Auto Create templates, 300 clip-art images, and 12 fonts. SuperPaint offers paint and draw tools for adding creative touches to your documents. The Deluxe CD includes 1,500 clip-art images. *Adobe, 800-888-6293, Mac disk, Deluxe CD, about $90, Deluxe Edition, $100.*
CLARISWORKS 4.0	Features seven page-creation Assistants, a word processor, spreadsheet, database, excellent paint and draw features, drag-and-drop clip art, and more. It has a better database than Microsoft Works. *Claris, 800-325-2747, Mac disk, about $130, Windows and Windows 95 disk, about $70.*
IMSI TURBO PUBLISHER	Includes 100 predesigned templates, eight layout assistants (Wizards), cue cards, 100 fonts, 1,200 clip-art images, and a spell checker. PowerText is roughly equivalent to Publisher's WordArt. *IMSI, 800-833-4674, Windows CD, about $30.*
MICROSOFT PUBLISHER CD DELUXE FOR WINDOWS 95	Create documents using PageWizards and templates ranging from banners to business cards. Includes borders, clip art, and a WordArt tool for manipulating text. *Microsoft, 800-426-9400, Windows 95, about $75.*
MICROSOFT WORKS 4.0	Includes a word processor, database, spreadsheet, WordArt tools, Clip Art Gallery, and a hotlink to the Microsoft Network. More than 30 TaskWizards and templates make creating newsletters, banners, brochures, business letters, and more a snap. *Microsoft, 800-426-9400, Mac and Windows 95 disk, about $55, CD, about $80.*

continues

Desktop Publishing Software

TITLES	DESCRIPTION
PERFECT WORKS 2.1	Includes a word processor, spreadsheet, database, draw and paint, and communications tools for Internet connection. Features QuickCorrect and Grammatik for fixing spelling and grammatical errors and 41 preformatted documents. *Novell, 800-638-9273, Windows disk, about $100.*
SERIF PUBLISHING SUITE	Includes publishing program, fonts, art, and a photo-editing tool. Offers three modes of use: Intro, Publisher, or Professional, each with more powerful editing and creation tools. Somewhat light on family-friendly features. *Serif, 800-489-6720, Windows and Windows 95 CD, about $80.*

Specialty Software

TITLE	DESCRIPTION
ADDRESS BOOK MAKER FOR WINDOWS PLUS	This easy-to-use program lets you keep track of all your addresses and phone numbers, format them to fit a variety of address book styles, and print labels and lists, including both sides of the page, if you so choose. Addresses can be imported from other programs or inputted manually. *Softkey, 800-227-5609 or 617-494-1200, Mac and Windows disk, about $20.*
ANNOUNCEMENTS 4.0	Create customized cards, posters, banners, and more with this creative package. Announcements comes with 200 clip-art images, and you can import your own graphics. *Parsons Technology, 800-223-6925, Mac, Windows and Windows 95 disk and CD, about $30.*
CALENDAR CREATOR PLUS	You can use this program to create calendars from a full sheet of paper down to credit-card size. There are a variety of predesigned templates from which you can make a calendar quickly, or you can design your own from scratch, importing your favorite photos or clip art. Other features include multiple ways to mark events (highlights, banners, etc.), the capability to enter repeating events just once, and file sharing over a network. *Softkey, 800-227-5609 or 617-494-1200, Mac and Windows disk and CD, about $50.*
CARDSHOP PLUS	You can make more than just cards (posters, stationery, and banners — just to name a few) with this software, which features 700 templates and 500 pieces of clip art. *Mindscape, 415-883-3000, Windows CD, about $20.*

continues

Specialty Software

TITLE	DESCRIPTION
COREL PRINT HOUSE	Print House is packed with 5,000 editable clip-art graphics, 1,000 phrases, 1,000 photos, 900 professionally designed samples, 572 templates from PaperDirect, 100 fonts, 70 borders, and 20 project types, including calendars, flyers, menus, signs and more. *Corel, 800-772-6735, Windows CD, about $100.*
FAMILY ATLAS FOR WINDOWS	Family Atlas is a specialized mapping program that lets you input pictures and information, and even link to genealogical information. The program, which comes with draw and text tools, comes with a variety of useful symbols that you can insert to create a visually exciting map of your family's history. *Parsons Technology, 800-223-6925, Windows disk, about $30.*
FAMILY ORIGIN FOR WINDOWS 4.0	Family Origin is a specialized program for creating family trees and for collecting and recording your family's roots to create your own database. You can then use the records to produce a variety of charts and reports. *Parsons Technology, 800-223-6925, Windows disk, about $30.*
GIFTMAKER	You can make more than 40 different personalized gifts — from mouse pads to baseball caps featuring your favorite art (even a family snapshot) and a fun slogan — using Giftmaker. Essentially, you use the software to design your gift; you send it to a professional printer, who then returns to you the finished product. *Maxis, 800-336-2947, Windows disk and CD, about $20.*
HALLMARK CONNECTIONS CARD STUDIO	With more than 1,000 finished cards to choose from, all of which can be customized by changing names, slogans, and art, this program is a veritable card shop right in your computer. Among specialty programs, this one rates at the top in print quality. *Micrografx, 800-733-3729, Windows CD, about $50.*

continues

Specialty Software

TITLE	DESCRIPTION
LABELPRO FOR WINDOWS	From the leader in labels comes this software, complete with 1,000 clip-art images, 100 fonts, more than 120 templates, and mail-merge functionality. *Avery Dennison, 800-252-8379, Windows disk and CD, about $60.*
LABELS FOR WINDOWS	This program, which features three draw tools that let you create custom designs, has more than 25 templates, 150 clip-art images, 120 label styles, a database, and an address book. It lets you create labels, envelopes, and even bar codes. *Expert Software, 800-759-2562 or 305-567-9990, Windows and Windows 95 disk and CD, about $15.*
MICROSOFT AUTOMAP ROAD ATLAS	This program features excellent routing capability and includes a nice variety of photos and videos so you can check out destinations long before you get there. *Microsoft, 800-426-9400 or 206-882-8080, Windows disk and CD, about $40.*
MICROSOFT ENCARTA 96	Encarta 96 is a top multimedia encyclopedia. It is a content-rich product that features a sophisticated link to online resources, and an easy-to-use search facility that lets you search any of the 26,500 articles by word, category, media, time, and place. *Microsoft, 800-426-9400 or 206-882-8080, Mac and Windows CD, about $55.*
PAPER ANIMAL WORKSHOP	This software features 3-D animations of 129 projects (origami animals, dioramas, and paper planes), all of which can be viewed from different angles, close up or far away, in forward or reverse, or frozen at any stage. *Strategic Alliance Partners, 800-711-0582 or 310-860-4029, Mac and Windows CD, about $25.*

continues

Specialty Software

TITLE	DESCRIPTION
PAPEROPOLIS	Whether it's cootie catchers or masks that you're trying to make, you're sure to find them on this CD-ROM, which features more than 600 projects. *Virgin Sound and Vision, 800-814-3530, Mac and Windows CD, about $20.*
PRINT ARTIST 3.0 CD EDITION	This instant printing program includes more than 6,500 graphics and layouts, 1,100 layouts fonts, 220 stock photos, and 100 type styles. There are also craft projects such as gift boxes, 3-D greeting cards, doll houses, and board games. *Sierra On-Line, 800-757-7707, Windows disk, about $45 or CD, about $60. Windows CD-ROM, about $55.*
PRINT PAKS SERIES	This series is made up of eight separate kits, including partyware (invitations, hats, banners, and more), iron-ons (for clothing, bags, and hats), pop-up greeting cards, and personalized pinwheels. Besides the necessary software, each kit includes the additional items that you'll need to complete the craft. *PrintPaks, 503-295-6564, Mac and Windows CD, about $20.*
PRINT SHOP DELUXE CD ENSEMBLE II SERIES	This program features loads of graphics and 73 fonts, as well as 3,500 text effects and ten types of projects. You can use it to make (among other projects) envelopes and labels for businesses and family affairs. *Brøderbund, 800-521-6263 or 415-382-4400, Mac and Windows CD, about $80.*
PUZZLE POWER	Puzzle Power includes a number of games such as crossword puzzles, word scrambles, and other word-type games. It also includes tools for creating your own games of the same type. *Centron Software, 800-848-2424, Mac and Windows CD, about $60.*

continues

Specialty Software

TITLE	DESCRIPTION
RAND MCNALLY STREETFINDER	StreetFinder is a guide listing every street in the country. It is the only street-map database available that has draw tools that let you map out a route, letting you easily create and print a map containing detailed directions. *Rand McNally, 800-671-5006 or 708-329-8100, Windows and Windows 95 CD, about $50.*
RAND MCNALLY TRIPMAKER 1996 EDITION	TripMaker is easy to use, has fast and accurate routing features, and includes flexible printing options. It helps you plan a trip from the route you take to the sights you see. *Rand McNally, 800-671-5006 or 708-329-8100, Windows and Windows 95 CD, about $50.*
STATIONERY STORE JUNIOR	You can make a variety of letterhead and matching envelopes using this program, which features 300 templates, 300 pieces of clip art, and an assortment of fun fonts. *Dogbyte Development, 800-936-4298, Mac and Windows CD, about $25.*
STREET ATLAS USA 3.0	Complete with paint tools that let you highlight your route on a colorful map, this program also features street address searches and a direct link to Phone Search USA. *DeLorme, 800-452-5931 or 207-865-1234, Windows and Windows 95 CD, about $80.*
STICKERSHOP PLUS	This program, which comes with templates for buttons, stickers and POGs, comes complete with adhesive paper and pre-cut cardboard. Stickershop Plus also comes with clip art and the capability to customize all the templates. *Mindscape, 800-866-5967 or 415-883-3000, Mac and Windows, about $40.*

continues

Specialty Software

TITLE	DESCRIPTION
WORLD'S EASIEST CERTIFICATES	This handy little program comes with ten different types of specialty paper on which you can print more than a dozen different types of certificates. *Deluxe, 800-730-3279, Windows and Windows 95 disk or CD, about $15.*
WORLD'S EASIEST INVITATIONS	This package contains invitation fonts, graphics, eight styles of decorated paper, and dozens of templates so that you can create invitations for any affair. *Deluxe, 800-730-3279, Windows and Windows 95 disk and CD, about $15.*
WORLD'S EASIEST PERSONAL BUNDLE IMAGE	A bundle made up of five separate programs, the Personal Image Bundle comes with everything you need to create calling cards, stationery, custom notes (Post-It style), stamps, memos, and notepads. *Deluxe, 800-730-3279, Windows and Windows 95 CD, about $35.*

Clip Art & Fonts

CLIP-ART PACKAGE	ART EXPLOSION Nova Development 800-395-6682	COREL GALLERY 2 Corel 800-772-6735	IMAGES WITH IMPACT SERIES 3G Services 800-456-0234
PLATFORM	Mac, Windows, and Windows 95 CD	Mac and Windows CD	Mac and Windows disk
FILE FORMATS	WMF, EPS, TIFF	CDR, CMX, CPT, TIFF, BMP, PCX, CDT	WMF, EPS
# OF IMAGES	40,000	15,000	About 100 per theme
CATALOG QUALITY	Fair printed, good on-screen	Excellent printed and on-screen	Good on-screen
QUALITY/ USABILITY OF ART	Good	Excellent	Good
PRICE	About $50	About $70	From about $25 to $50

continues

Clip Art & Fonts

CLIP–ART PACKAGE	MASTERCLIPS 35000 PREMIUM CLIP ART IMSI 800-833-4674	T/MAKER CLICKART INCREDIBLE 25000 IMAGE PAK T/Maker 800-986-2537	TASK FORCE CLIP ART "THE REALLY BIG EDITION" New Vision Technologies 800-387-0732
PLATFORM	Windows and Windows 95 CD	Mac and Windows CD	Windows
FILE FORMATS	WMF	WMF, EPS	WMF, CGM
# OF IMAGES	35,000	25,000	10,000
CATALOG QUALITY	Online only	Fair	Excellent
QUALITY/ USABILITY OF ART	Good	Good	Good
PRICE	About $50	About $50	About $35

Clip Art & Fonts

FONT PACKAGE	2000 FANTASTIC FONTS Expert Software 800-759-2562	ADOBE VALUE PACK Adobe 800-833-6687	ADOBE WILD TYPE Adobe 800-833-6687
PLATFORM	Windows CD	Mac and Windows disk	Mac and Windows disk
TRUETYPE OR POSTSCRIPT	Both	Type 1	Type 1
# OF FONTS	2,000	30	14
CATALOG QUALITY	Online only	—	—
QUALITY/ USABILITY OF FONTS	Good	Good	Good
PRICE	About $20	About $45	About $45

continues

Clip Art & Fonts

FONT PACKAGE	BITSTREAM 500 FONT CD Bitstream 800-522-3668	MONOTYPE TYPOGRAPHY FUN FONTS (three volumes sold separately) Monotype Typography 800-666-6897	PERSONAL FONT Signature Software 800-925-8840
PLATFORM	Windows CD	Mac and Windows disk	Mac and Windows disk
TRUETYPE OR POSTSCRIPT	TT, Type 1	Both	Both
# OF FONTS	500	25	1
CATALOG QUALITY	Online only	Good	Good
QUALITY/ USABILITY OF FONTS	Good	Good	Excellent
PRICE	About $50	About $20	About $100

continues

Clip Art & Fonts

FONT PACKAGE	SOFTKEY KEY FONTS Softkey 800-227-5609	SOFTKEY KEY FONTS PRO 3003 Softkey 800-227-5609	TYPECASE 2001 Expert/Swfte Software 800-237-9383
PLATFORM	Mac and Windows	Mac, Windows, and Windows 95 CD	Mac and Windows CD
TRUETYPE OR POSTSCRIPT	Both	Both	Both
# OF FONTS	Over 100	3,003	2,001
CATALOG QUALITY	Online only	Online only	Online only
QUALITY/ USABILITY OF FONTS	Good	Good	Good
PRICE	About $30	About $30	About $20

Digitizing Photos

PRODUCT	EASYPHOTO READER Storm Software 800-275-5734	EPSON PHOTOPC Epson 800-289-3776	KODAK DC40 Eastman Kodak 800-235-6325
PLATFORM	Mac and Windows	Mac and Windows	Mac and Windows
MAXIMUM IMAGE RESOLUTION	3 x 5 or 4 x 6 prints	640 x 480 pixels	756 x 504 pixels
FILE FORMATS (GIF, JPEG, TIF, BMP, etc.)	Various file formats*	Various file formats*	Various file formats*
QUALITY OF DIGITAL OUTPUT	Excellent	Good	Good
QUALITY OF PRINTED OUTPUT	Excellent	Good	Good
PRICE	About $250 (Windows) About $260 (Mac)	About $500	About $680

*Includes BMP, GIF, JPEG, EPS, PICT, PCX, TIFF, etc.

continues

Digitizing Photos

PRODUCT	KODAK DC50 Eastman Kodak 800-235-6325	QUICKCAM Connectix 800-950-5880	QUICKTAKE 150 Apple 800-538-9696
PLATFORM	Mac and Windows	Mac and Windows	Mac and Windows
MAXIMUM IMAGE RESOLUTION	756 x 504 pixels	320 x 240 pixels	640 x 480 pixels
FILE FORMATS (GIF, JPEG, TIF, BMP, etc.)	Various file formats*	AVI, BMP, TIFF	PICT
QUALITY OF DIGITAL OUTPUT	Excellent	Good	Good
QUALITY OF PRINTED OUTPUT	Excellent	Good	Good
PRICE	About $1,000	About $100	About $680

*Includes BMP, GIF, JPEG, EPS, PICT, PCX, TIFF, etc.

continues

Digitizing Photos

PRODUCT	SCANJET 4P Hewlett-Packard 800-752-0900	SNAPPY Play 800-306-7529
PLATFORM	Mac and Windows	Windows
MAXIMUM IMAGE RESOLUTION	Scalable	1500 x 1125 pixels
FILE FORMATS (GIF, JPEG, TIF, BMP, etc.)	Various file formats*	BMP, PCX, TIFF, TGA, and JPEG
QUALITY OF DIGITAL OUTPUT	Excellent	Excellent
QUALITY OF PRINTED OUTPUT	Excellent	Excellent
PRICE	About $500	About $190

*Includes BMP, GIF, JPEG, EPS, PICT, PCX, TIFF, etc.

Digitizing Photos

SERVICES	KINKOS COPY CENTER	KONICA www.konica.com	PHOTOCD Eastman Kodak 800-235-6325
PLATFORM	Mac and Windows	Mac and Windows	Mac and Windows
MAXIMUM IMAGE RESOLUTION	Customer specifies	600 x 400 pixels	Scalable from 128 x 192 pixels
FILE FORMATS (GIF, JPEG, TIF, BMP, etc.)	GIF, TIFF, PICT, PCX	BMP, PICT, JPEG	TIF/TIFF
QUALITY OF DIGITAL OUTPUT	Excellent	Good	Excellent
QUALITY OF PRINTED OUTPUT	Excellent	Good	Excellent
TURNAROUND TIME	1 day	3-5 days	2-3 weeks
PRICE	About $10 per image	About $15 per 25 exposures, including prints	About $20 per 25 exposures, including prints

continues

Digitizing Photos

SERVICES	PICTUREWEB www.pictureweb.com	SEATTLE FILMWORKS www.filmworks.com 800-345-6967
PLATFORM	Mac and Windows	Mac and Windows
MAXIMUM IMAGE RESOLUTION	800 x 640 pixels with custom resolution options	640 x 480 pixels
FILE FORMATS (GIF, JPEG, TIF, BMP, etc.)	JPEG, GIF	Various file formats*
QUALITY OF DIGITAL OUTPUT	Good	Good
QUALITY OF PRINTED OUTPUT	Good	Good
TURNAROUND TIME	1 week	1 week
PRICE	About $30 per 25 exposures, including prints	About $15 per 25 exposures including prints and replacement film

*Includes BMP, GIF, JPEG, EPS, PICT, PCX, TIFF, etc.

Paper Providers

COMPANY	AVERY 800-252-8379	BEAVER PRINTS 814-742-6070	PAPER ACCESS 212-463-7035
LABELS	Mailing, floppy disk, etc.	None	Basic mailing, floppy disk
SPECIALTY PAPERS*	E, F, IJ, L, N	B, C, L, E, N	B, C, F, G, H, L, E, N, P, PT, T
HOME OFFICE*	BC, CS	BR, BC, CS	BR, BC, CS
ENVIRONMENTAL/ RECYCLED STOCKS	None	None	Some
VALUE/PRICE	Good	Good	Good

*Paper Key: B=borders, BC=business cards, BR=brochures, C=certificates, CS=card stock, E=exotic, EN=envelopes, F=foil, G=gradations H=hot colors, IJ=ink-jet, L=letterhead, N=notecards, P=party, PT=pre-printed themes, T=textured

continues

Paper Providers

COMPANY	PAPER DIRECT 800-272-7377	QUEBLO 800-523-9080	STAPLES 800-333-3330
LABELS	Mailing, floppy disk, specialty	Mailing, floppy disk, file folder, specialty	Mailing, floppy disk, file folder, specialty
SPECIALTY PAPERS*	B, C, F, G, H, L, E, N, P, PT, T	B, C, F, G, H, L, E, N, P, PT, T	B, C, G, H, IJ, L, E, N
HOME OFFICE*	BR, BC, CS	BR, BC, CS	BR, BC, CS
ENVIRONMENTAL/ RECYCLED STOCKS	Some	Some	Minimal
VALUE/PRICE	Good	Excellent	Good

*Paper Key: B=borders, BC=business cards, BR=brochures, C=certificates, CS=card stock, E=exotic, EN=envelopes, F=foil, G=gradations H=hot colors, IJ=ink-jet, L=letterhead, N=notecards, P=party, PT=pre-printed themes, T=textured

continues

Paper Providers

COMPANY	OFFICE DEPOT 800-685-8800	OFFICE MAX 800-788-8080
LABELS	Mailing, floppy disk, file folder, specialty	Mailing, floppy disk, file folder, specialty
SPECIALTY PAPERS*	B, C, G, H, IJ, L, E, N	B, C, G, H, IJ, L, E, N
HOME OFFICE*	BR, BC, CS	BR, BC, CS
ENVIRONMENTAL/ RECYCLED STOCKS	Minimal	Minimal
VALUE/PRICE	Good	Good

*Paper Key: B=borders, BC=business cards, BR=brochures, C=certificates, CS=card stock, E=exotic, EN=envelopes, F=foil, G=gradations H=hot colors, IJ=ink-jet, L=letterhead, N=notecards, P=party, PT=pre-printed themes, T=textured

Miscellaneous Software

TITLES	DESCRIPTION
CLICKBOOK	A printer utility that creates booklets of any size and shape. *BookMaker, 800-766-8531 or 415-354-8161, Mac and Windows disk, about $50.*
MEDIAWRANGLER	A multimedia authoring program for combining elements into simple multimedia shows. *AltaVista, 800-480-2582, Windows and Windows 95 CD, about $60.*
STUDIO M	Multimedia authoring software for creating greetings, announcements, and albums. Includes tools for morphing and warping. *Gold Disk, 800-982-9888 or 408-982-0200, Windows and Windows 95 CD, about $50.*
STUFFIT DELUXE	A file compression program for the Mac and Windows. *Aladdin Systems, 408-761-6200, Mac and Windows disk, about $50.*
TYPE TWISTER	A utility for shaping and manipulating text. *Adobe, 800-888-6293 or 415-961-4400, Mac disk, about $45.*
WINZIP	An easy-to-use file compression program for Windows. *Nico Mak Computing, 713-524-6394, available for downloading from http://www.shareware.com, Windows and Windows 95 disk, about $30.*

Index

FREE ISSUE

Introducing **FamilyPC** — the new computer magazine for parents and kids! It's more colorful, more educational, more fun than you ever dreamed a computer magazine could be! That's because it's published jointly by Disney (the world's top expert on fun) and Ziff-Davis (the world's top publisher of computer magazines)!

Whether you have a DOS/Windows computer or a Macintosh, you'll find **FamilyPC** is packed with ideas on how to get the most value, use and fun out of your family computer. Every issue brings you:

Reviews:	The best hardware, software, online services, games & gear
Activities:	Dozens of creative art, music, science, craft & learning projects
Learning:	Effective ways to teach kids the computer skills they need
Help:	Troubleshooting tips and practical advice
PLUS:	A mini-magazine created by kids, for kids!

FamilyPC – it's just exactly what you need to make the most of your family's computer!

For fastest
service call
1-800-888-9688

☑ To receive your FREE trial issue of **FamilyPC**, simply mail this coupon or call **1-800-888-9688**. If you like **FamilyPC**, you'll receive 11 more issues (for a total of 12) for just $12.95 – you save 63% off the $35.40 annual cover price! Otherwise, simply write "cancel" on the bill, return it and owe nothing. The first issue is yours to keep or give to a friend.

NAME

ADDRESS

MAIL COUPON TO:
FamilyPC
P.O. Box 37089
Boone, IA 50037-0089

CITY

STATE   ZIP

Canadian and foreign orders, include U.S. funds and add $10 for GST/postage.
FamilyPC's annual cover price is $35.40. ©1996 FamilyPC   CBK1AA

Photo Credits

Jade Albert
Page 237

Mike Carroll
Pages 83, 153, 157, 159, 171, 195, 235

Guy Crittenden
Page 205

Danny Gonzalez
Pages 61, 133, 169

Brian Leatart
Pages 125, 177, 185

Lightworks Photographic
Pages 1, 24, 45, 57, 63, 64, 111,
137, 141, 143, 217, 218, 229

David Luttrell
Pages 3, 7, 11, 18, 21, 35, 38, 41, 51, 59, 71,
75, 80, 86, 94, 95, 97, 103, 127, 247, 248

Tamara Reynolds
Page 223

Shaffer/Smith Photography
Page 203

Sync Associates
Page 31